UNDERSTANDING
ITALIAN OPERA

UNDERSTANDING
ITALIAN OPERA

TIM CARTER

OXFORD
UNIVERSITY PRESS

OXFORD
UNIVERSITY PRESS

Oxford University Press is a department of the University of
Oxford. It furthers the University's objective of excellence in research,
scholarship, and education by publishing worldwide.

Oxford   New York
Auckland   Cape Town   Dar es Salaam   Hong Kong   Karachi
Kuala Lumpur   Madrid   Melbourne   Mexico City   Nairobi
New Delhi   Shanghai   Taipei   Toronto

With offices in
Argentina   Austria   Brazil   Chile   Czech Republic   France   Greece
Guatemala   Hungary   Italy   Japan   Poland   Portugal   Singapore
South Korea   Switzerland   Thailand   Turkey   Ukraine   Vietnam

Oxford is a registered trademark of Oxford University Press
in the UK and certain other countries.

Published in the United States of America by
Oxford University Press
198 Madison Avenue, New York, NY 10016

© Oxford University Press 2015

Library of Congress Cataloging-in-Publication Data
Carter, Tim, 1954– author.
Understanding Italian opera / Tim Carter.
    pages cm
ISBN 978-0-19-024794-2 (hardback: alk. paper)   1. Opera—Italy.   2. Monteverdi, Claudio,
1567–1643. Incoronazione di Poppea.   3. Handel, George Frideric, 1685–1759. Giulio Cesare.
4. Mozart, Wolfgang Amadeus, 1756–1791. Nozze di Figaro.   5. Verdi, Giuseppe, 1813–1901.
Rigoletto.   6. Puccini, Giacomo, 1858–1924. Bohème.   I. Title.
ML1733.C37 2015
782.10945—dc23
2015008480

This volume is published with generous support of the Lloyd Hibberd Endowment of
the American Musicological Society, funded in part by the National Endowment for the
Humanities and the Andrew W. Mellon Foundation.

9 8 7 6 5 4 3 2 1
Printed in the United States of America
on acid-free paper

Contents

List of Illustrations

Preface

"I am Music" (*Io la Musica son*), sings the character delivering the prologue in Claudio Monteverdi's opera, *Orfeo* (1607). "Who am I? I am a poet" (*Chi son? Sono un poeta*) is how Rodolfo introduces himself to Mimì in Giacomo Puccini's *La Bohème* (1896). We can rehearse the arguments made so often during opera's long history in terms of which matters most: music or words. But despite the almost three hundred years separating *Orfeo* and *La Bohème*, what remains constant is that Monteverdi's La Musica and Puccini's Rodolfo are each singing the same thing: Italian poetry. Their music is, of course, quite different: early Baroque declamation on the one hand, and late Romantic lyricism on the other. But their texts share similar poetic structures that have strong musical implications.

It is a fact of operatic life that words written for music will almost always be cast as poetry, not prose. The very first librettist, the Florentine poet Ottavio Rinuccini (1562–1621), established particular poetic procedures that endured in texts for Italian operas through to the early twentieth century and beyond. The musical styles that composers applied to such librettos changed, as did notions of adhering, or not, to the poetry's formal principles. These principles, however, allow for various approaches to understanding Italian opera both as a genre and in the case of individual works by providing a constant against which one can measure the musical setting. They also allow the asking of a very simple question: what happens when the music and the libretto somehow fail to coincide?

This gives easy access to a whole host of issues lying at the heart of any opera: the creative collusions and collisions involved in bringing it to the stage; the various, and varying, demands of its text and music; and the nature of its musical drama, to name just a few. In other words, it is as good a way as any—and perhaps better than most—to dig deeper into the workings of opera. In this book, I seek to show how these workings might be uncovered by way of a close reading of five Italian operas by Monteverdi, Handel, Mozart, Verdi, and Puccini. Two come from the Baroque era, one from the Classical, and two from the Romantic, at least in terms of the way in which music-historical periods are often identified. I chose them not just because they all sit squarely in the operatic canon, but also given that our familiarity with them may have blinded us to some of the remarkable, and remarkably surprising, things they do.

"Italian opera" is defined in terms of language rather than by the nationality of its creators: for example, Handel was German then British, and Mozart was born and lived in what we now call Austria. It is true, however, that native Italian librettists, composers, and performers for a long time dominated a repertoire with widespread international currency. Some of the more general remarks made in this book about poetic structures on the one hand, and musical forms on the other, would apply equally to opera in other languages (Czech, English, French, German, Russian). Likewise, my discussions of broader thematic issues (what kinds of subjects often appear in operas), of practical matters (how operas are brought to the stage), and of perennial questions concerning opera as drama apply across the entire genre. But sticking with one verbal and even musical language serves a historical purpose, and also an aesthetic one. Monteverdi's *L'incoronazione di Poppea* and Puccini's *La Bohème* might seem very different works, as indeed they are. But they also have common threads to do with shared linguistic and other values.

I imagine that readers of this book will already be fascinated by opera and its performance, whether live or by way of recording, but will want to know more about how it works: its tools and materials. In terms of navigating my text, it would make sense to start with chapter 1, but the subsequent chapters on single operas are able to stand on their own: each begins with a cast list (also noting the original singers, where known), details of the first performances, a comprehensive synopsis, and useful background information, before digging deeper. The quotations from opera librettos are taken from standard sources—usually those close to the music—save for minor editing to normalize spellings and punctuation. I do not expect fluency in Italian: everything is translated or paraphrased. There is no musical notation in this book, and technical terms are kept to a minimum. Four can be defined easily enough. The music I discuss is for the most part tonal, that is, based on one of twenty-four possible keys defined by way of a primary pitch and of two types of scales (major or minor) built upon it (so, F major, D minor, etc.): such keys exist in a network of relations that can be close or distant. Modulation is the process by which music moves from one key to another. If one thinks of a baseball diamond, the batter's box could be the tonic; first, second, and third bases represent related keys (in most cases, the dominant, four steps above the tonic, is the closest one); and the aim is to return to the home plate, or tonic. Cadences are a means of musical punctuation at the ends of phrases: they can be strong (like a period or full stop), weak (a comma), or somewhere in between (a colon or semicolon). Musical meter creates measures (bars) by way of grouping strong and weak beats: they usually fall into groups of twos (duple-time; 2/4), fours (common-time; 4/4 or C), or threes (triple-time; 3/4). These beats can be subdivided into twos or threes: for the latter, 6/8 (duple-time with a beat subdivided into threes), 9/8, and 12/8 (triple- and common-time subdivided in the same way) are common.

This book draws on several decades of my talking about opera to audiences of all kinds, whether in the university classroom, the pre-performance lecture, or the opera club. My gratitude to them for having listened is equal to their deep, abiding passion for an art form that in any logical world would be relegated to the realms of the absurd. It is a passion which, of course, I share.

UNDERSTANDING
ITALIAN OPERA

CHAPTER 1

What Is Opera?

ACT II, SCENE 6 of Giuseppe Verdi's *La traviata* (1853) ends with a typically heartrending moment for Violetta Valéry: "Love me, Alfredo, as much as I love you! Farewell!" Her story is taken from Alexandre Dumas's *La Dame aux camélias,* and the Italian libretto is by Francesco Maria Piave. She is a Parisian courtesan, a woman of easy virtue but who has fallen in love with the young Alfredo; his father, Giorgio Germont, breaks up the affair on the grounds of the dishonor it brings to the family; and Violetta shows her good side by realizing where her responsibilities lie, leaving the love of her life for his and society's greater good—*Amami, Alfredo, quant'io t'amo! Addio!* She then suffers the fate of many operatic heroines by way of a charming death.

Not for nothing did the film *Pretty Woman* (1990) turn a performance of *La traviata* into a cathartic moment for its own tart with a heart of gold, Vivian Ward (Julia Roberts), although she instead finds life and love with her Prince Charming, the millionaire Edward Lewis (Richard Gere). Seeing Julia Roberts in tears as Violetta dies is as good a way as any to capture something of the power of Italian opera, although there are many other films that make a similar point: *The Shawshank Redemption, Moonstruck,* and *Philadelphia* work equally well, if in very different ways. Even those that poke fun at the genre's absurdities—such as the Marx Brothers's classic *A Night at the Opera* (1935)—tend to remain in awe of such emotional moments where the voice holds sway over its audience.

As for Verdi in 1853, he milked *Amami, Alfredo* for all it was worth. The music pauses, then the soprano soars, and the powerful melody scarcely seems to need words to convey its meaning, turning the ones that are there into repetitive fodder: *Amami, Alfredo, amami quant'io t'amo, amami, Alfredo, quant'io t'amo, quant'io t'amo! Addio!* (to give a typically awkward singing translation designed to fit the musical notes: "Alfred, oh love me, / love me as I do love thee, / Alfred, oh love me, love me ever as I love thee, / now fare thee well"). That melody also becomes emblematic for the whole opera: Verdi made it the focal point of the opening orchestral prelude, meaning that we hear Violetta's musical declaration of love and her farewell even before we have met her. We take that music to heart.

There is plenty to say about how Verdi manages to make so powerful an effect. But one should start with the straightforward observation that Piave, the librettist, clearly did not mean for Verdi to do what he did with this part of his text. It comes from a separate *scena* (so called) between Violetta and Alfredo; the label prompts a "scene" without any extended aria or duet (for the latter, Violetta has just sung one with Giorgio Germont). She is certainly troubled by her as yet unannounced decision to leave her lover, and she knows she is terminally ill with consumption. Alfredo, on the other hand, is oblivious, and he rather complacently takes the typical male view that her *Amami, Alfredo, quant'io t'amo! Addio!* is proof that Violetta's heart "lives only for my love": he rounds off her line by turning it into a rhyming couplet—*Ah, vive sol quel core all'amor mio!* The text of the *scena* is in free-rhymed eleven-and seven-syllable lines (so-called *versi sciolti*). This is the closest Italian poetry comes to speechlike patterns, and the convention is that *versi sciolti* cue some manner of musical declamation called recitative. Closing a scene with a rhyming couplet in eleven-syllable lines is also typical. So far as the text is concerned, then, this exchange has no great poetic or even dramatic weight; it is Verdi who decides to put on the musical brakes. And who can resist? It is unlikely that Piave would have complained.

Such operatic moments where the music overtakes the text would seem to support the commonplace notion that it is the composer who puts the drama into opera. The no less common corollary is that poetry for (operatic) music must somehow be less than "great" poetry because it is servant to a musical master. My point is not—or at least, not yet—to disprove either statement, even if I shall be presenting enough arguments in favor of giving librettists credit where credit is due. Rather, I simply note that although we can feel Verdi's magical melting moment without understanding what Piave was doing in his libretto, we remain unaware of how it might have come about. The poetic structures within an opera libretto provide strong indications of what a composer should do with them. The composer can always choose to do something different—as Verdi did here—but identifying where such choices occurred allows speculation on why they were made.

Such speculation might seem futile were it not for the fact that it is likely to be grounded in something more concrete, and more tangible, than seems to be the case in much that passes for critical engagement in opera: wishful thinking about the music. It is an incontrovertible fact that Piave's *Amami, Alfredo, quant'io t'amo! Addio!* is a straightforward—if very elegant—eleven-syllable line in the context of *versi sciolti*. It is equally incontrovertible that Verdi treats this line in a manner different from other *versi sciolti* in the libretto of *La traviata*. What encouraged him to do so? Was it some attempt to bring Violetta to more vivid emotional life? Was it a grammatical imperative (*Amami*)? How about those lusciously singable alliterative As (all six of them) and final orotund Os (four, one after the other), and the mellifluous Ms (three), if with enough Ts and Ds for good vocal attack? Or did Verdi just think that his singer (Fanny Salvini-Donatelli) deserved the chance to exit on a strong musical note? These possible explanations engage with opera's drama, with its rhetoric, and with the fact that it is contingent on performance. They also enable us to penetrate something that might otherwise seem impenetrable.

SOME DEFINITIONS

In the preface to his *Albion and Albanus* (1685), the English poet John Dryden tried to define a genre relatively new to the English stage: "An *Opera* is a Poetical Tale, or Fiction, represented by Vocal and Instrumental Musick, adorn'd with Scenes, Machines, and Dancing." This definition was good enough to last nigh on a century: it was adopted wholesale through multiple editions of Samuel Johnson's *A Dictionary of the English Language* (1755). But one might usefully dissect Dryden's economical sentence. He defines opera by way of three elements presented in what seems to be a hierarchical order: poetry, music, and staging. This no doubt reflects Dryden's professional interest; there are plenty who granted music a higher status, and still would. We might also continue to argue over the relative importance of the scenes, machines, and dancing as fundamental to, or just an adornment of, the operatic "work" itself. As for Dryden's "tale, or fiction," assuming a deliberate distinction between them, then a "tale" is presumably taken from some existing source, whereas a "fiction" is newly invented. And if Dryden means by "represented" something other than just "performed," we need to worry about the mechanisms of representation, and therefore about the precise dramatic and other functions of opera's vocal and instrumental music. The key word in Dryden's definition, however, comes very early on: operas are first and foremost "poetical," a word which refers not just to the poetic imagination or to some heightened rhetorical style, but also to the nuts and bolts of poetry itself: meter and rhyme.

Later in his preface, Dryden develops his theme:

> If the Persons represented were to speak upon the Stage, it wou'd follow of necessity, That the Expressions should be Lofty, Figurative, and Majestical: But the Nature of an *Opera* denies the frequent use of those Poetical Ornaments: For Vocal Musick, though it often admits a Loftiness of Sound; yet always exacts an harmonious Sweetness: or to distinguish yet more justly, the Recitative Part of the *Opera* requires a more Masculine Beauty of Expression and Sound: The other, which (for want of a proper *English* Word) I must call *The Songish Part*, must abound in the Softness and Variety of Numbers; its principal Intention being to please the Hearing, rather than to gratify the Understanding.

Operas must be "poetical"—that is, their texts must be in poetry, not prose—but according to Dryden the presence of music denies lofty, figurative, or majestic poetic ornaments because while music may permit "loftiness of sound," it always requires "harmonious sweetness." He further notes the distinction between recitative, with its more "masculine" beauty, and what he finds himself forced, for lack of a better word, to call "the songish part"—his problem over the terminology is typical for the period. This "songish part" is more feminine (so Dryden implies); it requires "softness and variety" in its poetic meters ("numbers"); and it focuses less on understanding the words than on pleasing the ear.

Dryden then goes on to say that the best language for music is Italian, "the sweetest, the most harmonious, not only of any Modern Tongue, but even beyond any of the Learned" (i.e., Latin and Greek), one that "seems indeed to have been invented for the sake of Poetry and Musick," rich in vowels and "manly" on the one hand, and "sonorous" on the other. French cannot come close—which is what you would expect a British poet to say—and even English has too few of the feminine rhymes necessary for song, although Dryden allows that it is better for recitative. Moreover,

> we know that for some Centuries, the Knowledge of Musick has flourish'd principally in *Italy*, the Mother of Learning and of Arts: that Poetry and Painting have been there restor'd, and so cultivated by *Italian* Masters, that all *Europe* has been enrich'd out of their Treasury, and the other Parts of it in relation to those delightful Arts, are still as much Provincial to *Italy*, as they were in the time of the *Roman* Empire.

Italian opera, it seems, can hardly beaten, although in *Albion and Albanus* Dryden was willing to try.

IN PRAISE OF LIBRETTISTS

Most opera-lovers would reverse the order of Dryden's definition to put music at its head. Indeed, "First the music, and then the words" (*Prima la musica e poi le parole*) was a catchphrase enshrined in the title of a satirical *divertimento teatrale* (theatrical diversion) by Antonio Salieri (1786): Giambattista Casti's libretto begins with a hilarious scene where a composer forces a poet to come up with words for his completed musical score. For all that this is a procedural absurdity—which is the point of Salieri and Casti's satire—it reflects a common aesthetic presumption about the nature of opera. For that matter, most theater poets accepted, willingly or not, that when writing for music, compromises had to be made in terms of plot design and arrangement, and of poetic language, accent, and even vowel sounds (it is hard to sing a melisma on *u*). But there is an art to writing librettos, and it is worth uncovering what it might be.

A significant number of opera librettos merit high literary status, and some certainly gained it both within the canon and on their own terms. *Artaserse*, by Pietro Metastasio (1698–1782), was set in its original or some revised form by eighty composers ranging from Leonardo Vinci's opera of 1730 to Charles Lucas's of 1840, and his *Didone abbandonata* by sixty between 1724 (Domenico Sarro) and 1824 (Karl Gottlieb Reissiger). Other of his librettos—such as *Adriano in Siria* (1732), *Alessandro nell'Indie* (1729), *Demetrio* (1731), and *L'olimpiade* (1733)—also received large numbers of settings, and even his *La clemenza di Tito* had gained music by Antonio Caldara (1734), Johann Adolf Hasse (1735), Georg Christoph Wagenseil

(1746), Christoph Willibald von Gluck (1752), Niccolò Jommelli (1753, 1765), Baldassare Galuppi (1760), Pasquale Anfossi (1769), and numerous others well before Caterino Mazzolà reworked the text for Wolfgang Amadeus Mozart (1791). The poet involved in the first operas, Ottavio Rinuccini, published his librettos as "literary" texts—they also appeared in his posthumous *opera omnia* (the *Poesie* of 1622)—as did Giovanni Francesco Busenello (in his *Delle hore ociose* of 1656) and numerous other librettists during the seventeenth and eighteenth centuries, Metastasio included. Thus librettos could be read, studied, and appreciated independently of the music that had been attached to them. Indeed, such music—usually composed to suit local circumstances and needs—seems to have been incidental to their broader dramatic and literary stature.

It is true that certain, somewhat exceptional operas circulated in musical form during the genre's early history, whether because of the movement of composers (Monteverdi revived his *Arianna*, first performed in Mantua in 1608, in Venice in 1640) or by way of touring companies. For the latter, a good example is the group or groups known as the Febiarmonici (Musicians of Apollo) recorded as performing in Genoa (1644); Florence and Lucca (1645); Genoa and Florence (1646); Genoa, Bologna, and Milan (1647); Bologna, Turin, Reggio Emilia, Ferrara, and Rimini (1648); Milan (1649); and Lucca (1650), before ending up in Naples. They had a repertoire of operas such as Francesco Sacrati's *La finta pazza* and Cavalli's *Egisto* and *Giasone*, as well (at least in Naples) as his *Didone* and Monteverdi's *L'incoronazione di Poppea*. Singers could also take operas, or parts thereof (as so-called suitcase arias), from place to place. And some individual works gained sufficient reputation to earn widespread performance: Antonio Cesti's *Orontea* (Innsbruck, 1656), to a libretto by Giacinto Andrea Cicognini, was one of the most successful operas of its time—it was performed in Genoa (1660, 1661); Rome and Florence (1661); Turin (1662); Ferrara (1663); Milan (1664); Macerata (1665); Bologna (1665, 1669); Venice (1666); Bergamo, Brescia, and Palermo (1667); Lucca (1668); Portomaggiore (1670); Naples (1674); Reggio Emilia (1674); Hanover (1678); and Venice (1683). But the idea of a circulating musical repertoire, as distinct from circulating librettos, was in general a much later phenomenon developed by the international opera industry from the late eighteenth century on, as particular operas—and fewer of them—gained canonic status as fixed "works" to be performed musically more or less intact. Even then, however, one should not underestimate the willingness of opera houses through the nineteenth century and into the twentieth to adapt such works to suit their immediate circumstances, if only by cutting them down to size or otherwise adjusting them to suit the local vernacular. Nowadays we may have some belief in the integrity of "great" musical works, but when it comes to operas, not many are heard complete in the form envisioned by their creators, even if audiences are rarely kept informed of what has been removed.

It is important to keep that plural—creators—in mind. Save for the most literary librettists, most will have worked for the benefit of particular composers, and usually in some sense with them, writing texts to commission that would receive a one-time musical setting that might or might not be fortunate enough to enter the repertoire. This does not devalue their role as theatrical poets, nor should it lessen their status in our eyes. We may care more for Verdi's *La traviata* than Piave's, but the one could not exist without the other. Before Mozart, and often after, the libretto was normally complete before the composer put pen to paper, for all that it might then be revised according to the musical and other demands made upon it. Moreover, in early opera—and often later—poets were the prime movers in the operatic enterprise, not just by devising the subject and fleshing it out with appropriate words, but also given their often standard role as stage director. The libretto itself was usually the public face of opera in terms of the artifacts that survive to record a given performance: librettos were printed for general consumption inside or outside the theater, whereas musical scores were, on the whole, regarded as more ephemeral performance materials, to be adopted, adapted, and disposed of at will. Poets also acted as the chief ideologues of opera, promoting and defending the genre against its detractors and inserting it into broader literary and cultural debates. In a very real sense, the history of the libretto is the history of opera *tout court*.

Yet as countless librettists have complained, the words rarely come high on any operatic agenda. The music, singers, mise-en-scène, costumes, and choreography vie for the attention of the eye and the ear, while the text, if it is held in any regard at all, is dismissed as a trying necessity or a trifling irrelevance. The beauties of a poet's verse are as nothing compared with the beauties of a composer's music, and in some minds, both pall in favor of the beauties of a singer's high C. In this light, the history of the libretto is just one relatively minor branch of opera studies. But let us give credit where credit is due. Whether or not in collaboration with a composer, a librettist will identify or create a plot, pace the drama within (or sometimes outside) the genre-based conventions of the day, accommodate the requirements of staging, decide who sings what and where, and even, if the composer is lucky, come up with words worthy of taking wings of song.

ITALIAN VERSIFICATION

At least until the twentieth century, opera librettos in almost any language were always cast as poetry, not prose. Thus one needs to consider their meter, rhyme, and form. In terms of meter, two issues are of main concern for Italian verse: the number of syllables in a given line and the position of the final accent. In general, a line can be from three to eleven syllables in length (*ternario, quaternario, quinario, senario, settenario, ottonario, novenario, decasillabo,* and *endecasillabo*): the eleven-syllable line is the "classic" norm, with its chief component, the seven-syllable line, in second place. Syllable counts are affected by elisions (*sinalèfi*) and diphthongs (*sineresi*): respectively, the fusion into one syllable of the final and initial vowels of two consecutive words, and the similar fusion—permitted in specific contexts—of consecutive vowels in a single word. Thus

> Ve-/drò, / men-/tre io / so-/spi-/ro
>
> (*Le nozze di Figaro*, III.3)

is a seven-syllable line (a crass but metrical translation marking the stresses would be "Shall *I* see *while* I'm *sigh*ing"). Here the diphthong *io* is read as one syllable and is further elided with the end of *mentre*: were *io* (*mio, lui, due, sia, quei,* etc.) at the end of the line, it would almost invariably be two syllables. In practice, elisions and diphthongs can be handled with some flexibility by the poet, and also by the composer, who can also break them in a musical setting (an eleven-syllable line might be set to twelve or more notes).

This line from *Le nozze di Figaro* is a conventional *verso piano*, with the final accent on the penultimate syllable ("so*spi*ro"). An accent on the final syllable produces a "truncated" *verso tronco*: Leporello begins Mozart's *Don Giovanni* with "Notte e giorno fati*car*" ("Night and day I have to *work*"). One on the antepenultimate syllable produces a "sliding" *verso sdrucciolo*: "La donna è *mo*bile," sings the Duke of Mantua in Act III of Verdi's *Rigoletto* ("Woman is *mu*table"). But *versi tronchi* and *sdruccioli* are counted as modified *versi piani*. For example,

> Me-/tà / di / voi / qua / va-/da-/no
> e / gli al-/tri / va-/dan / là
>
> (*Don Giovanni*, II.4)

is a *verso sdrucciolo* followed by a *verso tronco* ("The half of you go *that*-a-way, / the others go down *there*"). The former has eight actual syllables, and the latter, six. But they are both reckoned as seven-syllable lines.

The different stress patterns at the end of each of these three types of Italian verse have not just poetic consequences but also musical ones. *Versi piani*, with the stress on the penultimate syllable, end in the manner of a trochee (strong–weak) or an amphibrach (weak–strong–weak). *Versi tronchi* end with an iamb (weak–strong) or anapest (weak–weak–strong), and *versi sdruccioli* end with a dactyl (strong–weak–weak). Musical meter also has strong and weak beats, as in the quadruple-time march (strong–weak–strong–weak) or the triple-time waltz (strong–weak–weak). So verbal and musical stresses should ideally either coincide according to the beat or match in other ways (e.g., with a longer musical note). Furthermore, musical cadences—the equivalent of punctuation—tend to go from weak beat to strong. Therefore it is easier to provide such cadences on *versi tronchi* (ending weak–strong) than on *versi piani* (ending strong–weak), meaning that the *versi tronchi* that often close off stanzaic texts in Italian librettos help determine musical articulation.

The position of internal accents and caesuras in these lines is to some extent free, although each line length has standard patterns. Lines with an even number of syllables—*versi parisillabi*—tend to be particularly clear-cut, while the eleven-syllable line is the most flexible of all, although its length sometimes creates problems in other ways. These patterns also produce characteristic rhythms associated with specific line lengths. Thus Cherubino's "Non so più cosa son, cosa *faccio*" in Mozart's *Le nozze di Figaro* (I.5) derives much of its breathless character from Lorenzo da Ponte's ten-syllable lines ("I don't know who I am, what I'm *doing*"). All this has obvious ramifications for musical setting; it further helps explain the obvious differences between music setting Italian verse and that for some other language.

The *verso piano* is the standard form; *versi sdruccioli* and *tronchi* can be used for special effects. For example, in librettos *versi sdruccioli* often invoke pastoral resonances (on the precedent of Sannazaro's *Arcadia*, first published in 1504). They also have a long history of association (often in five-syllable lines) with infernal, demonic, or magic scenes, as with Medea's "L'armi appre*statemi*" in Cavalli's *Giasone* (1649), Act III, scene 9; the infernal chorus "Chi mai dell'Erebo" in Gluck's *Orfeo ed Euridice* (1762), Act II, scene 1; or the witches' "Tre volte *miagola*" in the opening of Act III of Verdi's *Macbeth* (1847). The *verso tronco*, on the other hand, can be comic (and is sometimes associated with nonsense syllables), although, as noted above, it also has other functions in terms of articulating closure.

Italian opera librettos draw only rarely upon the standard poetic forms of Renaissance Italian (Tuscan) hendecasyllabic verse, such as Dante's *terza rima* (rhyming *ABA BCB CDC* . . .), Petrarch's fourteen-line sonnet (with two quatrains—*ABAB ABAB*—and two tercets, e.g., *CDC DCD*), or the *ottava rima* stanzas of Ariosto and Tasso (*ABABABCC*).[1] When librettists choose such hallowed forms, it is often for special (archaic, moralizing, etc.) effect, as with Orpheus's "Possente spirto, e formidabil nume" in *terza rima* in Act III of Monteverdi's *Orfeo* (1607); Don Alfonso's *ottava rima* "Tutti accusan le donne, ed io le scuso" in Mozart's *Così fan tutte* (1790), Act II, scene 13; and the sonnets in Verdi's *Falstaff* (1893), Act III, scene 2, and in Act III of Puccini's *Tosca* (1899). Special effects are also often associated with line lengths and forms invoking "popular" poetry, such as the nine-syllable line and, in some contexts, eleven-syllable lines in rhyming couplets (in the case, as we shall see, of Susanna's "Deh vieni non tardar, o gioia bella" in *Le nozze di Figaro*, IV.10).

Instead, the basis of early librettos—as of the late Renaissance pastoral plays that provided their most immediate precedent—was a mixture of free-rhyming eleven- and seven-syllable lines, producing *versi sciolti* ("loose" or "free" verse). More regular rhymes and/or metric consistency could define structural units within this flow; and lines could be divided between characters to enhance the effect of dialogue. However, one major exception—and it is a crucial one—is the strophic canzone/canzonetta, generally in other than mixed seven- and eleven-syllable lines, which appears even in the earliest operas. For example, Ottavio Rinuccini introduced strophic groupings of eight-syllable lines (sometimes combined with four-syllable ones), five-syllable lines, and so forth in the "first" operas, *Dafne* (1598) and *Euridice* (1600), specifically for the end-of-"scene" choruses. His model was the strophic arrangement characteristic of some such choruses in Renaissance drama; he also drew on the anacreontic verse introduced (in part, on French precedent) by the poet Gabriello Chiabrera, who said that he was catering specifically to composers of the "new music" and their "arias." Rinuccini also cast some of his poetry for individual characters in strophic forms when they could plausibly "sing" rather than just "speak." In another very early opera, Monteverdi's *Orfeo*, the librettist Alessandro Striggio (the younger) made even greater play of formal songs that stand apart from the prevailing

---

1. In this book, I adopt the convention in indicating rhyme-schemes that eleven-syllable lines are in upper case, seven-syllable ones are in lower case, and superscript numbers show other meters. So, *ABA* indicates three eleven-syllable lines of which the third rhymes with the first; *ABa* has the same rhyme-scheme but the third line has seven syllables; while $a^8b^4a^8$ has two rhyming eight-syllable lines separated by a four-syllable one. *Versi tronchi* (with the accent on the final syllable) are indicated with "t"; *versi sdruccioli* (accent on the antepenultimate syllable) have an "s."

versi sciolti for the recitative: Orpheus's celebratory "Vi ricorda, o boschi ombrosi" (four four-line stanzas in eight-syllable lines) near the beginning of Act II is an obvious example. Such songs are marked as separate both dramatically and musically, not just by their strongly melodic style but also by the presence of an instrumental ensemble (here playing ritornellos before and between each stanza) as distinct from the harmonic "continuo" group (a harpsichord, theorbo, etc.), which improvises a simple chordal accompaniment over a notated bass line for the declamatory recitative. It was a distinction of profound significance that would shape both the poetic and the musical form of opera for the next four centuries.

POETIC STRUCTURES AND MUSICAL CONSEQUENCES

Versi sciolti in eleven- and seven-syllable lines remained standard for recitative (and variants thereof) through the nineteenth century and beyond: their fluidity was well suited to its dramatic function and musical style. However, arias and ensembles favored shorter poetic lines in clear-cut patterns with regular rhymes. It is hard to set uneven *versi sciolti* to balanced musical phrases, while more regular poetic patterns do not offer the flexibility associated with recitative. From early opera on, such structural and therefore dramatic shifts were essentially cued by the librettist, whom the composer could ignore only at the cost of potential risk to the musical outcome.

The relative weight in a libretto of *versi sciolti* versus other metrical schemes therefore became contested ground in terms of which style—declamatory recitative or songful aria—was considered most appropriate for drama through music. The seventeenth century reveals the shifts as the canons of opera were forged in changing social, political, and even literary contexts. Lodovico Zuccolo's treatise entitled *Discorso delle ragioni del numero del verso italiano* (Discourse of the Reasons for the Meter of Italian Verse; 1623) showed clear contempt for the new canzonetta, claiming it to be a mere sop to musicians. Even more sympathetic theorists of the second quarter of the century, such as Giovanni Battista Doni and the anonymous author of *Il corago* (The Theater Director), felt ambivalent about shifts away from *versi sciolti*: they approved the variety thereby achieved but warned against anticlassical improprieties. At the heart of the debate lay the threat to dramatic verisimilitude posed by song, rather than sung speech. But as opera moved from the north Italian courts to enter more public domains—starting in Venice from 1637 on—the rising fortunes of the aria could scarce be resisted. By the mid seventeenth century, Francesco

Cavalli and his favored librettist, Giovanni Faustini, confirmed Rinuccini's principle that arias (duets, etc.) should on the whole be set apart in poetic terms by a change in line length, by the use of regular metrical and rhyming structures, and/or by the use of refrains. But they introduced an increasing number of such structured passages, forcing the greater presence of lyrical, rather than declamatory, music in their operas. Thus, Giacomo Francesco Bussani's libretto for Antonio Sartorio's *Giulio Cesare in Egitto* (1676)—the model for Handel's later opera—has some sixty "aria" texts kept distinct in various ways from the *versi sciolti* for the recitative.

Various reform movements in the late seventeenth and early eighteenth centuries sought to bring some order to the proceedings by rationalizing the typical number and form of arias. The trend within so-called serious opera (*opera seria*) was for aria texts to be in two strophes. Each strophe matches in the number of lines (usually four) and their meter; each has the same rhyme-scheme (and sometimes the same rhymes); and each ends with a *verso tronco* most often rhymed with its partner. This reflected the classicizing program of the so-called Arcadian Academy (including such poets as Apostolo Zeno and then Pietro Metastasio) to purify the libretto of perceived earlier abuses. It also meshed with the then preferred musical structure, the *da capo* aria, with a strophe each for the A and B sections, the latter followed by a reprise of the former.

Eighteenth-century comic opera (*opera buffa*) could make freer play of these aria forms—albeit within the same broad parameters—for dramatic or humorous effect. For example, Carlo Goldoni (1707–1793) and his successors stretched to longer aria texts with, say, one or two strophes stating a position, a longer middle section containing comic "patter," and a final couplet or quatrain rounding off the argument. Such arias might also include one or more changes of line length; and the recurring *verso tronco*, generally rhymed, grew increasingly important for structure and unification. This extendible technique also proved useful for the ensembles that were fast becoming a characteristic of *opera buffa*. In the work of Lorenzo da Ponte, these movements can generate complex, sectional verse structures (but simple ones are still possible); they nevertheless present clear instructions to the composer, with changes of poetic meter articulating dramatic shifts and prompting changes of musical style, tempo, key, and the like.

Even in *opera seria* toward the end of the eighteenth century, two-strophe aria texts started to lose ground, whether to three-strophe ones—characteristic of the aria form known as the *rondò*—or to other more flexible poetic forms, also with changing meters. Part of the impulse was a search for greater naturalism in opera, or at least an attempt to mitigate opera's patent antinaturalism: comparing Mazzolà's reworking of *La clemenza di Tito* for Mozart with Metastasio's original of fifty-seven years earlier reveals some important trends. But the shift to "through-composed" opera in the nineteenth century, which tried to generate a near-continuous musical flow with constant orchestral accompaniment from the beginning to the end of each act, had surprisingly little effect on approaches to versification in librettos, at least initially. Thus recitatives, arias, and ensembles can still be distinguished in conventional poetic ways, as can formal subdivisions within arias and ensembles. The continued significance of these structures is clear from Verdi's correspondence with his librettists: the composer had an acute sense of what was necessary for his poetry, often making quite specific demands of his collaborators.

However, a change can be discerned at least from his *Aida* (1871) on, if not before. Verdi's former preference for clear structures—and often for *versi parisillabi*—shifts in favor of longer lines. These include *versi doppi*, "double" verses that treat two lines of a given meter as a single metrical unit. This, coupled with a tendency for irregular groupings of lines and flexible changes of line length, produces a striking asymmetry that reflects a changing musical style, but also a renewed search for greater naturalism on the stage: Verdi's letters to his librettists Antonio Ghislanzoni (for *Aida*) and Arrigo Boito (for *Otello* and *Falstaff*) make both points clear. However, even supposedly more "naturalistic" operas of the Verismo (Realism) school such as Mascagni's *Cavalleria rusticana* (1890) and Leoncavallo's *Pagliacci* (1892) have surprisingly conservative librettos in terms of their poetic structures. Likewise, the libretto of Puccini's *La Bohème* (1896) certainly falls into regular (if highly flexible) groupings of conventional line lengths—this is by no means prose—even if their effect on the musical flow often seems exiguous. Prose librettos were instead to become a feature of (some) operas in the twentieth century, though there are not many of them in Italy, where librettos have tended to remain in some or other form of poetry, however loose the definition of the term might have become.

TWO EXAMPLES FROM MOZART

The obvious question is why all this matters, and the answer is best provided by examples not so much of standard poetic and musical forms—we shall see plenty of those in the following chapters—as of operatic moments where poetic and musical form appear to deviate one from the other.

The opening of Mozart's *Don Giovanni* (1787) moves quickly from Leporello's complaints over his hard life as a servant, through Donna Anna's entrance as she flees Don Giovanni's amorous advances, to the Don's killing of her father. After a change of scene, Don Giovanni and Leporello argue over the recent events, and then a new character enters, as yet unrecognized and unnamed. She complains of having been abandoned by her lover: she will tear out his heart when she finds him. Giovanni and Leporello observe from the side, and the Don assumes that here is another woman who needs some "consolation," while Leporello sees history repeating itself. But when Giovanni moves into the open to greet her, he realizes that she is his former lover Donna Elvira (and of course, the Don is the subject of her complaint).

A mere twelve measures of orchestral introduction are sufficient to establish Elvira's character—relatively noble, somewhat sentimental, yet also slightly unstable—by way of the musical conventions of the day such as the choice of key, the musical meter, and the orchestration. The stage seems set for an entrance aria, which is what the librettist Lorenzo da Ponte provides:

DONNA ELVIRA

	Ah! chi mi dice mai	7	Ah! who will tell me
	quel barbaro dov'è,	7t	where that barbarian is,
	che per mio scorno amai,	7	whom to my shame I loved,
	che mi mancò di fé?	7t	who betrayed my trust?
5	Ah! se ritrovo l'empio,	7	Ah! if I find the traitor
	e a me non torna ancor,	7t	and if he does not return to me,
	vo' farne orrendo scempio,	7	I will slaughter him most horribly,
	gli vo' cavar il cor.	7t	I will tear out his heart.

DON GIOVANNI

	Udisti? Qualche bella	7	Did you hear? Some beauty
10	dal vago abbandonata. Poverina!	11	abandoned by her lover. Poor thing!
	Cerchiam di consolare il suo tormento.	11	Let us try to console her torment.

LEPORELLO

	(Così ne consolò mille e ottocento.)	11	(So has he consoled one thousand eight hundred.)

DON GIOVANNI

	Signorina!	→	My lady!

ELVIRA
    Chi è là? → Who is there?

DON GIOVANNI
    Stelle! che vedo! 11 Heavens! what do I see?

Da Ponte gives Donna Elvira two four-line stanzas alternating seven-syllable *versi piani* and *versi tronchi,* and then the text moves to *versi sciolti* (as Don Giovanni "speaks"), with a final line divided into three statements (the scene then continues in *versi sciolti*). The structure suggests an aria followed by a recitative. Yet Mozart turns this into a trio (although in the nineteenth century it might have been called an *aria con pertichini*): he brings Giovanni's and Leporello's first lines (9–12; *Udisti? . . . ottocento*) into what would seem by rights to be Elvira's musical domain. The trio then starts to dissolve as the Don addresses Elvira directly with a wheedling *Signorina!* The orchestra stops just before her *Chi è là?*

Turning what should be an aria into a trio makes dramatic sense even if it does not quite fit da Ponte's grammar: Giovanni's question to Leporello, *Udisti?* (Did you hear?), is in the remote past tense, so Elvira has stopped singing, but making her continue forces the two men to listen some more, while Leporello can also mutter his aside. Likewise, stopping the would-be aria and starting the recitative at Elvira's *Chi è là?* mark the moment where she speaks not to herself but to another character ("Who is there?"). Furthermore, the musical overlap maintains the dramatic momentum (which seems to have been Mozart's concern right from the start of the opera); it prevents the audience from applauding the singer's virtuoso display; and it allows Elvira to stay on stage for the rest of the scene (we shall see that arias often cue a character's exit). But undercutting her musical moment by way of an aria-as-trio also has an impact on our reading of the character: Elvira is consistently represented as having insufficient power to turn the plot of *Don Giovanni* to her advantage.

While Mozart's construction of "Ah! chi mi dice mai" may not have been da Ponte's intention, his text does not prevent it: if it had, Mozart would presumably have gone back to the librettist to ask for different poetry. In other words, there is usually some leeway within or beyond a libretto's poetic structures for the composer to make creative choices. As for why Mozart did what he did, we do not have much evidence of his thought processes as he composed this or any other part of *Don Giovanni,* but we can reasonably infer that they went along one or other of the lines suggested above. Even if he did not think about it at all, his instincts are open to similar consideration. Of course, there is always an obvious danger of circularity in such argument: Mozart's decisions must always be shown to be good ones because he is, well, Mozart. But what happens if he made a choice that, while not exactly bad, had somewhat dangerous consequences?

In the case of "Ah! chi mi dice mai," Mozart seems anxious to keep the plot moving forward. At a particular moment early in Act I of his *Così fan tutte* (1790), on the other hand, he decides instead to slow things down. Guglielmo and Ferrando have been persuaded by their philosophical friend Don Alfonso to test the fidelity of their fiancées, Fiordiligi and Dorabella. They pretend to be going off to war, which inevitably causes the women great distress:

DON ALFONSO		
Non v'è più tempo amici: andar conviene	11	There is no more time, friends: you must go
ove il destino, anzi il dover v'invita.	11	whither destiny, nay duty calls you.
FIORDILIGI		
Mio cor . . .	→	My heart . . .
Dorabella		
Idolo mio . . .	→	My dearest . . .
FIORDILIGI		
Mio ben . . .	→	My love . . .
DORABELLA		
Mia vita . . .	11	My life . . .
FIORDILIGI		
Ah, per un sol momento . . .	7	Ah, just for a moment . . .
DON ALFONSO		
5 Del vostro reggimento	7	Your regiment's
già è partita la barca.	7	ship has already left.
Raggiungerla convien coi pochi amici	11	You must join it with those few friends
che su legno più lieve	7	who on a smaller boat
attendendo vi stanno.	7	stand waiting for you.
FERRANDO, GUGLIELMO		
10 Abbracciami, idol mio!	→	Embrace me, my dearest!
FIORDILIGI, DORABELLA		
Muoio d'affanno.	11	I die of torment.

FIORDILIGI			
Di scrivermi ogni giorno	7	That you will write every day
giurami, vita mia!	→	promise me, my life!

DORABELLA			
Due volte ancora	11	Twice over
tu scrivimi, se puoi.	→	write to me, if you can.

FERRANDO			
Sii certa, o cara.	11	Be certain, beloved.

GUGLIELMO			
Non dubitar, mio bene.	7	Do not doubt it, my dearest.

DON ALFONSO

15   (Io crepo se non rido!)   7   (I'll burst if I don't laugh!)

FIORDILIGI			
Sii costante a me sol . . .	→	Be constant just to me . . .

DORABELLA			
Serbati fido.	11	Keep faithful.

FERRANDO			
Addio!	→	Farewell!

GUGLIELMO			
Addio!	→	Farewell!

FIORDILIGI, DORABELLA			
Addio!	7	Farewell!

FERRANDO, GUGLIELMO, FIORDILIGI,
    DORABELLA

Mi si divide il cor, bell'idol mio.   11   My heart is torn in two, my fair
                                                beloved.

Da Ponte constructs this entire episode in verse for recitative, presumably in a declamatory style over a simple continuo accompaniment (just as Mozart begins it). However, Mozart takes the women's *Muoio d'affanno* (I die of torment; line 10)—closing a rhyming couplet—as the cue to bring in the orchestra for what becomes an ensemble for all five voices: the so-called Letter Quintet ("Di scrivermi ogni giorno"). The pace slows drastically, and for Fiordiligi and Dorabella, at least, this becomes a deeply moving musical moment. Guglielmo and Ferrando are engaging in deception, and Don Alfonso is bursting to laugh; but the two women are desolate.

This is one of a number of seemingly intense emotional statements in *Così fan tutte*: another is the sublime E major trio "Soave sia il vento" as Fiordiligi and Dorabella (and Don Alfonso) bid safe voyage to their now-distant lovers. As for the Letter Quintet, it might seem wholly reasonable for Mozart to take the torment of parting as a cue to move from simple recitative to something more passionate so that his music can in effect (and affect) take over. But only the women are suffering; the men—and we in the audience—know that this is all a rather nasty game. Treating it as a musically serious moment, if that is what Mozart does, threatens to turn bathos into pathos, and therefore to tip the balance away from comedy. This seems to be a problem in *Così fan tutte* as a whole, where Mozart's musical depth appears to add a weight and seriousness lacking in da Ponte's libretto, perhaps because the composer missed its complex literary intertextualities; it also explains Eduard Hanslick's oft-echoed complaint (1875) about the opera's mismatch between Mozart's divine score and the tawdry plot. Of course, E. T. A. Hoffmann may have come closer when he wrote in 1813 about the music conveying "the most delicious irony": by this reading, Mozart's handling of "Di scrivermi ogni giorno" is not so much deep as ironic (or, perhaps better, it is ironic precisely because it is so deep). But this creates a problem for opera directors: musical irony is very hard for performers to handle, and for listeners to understand, given our tendency to trust what the music seems to be telling us.

One suspects that if Antonio Salieri had set *Così fan tutte* to music, as da Ponte originally intended, he would have taken a more straightforward approach. Moreover, while Mozart's decision here to treat a recitative text as something else may have brought him benefits, so he thought, it also involved a trade-off. He makes the text flow quite naturally up to the three statements of *Addio!* (Farewell!) and its rhyming partner, *Mi si divide il cor, bell'idol mio* (My heart is torn in two, my fair beloved). But he then indulges, reasonably enough, in some text repetition to extend the moment. This works beautifully for the two women and their fiancés, who are singing the same words at the same time, in harmonious homophony. But Don Alfonso is left just with his single line (15), *Io crepo se non rido* (I'll burst if I don't laugh), an aside not meant to be heard by the other characters. He has already said it twice in the quintet, but now he must say it thrice more (plus *se non rido* a further two times) to fill out the musical space. One might read this as Mozart's instruction to the audience: to die laughing at his opera. But if this had been designed as a real ensemble, da Ponte would probably have given Don Alfonso something more, and better, to sing.

While these two examples from Mozart further reveal the benefits of the approach advocated in this book—that demonstrable musical deviations from the poetic structure of a libretto open a door to critical inquiry that might otherwise be left closed—it is important to note that such instances are relatively rare in his operatic output, and more so than one might expect from a free-spirited "great" composer. For the most part, Mozart (as well as Monteverdi, Handel, Verdi, and even to some degree Puccini) were willing to do precisely what their librettos told them to do, meaning that the poet's instructions, and the ways in which they were conveyed, were more often musically convenient than not. In other words, there is no less value in considering why particular kinds of poetic structure worked for particular kinds of music than in worrying about moments where the composer and librettist seem to have disagreed. In the following chapters, we shall look at things both ways.

An "exotic and irrational entertainment"?

The idea of a drama in music is no more absurd than that of a drama in iambic pentameters—unless one happens believe that Julius Caesar did indeed address Mark Antony in five-feet lines—or, for that matter, one in Elizabethan English purporting to represent life in ancient Rome. Of course, Shakespeare has conditioned most of us to accept the convention with nary a question, and a willing "suspension of disbelief" is part of the contract required to gain admission to the theater. But while we can believe—or at least, temporarily agree not to disbelieve—in pentameters, music may seem one step too far. The fundamental question posed by opera is quite simple: why should people sing?

Part of the issue hinges on verisimilitude, which is one subtext of Dr. Johnson's famous characterization of opera as "an exotic and irrational entertainment." This was a somewhat throwaway, and anti-Italian, remark in Johnson's *Life of Hughes* (one of his set of biographical sketches of English poets written between 1777 and 1781); for the definition of the term "opera" in his dictionary, Johnson borrowed Dryden's "a poetical tale, or fiction …" Yet suspicion of, if delight in, the exotic and the irrational have always animated the history of opera since it emerged in Florence at the end of the sixteenth century.

It was not at all uncommon for the tale or fiction that Dryden defined as the typical basis for opera to be drawn from some prior source. All five operas discussed in this book, and many others, drew on material first developed in other contexts and manipulated to suit the genre, and we shall see that those manipulations reveal a great deal about how opera differs from other dramatic or literary forms. But operatic subjects also faced special constraints. Dryden articulated the issue in characteristically Baroque ways. His opening one-sentence definition of opera continues thus:

> The suppos'd Persons of this Musical *Drama* are generally supernatural, as Gods, and Goddesses, and Heroes, which at least are descended from them, and are in due time to be adopted into their Number. The Subject therefore being extended beyond the Limits of Humane Nature, admits of that sort of marvellous and surprizing Conduct, which is rejected in other Plays.

This explains the subject matter of the earliest operas in the north Italian courts around 1600, drawn chiefly from Greco-Roman myth, where supernatural gods and goddesses could reasonably be expected to differentiate themselves from mere mortals by way of music. It also accounts for their standard setting in the pastoral utopia of Arcadia, where poetry, and therefore music, are a natural condition of an idealized life. Thus for Dryden the presence of gods, goddesses, and heroes

> hinders not, but that meaner Persons may sometimes gracefully be introduc'd, especially if they have relation to those first Times, which Poets call the *Golden Age*: wherein by reason of their Innocence, those happy Mortals were suppos'd to have had a more familiar Intercourse with Superior Beings; and therefore Shepherds might reasonably be admitted, as of all Callings the most innocent, the most happy, and who by reason of the spare Time they had, in their almost idle Employment, had most Leisure to make Verses, and to be in Love; without somewhat of which Passion, no *Opera* can possibly subsist.

In other words, Dryden seeks to rationalize opera by the argument that in some cases, at least, its amorous subject matter justifies the presence of music not just as the food of love, as it were, but also as its language. His notion that opera engages with the "marvellous and surprizing conduct" of "gods, and goddesses, and heroes," or of shepherds and nymphs in an Arcadian golden age, not only explains the genre's potential for princely propaganda, but also invokes the genre's fascination for the exotic. Thus Dryden calls not just on mythology but, in addition, on epic on the one hand, and pastoral on the other; and both of these literary modes and their typical subject matters have a long-established presence in opera. The game changes, however, in the case of operas drawing on the actions of "real" historical characters—Nero and Poppaea Sabina, say—or of those closer to some notion of contemporary life such as a Figaro and a Susanna, or a Rodolfo and a Mimì. It is easier to explain why Orpheus sings than it is in the case of a Roman emperor, the servants of an eighteenth-century count, or bourgeois lovers in mid-nineteenth-century Paris.

While one might as well just accept that opera can never be verisimilar in any literal sense of the term (nor, of course, can most theater), the matter has tended to bring to the surface a complex set of anxieties both in operatic works themselves and in commentaries upon them. The latter often engage in some form of special pleading, as in the argument that despite the unreal nature of music, its range and depth somehow make opera true to emotional life. Whether one views operatic characters as puppets guided by an authorial mastermind or as creating and voicing their own fates—modern opera criticism generally makes some kind of choice between the two—there is a great deal invested in notions of insight and truth. This might not stand up to close scrutiny: it is always dangerous to submit operatic characters to any form of psychoanalysis, musical or otherwise. But opera-lovers are more likely to prefer the convenient fictions inherent in this reading over its opposite: that opera's patent absurdity creates the alienation effect that Brecht argued was essential for any theater that claimed to be politically and socially aware.

As for opera's own anxieties—as distinct from those of its supporters—they are manifest all around. They help explain the potential for operas with musicians at their head, be it Orpheus, a troubadour, or even a singing barber. But in the case of Monteverdi's *Orfeo* (1607)—and even with so prominent a musical figure in the title role—there is a careful separation of song and musical speech, with the songs coming at plausible moments: Orpheus sings before his wedding, at the gates of Hades, in praise of his lyre, and so forth. Thus verisimilitude is granted not just by the character but also by the occasions on which singing, rather than musically speaking, occurs.

Some would call these songs "diegetic"—although the term is problematic given that Plato meant something different by it—as distinct from the other music we hear throughout an opera but to which the characters usually appear deaf.[2] (A third category of operatic music—invoking natural sounds audible to those onstage such as birdsong or a storm—is a very special case.) The use of "real" music on the stage—that is, performances that characters can themselves be reckoned to hear—usually provides an excuse for a lyric interlude that may or may not have a dramatic point: Cherubino's "Voi che sapete" in Act II of *Le nozze di Figaro*, with Susanna "playing" her guitar to accompany him; Alfredo's *brindisi* (drinking song) toward the beginning of *La traviata*; Musetta's waltz in Act II of *La Bohème*. Likewise, representing actual music making and dancing with onstage musicians became a virtuoso (for the composer) cliché, and Mozart's ingenious dance music in the Act I finale of *Don Giovanni*—providing a background to onstage action—had a strong influence on nineteenth-century opera, including the opening of Verdi's *Rigoletto*. Similar motives underpin hunters' or sailors' choruses, military marches, spinning songs, and lullabies, for which excuses can usually readily be found assuming the right subject matter.

Moving away from the diegetic but still plausibly within its boundaries are standard set pieces with which "real" music conventionally becomes associated, such as prayer-scenes, on the one hand (Desdemona in Verdi's *Otello*, IV.2), and magical incantations, on the other (Alcina's "Ombre pallide" in Handel's eponymous opera), given that music is often associated with heightened invocation. The principle may extend to exhortations, whether in person (the chorus of Hebrew slaves in Verdi's *Nabucco*) or by letter, and also to mad-scenes (Donizetti's *Lucia di Lammermoor*) where the recourse to music further gains verisimilitude by virtue of the situation given that sane people do not normally hear flutes twittering in the air around them. Exhortation and madness usually also combine in another typical set piece, the lament, although there was some debate at least in the Baroque period over whether laments were better framed as musical speeches (so, in an impassioned recitative, as in the only surviving part of Monteverdi's *Arianna*) or as formal arias (we shall see the case of Cleopatra in Handel's *Giulio Cesare in Egitto*).

These tropes or their derivatives can usually be found to some degree woven by librettists and composers in any opera, even those that seemingly eschew conventional set-pieces to seek a more "natural" form of musical drama: the two operas primarily associated with the Verismo school of

---

2. Plato uses the terms "diegetic" and "mimetic" in relation to epic poetry to distinguish when Homer speaks as Homer (i.e., the poet as narrator) and when he voices a character within the narration (Odysseus, etc.).

Italian opera in the 1890s, Mascagni's *Cavalleria rusticana* and Leoncavallo's *Pagliacci*, variously have their folk songs, prayer-scenes, and *brindisi*. Other conventions include the "I"-songs where characters introduce or explain themselves to each other or to the audience (Leporello's "Notte e giorno faticar" at the beginning of *Don Giovanni*; Rodolfo's "Chi son? Sono un poeta" in *La Bohème*); narrative songs where a character offers an account of prior events that provide the backstory necessary to understand the action; or songs that simply set a time and a place. A special form of the "I"-song is the monologue where the character alone on stage muses on matters of life or death, somewhat in the manner of the formal soliloquy in spoken plays. One might also add other song types to this list, such as the revenge aria, the love-duet, and so on. Although such settings are rarely diegetic, strictly speaking, they tend to have a formality that makes them appear nearly so, while also somehow distinguishing them from the other dramatic and musical action. When in Verdi's *Rigoletto* (I.1) the Duke of Mantua sings a strophic *ballata* (so labeled) about dispensing his favors to this or that woman—they are all the same to him ("Questa o quella a me pari sono")—it may not be clear whether this is a "real" song or not, but it functions as if it were.

Of course, this leaves a great deal of operatic music unexplained, at which point the argument tends to return once more to notions of emotional truth or psychological penetration. But how a given opera moves between episodes of greater or lesser verisimilitude—or, if you prefer, different versions of verisimilitude—can be very revealing. So, too, is the tendency to play on whether operatic characters hear only each other's words or also their music: Don Giovanni's question to Leporello as they spy on Donna Elvira—*Udisti?* (Did you hear?)—is endlessly intriguing in terms of what precisely is being heard.

Much depends on an individual opera's subject matter: mythical deities, Arcadian shepherds and shepherdesses, ancient Egyptian rulers, and exotic non-Western others pose fewer problems than characters from European history or from "real" life contemporary to the opera. Much also depends on the period in terms of whether opera is just accepted as a theatrical norm—as it was for the most part in the seventeenth, eighteenth, and nineteenth centuries—or requires some manner of special pleading. However, the genre can often appear skittish about its raison d'être. Early operas usually had prologues to justify their aesthetic premises, and the technique returned in the late nineteenth and early twentieth centuries as the genre once more came under suspicion: thus Leoncavallo's *Pagliacci* has the protagonist,

Tonio, first appear as the "Prologo" to emphasize the claims of Verismo. Similar is the use of other framing devices that somehow distance the plot from the lives it represents, whether by establishing it as a lesson-bearing exemplar (the power of Amor in Monteverdi's *L'incoronazione di Poppea*; the "school for lovers" in Mozart's *Così fan tutte*), as the telling of a "story," or as part of an overtly theatrical exercise or debate. The technique has been extended still further to the rather self-conscious trick of making an opera be "about" opera, whether in purely practical terms—as with the aforementioned *Prima la musica e poi le parole* by Casti and Salieri and also the piece paired with it at the time, Mozart's *Der Schauspieldirektor*—or in more philosophical ones (Luciano Berio's *Un re in ascolto*). Such narrower self-reflexivity, which can also extend to a rather knowing self-parody, seemingly stands in contrast to more grandiose claims for opera's universality, though, as *Un re in ascolto* makes clear, they are two sides of the same coin. Opera composers may have variously sought in different ways, times, and places to prove the eminent Dr. Johnson wholly wrong—that opera is not "irrational"—but we all know, deep down, that he was exactly right.

FURTHER READING

There are numerous general surveys of opera, one of the more accessible of which is *The Oxford Illustrated History of Opera*, edited by Roger Parker (Oxford and New York: Oxford University Press, 1994). Herbert Lindenberger, *Opera in History: From Monteverdi to Cage* (Stanford, CA: Stanford University Press, 1998), takes a more thematic view. Thomas Forrest Kelly, *First Nights at the Opera* (New Haven, CT: Yale University Press, 2004), focuses more on historical contexts than on the musical and poetic issues covered in the present book; one of his case studies (Handel's *Giulio Cesare in Egitto*) overlaps with mine to complementary effect. Important aesthetic questions are raised in Joseph Kerman, *Opera as Drama*, rev. ed. (Berkeley and Los Angeles: University of California Press, 1988), which remains a controversial classic, as well as in Carolyn Abbate, *Unsung Voices: Opera and Musical Narrative in the Nineteenth Century* (Princeton, NJ: Princeton University Press, 1991), and in Gary Tomlinson, *Metaphysical Song: An Essay on Opera* (Princeton, NJ: Princeton University Press, 1999). John Rosselli, *Singers of Italian Opera: The History of a Profession* (Cambridge: Cambridge University Press, 1992), remains useful for more practical concerns. Two studies of the opera libretto tend to deal more with subject matter than with questions of poetics: Gary Schmidgall, *Literature as Opera* (Oxford and New York: Oxford University Press, 1977); and Patrick J. Smith, *The Tenth Muse: A Historical Study of the Opera Libretto* (New York: Knopf, 1970). *The New Grove Dictionary of Music and Musicians*, rev. ed. (London: Macmillan, 2001) mostly incorporates, and sometime supersedes, the entries in *The New Grove Dictionary of Opera* (London: Macmillan, 1992), although the latter is still useful for entries on individual operas. These two dictionaries are conflated in *Grove Music Online*, available on subscription from Oxford University Press (www.oxfordmusiconline.com/public/), although free access may be possible from university and public libraries. The *New Grove* articles on composers, librettists, performers, and others are very convenient sources of biographical information, work lists, and bibliographies.

Chapter 2

Giovanni Francesco Busenello and Claudio Monteverdi, *L'incoronazione di Poppea* (Venice, 1643)

CLAUDIO MONTEVERDI (PORTRAIT BY BERNARDO STROZZI, CI640)

Monteverdi wrote a large amount of theatrical music, both during his employment at the court of Duke Vincenzo Gonzaga of Mantua and then after he moved (in 1613) to become maestro di cappella *at St. Mark's Basilica in Venice.*
Innsbruck, Ferdinandeum. AKG-IMAGES.

Fortuna [Fortune] (soprano)
Virtù [Virtue] (soprano)
Amore [Amor/Cupid] (soprano)
Poppea [Poppaea], most noble lady, mistress of Nerone, raised by
    him to the seat of empire: Anna di Valerio (soprano)

Nerone [Nero], Roman emperor: ?Stefano Costa (soprano castrato)

Ottavia [Octavia], reigning empress, repudiated by Nerone: Anna Renzi (mezzo-soprano)

Seneca, a philosopher, preceptor to Nerone: ?Giacinto Zucchi (bass)

Ottone [Otho], most noble lord: ?Fritellino (alto castrato)

Drusilla, lady of the court (soprano)

Arnalta, aged nurse and confidante of Poppea (alto)

Nutrice [Nurse], nurse of Empress Ottavia (alto)

Lucano [Lucan], a poet, intimate of Nerone, nephew of Seneca (tenor)

Valletto, a page of the empress (soprano)

Damigella, a lady-in-waiting to the empress (soprano)

Liberto, a captain of the Praetorian Guard (bass)

Littore [a Lictor], an officer of imperial justice (bass)

Pallade [Pallas Athene], goddess of wisdom (soprano)

Mercurio [Mercury], the gods' messenger (bass)

Venere [Venus] (soprano)

Two soldiers of the Praetorian Guard (tenors)

Friends (*famigliari*) of Seneca,[1] consuls, tribunes, cupids

SETTING: Rome, conflating and reworking events of 58–65 CE.

SOURCE: Tacitus (*c*56–after 117 CE), *Annals*, XIII–XVI, etc.

FIRST PERFORMED: Venice, Teatro SS. Giovanni e Paolo, Carnival 1642–43.[2] Revived in Naples in 1651 with a somewhat different version of the score; there may also have been performances in Venice in 1646 and in Paris in 1647. The first modern staging was probably the one of the drastically cut version prepared by Vincent d'Indy done in Paris on 5 February 1913 (there had been a concert performance in 1905); the first U.S. performance was at Smith College on 27 April 1926 (using the d'Indy edition), and the first U.K. one at Oxford University on 6 December 1927. In some early

---

1. The term *famigliari* means "familiars," in the sense of those who might often be in, or even reside in, a household without necessarily being "family" in the genetic sense. Thus Seneca's *famigliari* can be interpreted as his friends or pupils.

2. Strictly speaking, Carnival runs from 26 December to Shrove Tuesday (the date of which varies by year), so a single Carnival season spans two calendar years. Matters are also complicated by one form of Venetian-style dating where the "new" year begins on 1 March. This explains the preferred styling of Carnival 1642–43: referring to just Carnival 1643 would be ambiguous.

sources, the opera is styled *La coronatione di Poppea* and *Il Nerone*. The synopsis, below, follows the materials probably, if not always clearly, associated with the Venice performance(s) and most often used today.

PROLOGUE. (*An aerial scene.*) Fortuna, Virtù, and Amore, in clouds, dispute their respective powers. Amore claims to be master of the world, as the story of Nerone and Poppea will prove.

ACT I. (Scenes 1–4: *Poppea's palace.*) Ottone arrives at the house of his beloved Poppea ("E pur io torno qui, qual linea al centro") and sees Nerone's soldiers outside, asleep. He realizes that she is together with Nerone and curses her faithlessness. The soldiers are aroused and complain about their job and the decline of Rome ("Sia maledetto Amor, Poppea, Nerone"); they feel sorry for Empress Ottavia being so badly treated. Nerone enters with his mistress: they take a sensuous farewell as Poppea emphasizes her love for him ("Signor, sempre mi vedi") and seeks to guarantee their marriage. She is left alone with her nurse, Arnalta, to discuss tactics, and she ignores Arnalta's commonsense warnings, for Amore and Fortuna are on her side ("Per me guerreggia Amor e la Fortuna"). Arnalta is left to grumble at her mistress's folly ("Ben sei pazza, se credi"). (Scenes 5–13: *City of Rome.*) Ottavia despairs at her humiliation ("Disprezzata regina") while her nurse (Nutrice) suggests that she should take a lover ("Se Neron perso ha l'ingegno"). Seneca, shown in by Ottavia's page, Valletto, urges restraint and appeals to her dignity: Valletto responds by mocking Seneca's pedantry. As Seneca reflects on power and the transitory nature of life ("Le porpore regali e imperatrici"), Pallade (Pallas Athene) appears to warn him of his impending death. Seneca welcomes the news. Nerone enters and discusses with Seneca his plans to repudiate Ottavia and wed Poppea ("Son risoluto insomma"). The philosopher urges reason, but Nerone is inflamed to anger. Poppea then calms him down ("Come dolci signor, come soavi"), suggesting that Seneca must be killed. Ottone confronts Poppea over her infidelity ("Ad altri tocca in sorte"), but she dismisses him, although Arnalta feels somewhat sorry for the poor man ("Infelice ragazzo!"). He tries to come to his senses ("Otton, torna in te stesso") and vows revenge. Then he turns to Drusilla, who has always loved him, and swears that he will favor her over Poppea, although he knows that his words contradict his heart.

ACT II. (Scenes 1–3: *Seneca's villa.*) Seneca praises stoic solitude. The god Mercurio (Mercury) appears, warning him again of death, which the philosopher accepts happily ("Oh me felice, adunque"). Liberto enters with Nerone's command that Seneca must die by the end of the day, and is impressed by the philosopher's calmness in response to it ("Mori, e mori felice"). Seneca gathers his *famigliari* around him; they urge him not to die ("Non morir, Seneca") but he is determined, and they leave to prepare the bath in which he will open his veins. (A scene for Virtù, a chorus of virtues, and Seneca is omitted, or was added later to the libretto.) (Scenes 4–9: *City of Rome.*) Following a flirtatious scene between Valletto and Damigella, Nerone and Lucano celebrate the news of Seneca's death with wine and song ("Hor che Seneca è morto"), praising Poppea's beauty ("Son rubini pretiosi"). (A scene for Nerone and Poppea is omitted, or was added later to the libretto.) Ottone realizes that he still loves Poppea ("Sprezzami quanto sai"), but Ottavia orders him to assume female garb and kill her: he cannot refuse. Drusilla delights in her love for Ottone ("Felice cor mio"), and Ottavia's nurse wishes she were in her place ("Il giorno femminil"). Ottone explains to Drusilla his plan for Poppea, and she gives him her clothes. (Scenes 10–12: *Poppea's garden.*) Poppea rejoices in Seneca's death ("Hor che Seneca è morto") and prays for Amore to support her; Arnalta then lulls her to sleep ("Oblivion soave"). Amore watches overhead, proclaiming his power to protect humankind ("O sciocchi, o frali"), as Ottone enters dressed as Drusilla and tries to kill Poppea. Amore prevents the deed; Poppea wakes and gives the alarm as Ottone escapes. Amore vaunts his success ("Ho difeso Poppea").

ACT III. (Scenes 1–7: *City of Rome.*) Drusilla joyfully anticipates Poppea's death ("O felice Drusilla, oh che sper'io"), but Arnalta identifies her as the would-be assassin, and she is arrested. Nerone sentences her to death, but Ottone, in turn, confesses his guilt, despite Drusilla's persistent attempts to protect her beloved. Nerone banishes Ottone while praising Drusilla as a model of womanly behavior, and she asks to go into exile with him. Ottone accepts the punishment with glad heart ("Signor, non son punito, anzi beato"). Now that Ottone has implicated Ottavia in the affair, Nerone has the excuse he needs, and he banishes her, too. He and Poppea rejoice that the way is clear to their marriage ("Non più s'interporrà noia o dimora"). Ottavia enters and, in a lament, bids a halting farewell to her home and friends ("Addio Roma, addio patria, amici addio"). Arnalta revels in the exaltation of her mistress as empress of Rome ("Oggi sarà Poppea"). (The Ottavia and Arnalta scenes are reversed in some sources.) (Scene 8: *Nerone's palace, with gods in the heavens.*) Nerone crowns Poppea ("Ascendi, o mia diletta"), and the consuls and tribunes pay homage. Amore proclaims his triumph to the approval of his mother, Venere ("Io mi compiaccio, o figlio"), and a chorus of cupids celebrates the marriage. Nerone and Poppea have a final ecstatic duet ("Pur ti miro, pur ti godo").

CLAUDIO MONTEVERDI (1567–1643) was well into his seventies when he composed *L'incoronazione di Poppea*. It was the third of three operas that he wrote for Venice late in his life, and his first collaboration with Giovanni Francesco Busenello (1598–1659). As such it reveals a particular stage of

MAP OF VENICE (ENGRAVED BY MATTHAEUS MERIAN; NUREMBERG, 1650)

"Public" opera in Venice took advantage of the city's tourism industry that was well developed even in the seventeenth century by way of the Grand Tour. The Teatro SS. Giovanni e Paolo, where L'incoronazione di Poppea *was first performed, was located in the piazza on the north side of the city (north-northeast of St. Mark's Square in the center of the map).*
AKG-IMAGES/Historic-maps.

early opera as the genre left the princely courts of northern Italy and entered more public domains. *L'incoronazione* also takes a historical subject rather than a mythological or pastoral one, and it is probably the first opera—or at least, the first by a "great" composer—to raise the classic moral dilemmas posed by not-so-nice characters singing the most beautiful music.

The surviving sources for *L'incoronazione* are complex. The earliest datable one is a *scenario* (synopsis) associated with the first performances in Venice of what it styles an *opera regia* (royal opera). Then we have a printed libretto for a performance by the touring opera company known as the Febiarmonici in Naples in 1651, plus at least seven manuscript librettos of uncertain date (although one of them may be close to the version of the opera heard at the premiere). Busenello also included the libretto in his collected works, published as *Delle hore ociose* (Hours of Leisure) in 1656. Given that this edition was presented for literary consumption, the differences between the libretto here and in the other sources may not relate to any musical performance—although it is possible that the 1656 version in some way reflects what Busenello first gave to Monteverdi for musical setting, that is, prior to the composer's handling of it. The music survives in two manuscripts: one akin to a presentation copy now surviving in Naples and perhaps associated with the 1651 performance, the other more a performing score now in Venice, copied in the early 1650s in circles associated with the opera composer Francesco Cavalli (1602–1676). Although its preparation might also have had something to do with the Naples production, the Venice score seems closer to the original one. But none of the musical sources dates from around the time of the first performance.

It is now commonly accepted that *L'incoronazione* as it survives combines the work of various composers, although opinions vary on the precise nature of that mix. A version of the text of the final duet between Nerone and Poppea had already been used in a revival in Bologna in 1641 of Benedetto Ferrari's *Il pastor regio* (Venice, 1640)—Ferrari's music does not survive—and the words later appeared in an entertainment, *Il trionfo della fatica*, by Filiberto Laurenzi (1647). There is music almost certainly by Cavalli (the opening sinfonia is reworked from his *Doriclea* of 1645) and by Francesco Sacrati: the sinfonias in the consul scene in Act III appear in a touring version (1644–45) of the latter's *La finta pazza* (first performed in Venice in 1641; the score for the premiere is lost). The consensus is that at least some of the final scene and also some of the music for Ottone (perhaps as it was reworked for another singer) involve one or more other hands, whether or not acting under Monteverdi's direction until he died. Parts of

POPPAEA SABINA (FONTAINEBLEAU
SCHOOL, C1560)

*Emperor Nero's second wife (d. 65 CE)
remained a source of fascination: this
much later "portrait" clearly shows what
attracted early modern artists to her.*
Geneva, Musée d'Art et d'Histoire. AKG-IMAGES/
André Held.

the music in the Naples score also appear to come from later still. But a fair amount of the music in *L'incoronazione* rings true to the style of late Monteverdi, and even the final love-duet, "Pur ti miro, pur ti godo"—over which there has been considerable debate—is close enough to music known to have been composed by him that it is at least in keeping with it.

It would help if we had more information about the first performances of *L'incoronazione* during the Carnival season of 1642–43. The opera was staged at the Teatro SS. Giovanni e Paolo coterminously with Laurenzi's *La finta savia* (libretto by Giulio Strozzi), which also had music by other composers. Piecing together information on that production and from other sources permits a decent stab at identifying at least some of the singers used in both operas. We already knew that the Roman soprano Anna Renzi (*c*1620–after 1661; she was Laurenzi's student) was Ottavia—her performance in that role was celebrated in contemporary poetry—although it emerges that she may originally have been intended for Poppea, who in the end was almost certainly played by Anna di Valerio. Various sources associate at least eight other singers with the theater in the 1642–43 season, including Stefano Costa (probably Nerone) and two other castratos nicknamed Fritellino (Ottone?) and Rabacchio, and the bass Giacinto Zucchi (Seneca?). This gets reasonably close to the thirteen or so singers that would seem to be the minimum needed to cover the twenty-eight separate roles in *L'incoronazione* (including each chorus part as a single role). Clearly such doubling occurred—it would have been grossly inefficient for it not to—in ways that may also have had an impact on the design of the opera; further, the Naples production seems to have treated Arnalta and (Ottavia's) Nutrice as the same character.

Having three castratos in the cast (Nerone, Ottone, and probably Valletto) was not unusual for opera at the time. Such singers had become a feature of church choirs in Italy, Spain, and parts of southern Germany in the second half of the sixteenth century. The advantages were obvious: the boys used in such choirs had only short-term prospects (prior to puberty) that lessened the value of any investment in their training, and women were not allowed by virtue of St. Paul's dictum that they should keep silent in church (I Corinthians 14:34). However, for boy singers with obvious musical talent, castration (normally, removal of the testes) could offer a path to fame and fortune. Although it was officially banned by the church and by secular authorities, it was accepted when cast as a consequence of necessary medical intervention, perhaps as a result of a real or feigned accident (e.g., falling off a horse). For it to be effective for musical purposes, it needed to occur before puberty and the bodily changes associated with it, including those affecting the voice, so it was done normally around the age of ten or eleven. Castratos grew to normal size and suffered few other abnormalities apart from unusually elongated limbs and a tendency to portliness. They were often reported to be prodigious lovers, although the physiological realities would seem to suggest otherwise.

In the developing opera industry in seventeenth-century Italy, castratos soon took over the leading role of the *primo uomo*. By virtue of their prolonged training and extended lung capacity, their voices were penetrating, flexible, wide-ranged, and capable of extraordinarily virtuosic coloratura. Having the *primo uomo* sing in the same register as the *prima donna* also allowed for thrilling musical effects, with closely spaced dissonances rubbing erotically together and the consonances harmonizing with a sexual charge. Castratos dominated Italian *opera seria* until the early nineteenth century, when taste and distaste prompted a shift in favor of the heroic tenor, although the last castrato in the papal chapel, Alessandro Moreschi, died in 1922 (some of his recordings made in the early 1900s—well beyond his prime—can be found on YouTube). The obvious problem nowadays, however, is to find singers able to sing castrato roles. There are three options: transposing the music down an octave for a tenor or baritone; having a female singer take on a so-called trouser role; or using a male countertenor singing falsetto. The last tends to be preferred now that music conservatories accept the feasibility of catering for such voices: indeed, the rise of well-trained countertenors able to hold their own on the operatic stage has been one of the more striking developments of recent decades, and has transformed the production of Baroque opera.

In terms of the 1643 *L'incoronazione*, we could also do with more details of its staging. The sets listed in the *scenario* (and given in the synopsis, above) would seem to be fairly straightforward save for the cloud machines needed for the prologue, the final scene, and perhaps the various appearances of the gods in Acts I and II. However, the predominant "City of Rome" set (I.5–13, II.4–9, III.1–7) leads to the apparent oddity of "private" scenes that one would expect to be located indoors (e.g., in Ottavia's and Nerone's separate rooms in the imperial palace) seemingly being done instead in an outdoor "public" space, unless the rubric means something different. Modern productions will usually seek to remedy the defect, if it is. But this has a bearing on the apparent erotic intensity of at least some of those scenes (e.g., between Nerone and Poppea, and, as often played nowadays, between Nerone and Lucano), although it makes perfect sense in theatrical terms: one can only bring in successive, often antagonistic, characters on neutral ground, as it were.

Other problems need to be solved, and gaps filled, in the surviving musical materials, not least in terms of the instrumental parts. Baroque opera generally employs instrumentalists in two different ways. First is the group of basso continuo instruments that accompany the voice throughout, improvising harmonies over a notated bass line that may in addition have figures or other symbols to indicate the chords needed (hence the term "figured bass"): typical continuo instruments include harpsichords, larger members of the lute family (the chitarrone, theorbo, archlute, etc.), portative organs, and the like. They may play together for a fuller sound, or may be variously used to distinguish characters, settings, and moods. Although it is common today for the continuo group to include a string instrument (such as a violoncello) playing the bass line—and although that undoubtedly occurred at the time in certain circumstances (for instance, perhaps for acoustic reasons)—it is neither necessary nor necessarily "authentic," and there has been a recent trend to do away with it so as to give the continuo players more flexibility.

The second instrumental group is made up of the ensemble that provides ritornellos between the stanzas or sections of an aria, and sinfonias at the beginning or end of scenes, or that otherwise covers for scene changes and the like. For much of the Baroque period, this ensemble would be made up of members of a single instrument family (e.g., a string consort made up of various forms of violins, violas, cellos, and double basses): only later do we get mixed-family ensembles—that is, what we would now call an orchestra—comprising wind, brass, percussion, and string instruments, although it is clear that even in the earlier period, instrumentalists could switch from one instrument to another if needed. For much of the period, too, this ensemble will not play over the vocal line, although such instrumental accompaniments do start to appear later in the seventeenth century and are very common thereafter. One problem in *L'incoronazione* is that the instrumental ensemble (as distinct from the continuo group) is used fairly infrequently in the opera, and therefore somewhat uneconomically in terms of paying performers to do nothing. Another is that the musical sources often mark the presence of a ritornello or sinfonia but do not notate it whole or even in part. Some creative composition is needed just to flesh out what the sources seem to require, and once one starts down that route, it is hard to know where to stop. While few will now condone Raymond Leppard's pioneering (for its time) edition of *L'incoronazione* as "realized" for the Glyndebourne Opera House in 1962—with its lavish string accompaniments and other alterations—it is rare even nowadays to find a totally "clean" version of the opera without some additional instrumental writing and other adjustments.

MONTEVERDI IN VENICE

We would probably be less worried about *L'incoronazione* if it were not Monteverdi's last known composition: he died on 29 November 1643 at the grand old age of seventy-six. He had been baptized in Cremona on 15 May 1567, and after studying with Marc'Antonio Ingegneri, *maestro di cappella* at the cathedral there, he found his first position at the court of Duke Vincenzo Gonzaga of Mantua, where he rose to become *maestro della musica* in 1601. As such, his responsibilities extended to music for court entertainments, including ballets and the newly emerging genre of opera: his *Orfeo*, to a libretto by the poet and court functionary Alessandro Striggio the younger, was performed at the end of Carnival 1606–7 (on 24 February and 1 March 1607), and his *Arianna* (now lost), to poetry by the Florentine Ottavio Rinuccini, was included in the celebrations of the wedding of Prince Francesco Gonzaga and Margherita of Savoy in May–June 1608. However, following the death of Duke Vincenzo in early 1612 and the succession of Prince Francesco, Monteverdi was discharged from court service in late July: this was not so unusual in the case of a change of rulers, although intrigue from rivals may have played a part, or Monteverdi may even have engineered things himself given that he had evidently been unhappy with his service in Mantua for some time. He was fortunate, however, that in the summer of 1613, the position of *maestro di cappella* at St. Mark's Basilica in Venice fell vacant. Monteverdi was appointed in August—the first non-Venetian to hold the position in fifty years.

Monteverdi remained a Mantuan citizen and so continued to have obligations to the Gonzagas, and they maintained a hold over him by way of an annual pension that he had been promised but was rarely paid. Thus, in addition to his duties at St. Mark's and his work for other Venetian institutions, he continued, at least sporadically, to compose theatrical and similar music for Mantua (much of which is lost). He also provided musical entertainments for notable Venetian patricians, including the *Combattimento di Tancredi e Clorinda* for Girolamo Mocenigo in Carnival 1624 (probably 1623–24) and *Proserpina rapita* (1630) for the wedding of Mocenigo's daughter Giustiniana and Lorenzo Giustiniani. Furthermore, it is clear from Monteverdi's letters that he was in contact with the theatrical troupes that periodically visited Venice. That theatrical scene changed significantly in early 1637, however, after the Teatro S. Cassiano, which had burnt down in 1629, was rebuilt and initiated the practice of performing operas during Carnival for subscribers and a ticket-buying public. The pattern was quickly followed by the Teatro SS. Giovanni e Paolo (1639), the Teatro S. Moisè (1640), and the Teatro Novissimo (1641). This commercial expansion, and the competition that ensued, made their effects quickly felt: five new operas were staged in Venice in the three seasons following the opening of the Teatro S. Cassiano, and some fifty had been performed by 1650.

Despite his advanced age, Monteverdi was prompted to enter the market by reviving his *Arianna* from 1608 (Teatro S. Moisè, Carnival 1639–40) and composing *Il ritorno d'Ulisse in patria* for the same season, probably at the Teatro SS. Giovanni e Paolo. *Il ritorno* was repeated the next year, when Monteverdi also provided a new opera, *Le nozze d'Enea in Lavinia* (or . . . *con Lavinia*) again for SS. Giovanni e Paolo (the music is lost). *L'incoronazione* came two years later at the same theater. Although he was surrounded by younger, more active colleagues—not least Francesco Cavalli—Monteverdi must have been regarded with something akin to veneration. Just how well he was able or wanted to capture the new operatic styles developed for Venetian audiences, however, remains a matter of debate.

The year 1637 is usually deemed to mark the emergence of "public" opera, distinct from the previous "court" operas and related music-theatrical entertainments that were essentially one-off events. We can argue over the extent to which Venetian opera was, in fact, "public"—it still relied on noble patronage to provide the large financial resources needed to put such works on the stage—although it is clear that production infrastructures changed to meet the evident demand, with impresarios, librettists, composers, singers, dancers, set and costume designers, and so forth working within what one might start to call an opera industry that operated with remarkable efficiency. The market to which this industry catered was formed not just by Venetians, but also by the large numbers of visitors to the city during Carnival undertaking various forms of the European Grand Tour, seeking to admire Venice's architecture and art, and, still more, to revel in its libidinous pleasures, which explains the fascination with attractive singers and appealing music. Many in the audience would have associated the title role in *L'incoronazione di Poppea* with the city's famous courtesans. It is also clear, however, that in some cases at least, opera provided a forum for Venetian political statement or even propaganda. Venice was, of course, one of the last independent republics in the Italian peninsula, and one reading of *L'incoronazione* rests heavily on the issue.

THE FIRST OPERAS

The first through-composed *favole in musica* (plays in music)—the generic term for what later came to be called "opera"—appeared in Florence: *Dafne* (1598) and *Euridice* (1600). Both had librettos by Ottavio Rinuccini and music by Jacopo Peri. They drew on earlier traditions of Florentine entertainments, not least the spectacular *intermedi* staged between the acts of spoken plays, particularly at moments of court celebration: the famous example is the *intermedi* accompanying Girolamo Bargagli's comedy *La pellegrina* for the wedding of Grand Duke Ferdinando de' Medici and Christine of Lorraine (May 1589). But *Dafne* was essentially a small-scale piece presented in the private household of its patron, Jacopo Corsi (who composed some of the music), and *Euridice* was not much larger, even if the production was Corsi's contribution to the next big wedding festivities in Florence, for Maria de' Medici and King Henri IV of France (October 1600; however, *Euridice* was previewed at court in May). According to Peri's preface to the printed score of *Euridice*, the opera was at least partly motivated by an attempt to recreate the reputed, and reputedly powerful, performance practices of ancient Greek and Roman tragedy, understood as a heightened recitation tending toward the musical. Thus early opera formed part of the broader humanist revival typical of the Renaissance, and also responded to complaints about contemporary musical styles that were repeatedly accused of lacking rhetorical and expressive power because they obscured the delivery of the words. The typical texture of Renaissance polyphony—contrapuntal writing for multiple voices—needed to be replaced by something much simpler: music for solo voice and basso continuo. As for the vocal line, it should be declamatory rather than lyrical, should respect the natural accents of the text, and should occupy a narrow range, all in a manner cultivating (so Peri said) a middle ground between speech and song. This style soon became known as the *stile recitativo*, or recitative.

Perhaps it is inevitable that what was said about early opera did not always square with what it did. Peri himself admitted that his new style of recitative had little to do with the ancient Greeks and Romans—even if it was, he said, the best way to meet the needs of the modern Italian language—and neither *Dafne* nor *Euridice* is a tragedy in any technical sense of the term. Rather, their stories draw on Greek myth as transmitted by Roman sources such as Ovid's *Metamorphoses*, and they are firmly situated within the realm of the pastoral. Nor do *Dafne* and *Euridice* consist wholly of recitative. Choruses punctuate the action, also dividing it into a classical five-part structure (the three-act division found in *L'incoronazione* is a more modern one). Rinuccini also finds periodic opportunities for at least some of the main characters to break out into "real" song at plausible moments.

The pattern is followed in Monteverdi's *Orfeo* (1607): its librettist, Alessandro Striggio, certainly knew Rinuccini's text (he probably saw the opera in Florence in 1600), and Monteverdi had seen not only Peri's score but also perhaps the rival setting published by Peri's competitor in Florence, the singer Giulio Caccini: Caccini had incorporated some of his own music (sung by the singers from his studio) in the October 1600 performance of Peri's *Euridice*, and he preempted by some three months the printing of the latter's score, although Caccini's opera was first performed complete only in December 1602. Acts I and II of Monteverdi's *Orfeo* have songs and dances celebrating the wedding of Orfeo and Euridice prior to the entrance of the messenger (a classical device) reporting her untimely death. And when Orfeo reaches the gates of Hades to recover his bride, his plea to the gods is in an appropriately structured, and highly virtuosic, musical style: it is song rather than sung speech. That difference is also made clear by the poetry. For the "songs" (and choruses), both Rinuccini and Striggio turn from the *versi sciolti* (free-rhyming eleven- and seven-syllable lines) designed for recitative to regular stanzaic structures often using other line lengths (e.g., four-, five-, six-, or eight-syllable lines). Or they adopt one or another of the fixed forms typical of Italian poetry: thus Striggio constructs Orfeo's plea, "Possente spirto, e formidabil nume," in the *terza rima* typical of Dante. These structured texts generate repetitive musical structures (the same music repeated exactly or with variation for each stanza) that are called arias in the early seventeenth-century sense of the term, that is, a strophic setting of a strophic text.

As one might expect, the creators of early opera were somewhat nervous about the genre's raison d'être and sought to justify, or at least explain, it by way of formal prologues preceding the main action: *Dafne* is introduced by Ovid, *Euridice* by the personification of Tragedy, and *Orfeo* by that of Music. They also relied on characters famed for their musical skills (Apollo, Orpheus) to justify the new medium. Matters became more problematic, however, as other types of characters took to the stage. In Monteverdi's *Arianna*, for example, the protagonist is more likely to "speak" than to sing: thus, when Arianna is abandoned on the island of Naxos by her lover Teseo (Theseus), the poetry of her lament is in *versi sciolti*, and the music is recitative, albeit in a very powerful version thereof. Save for the prologue delivered by Apollo, only the chorus "sings" in that opera, whether representing the simple fisherfolk on the island or as generic commentators on the action. The same problems of singing versus speaking continue in the mythological operas performed infrequently in the north Italian courts in the first few decades of the seventeenth century, and also in the sacred operas on the lives of saints that came into fashion in Rome in the 1630s under the patronage of members of the Barberini family, at the head of which stood Maffeo Barberini, Pope Urban VIII.

Orfeo was performed by an all-male cast (with castratos playing the female roles) made up of the nine singers of the Mantuan court musical establishment (although a Florentine castrato replaced one of them) as well as the virtuoso tenor Francesco Rasi in the title role. In the case of *Arianna*, the title role was taken by a renowned actress from the *commedia dell'arte*, Virginia Andreini, who reportedly moved the ladies of the audience to tears by her rendition of Arianna's lament. No doubt it was the combination of her singing and acting skills that made such an impact, although the piece itself had its attractions: it became very popular in its time and is the only part of the opera to survive. However, other comments on the *stile recitativo* were more negative: "too much like the chanting of the Passion," said one observer at the wedding festivities in Florence in 1600, while others often commented on the "tedium" of recitative. This is one reason opera never established a strong foothold in the courts of northern Italy in the early part of the century; another was that opera inhibited the participation of these noble audiences in their entertainments, for example, by way of courtly dancing.

The resulting tensions would end up animating the whole history of opera: how to reconcile the differing needs and justifications for musical speech versus song. Early librettists found various ways around the problems: keeping gods or allegorical characters in the dramatic frame who could use music as a sign of their superhuman powers; introducing shepherds or other lower-class characters (servants, etc.) who might plausibly sing in their daily lives; establishing formal conventions where singing could be expected (prayer-scenes, incantations, lullabies); or having characters adopt some disguise (enhanced by their use of music). All these tricks, and more, are apparent in Giacomo Badoaro's libretto for Monteverdi's *Il ritorno d'Ulisse in patria*. But even here, music still needs to break out of the mold. The heroine of the opera, Ulisse's long-suffering wife, Penelope, is in effect imprisoned in recitative throughout the opera until the very end, when she is reunited with her husband: her aria, "Illustratevi, o cieli," is only minimally cued by the repetitive patterns and occasional *versi sdruccioli* in the text, but it is a glorious moment of musical and emotional release. The genie had been let out of the bottle.

"BUT HERE THE MATTER IS REPRESENTED DIFFERENTLY"

Singing gods, shepherds, or even saints are one thing, but "real" people are another. Giovanni Francesco Busenello's first libretto for the new Venetian opera houses, *Gli amori di Apollo e di Dafne* (1640; music by Francesco Cavalli) played the typical mythological/pastoral games, while in his second, *Didone* (1641), also for Cavalli, he turned to epic. In his third libretto, for Monteverdi, he shifted ground again, or so it would seem. *L'incoronazione di Poppea* has often been identified as the first opera on a historical subject—which is more or less true if one accepts that saints are not historical figures—and thus lauded for bringing opera down to earth. Yet obvious problems ensue not just because of the question of verisimilitude, but also given the didactic role and responsibilities of history.

One might argue that all history is fiction, and that operatic histories are still more fictional than most. But while there is no reason, in principle, for an operatic Mary Stuart to bear much relation to the actual Queen of Scots, we will tend to compare her representation with what we know of her ill-fated life and judge matters in terms of any fidelity, or lack thereof, to the historical record. We will also bring to bear on our reading of such representations our awareness of matters extrinsic to them, even though we should admit—*pace* Stanislavski—that operatic characters do not have a life outside the boundary of their performance, nor much of one within it. In the case of *L'incoronazione*, for example, we know that soon after the real Nero's wedding with Poppaea, he had a hand in her death (in 65 CE)—reportedly kicking her in the abdomen while she was pregnant—and himself came to a sticky end, and that Otho (Ottone) eventually, albeit briefly, himself became emperor of Rome. This offers the satisfaction of believing that Nerone and Poppea will in the end receive just punishment for their evident transgressions in the opera: their triumph at its end comes shortly before a fall. Whether it is a viable critical strategy for dealing with the moral problems of *L'incoronazione* remains unclear.

Busenello certainly knew his Roman history, drawing for his libretto on Tacitus's (*c*56–after 117 CE) *Annals* (XIII–XVI), Suetonius, and Dio Cassius, and also the pseudo-Seneca tragedy *Octavia*. But he reordered and reconstituted historical events: the beginning of Nero's relationship with Poppaea in 58 CE and the transfer of Otho to Lusitania that same year; Nero's marriage to Poppaea and the exile (then death) of Octavia in 62 CE; and the death of Seneca for his involvement in the Pisonian Conspiracy against the emperor in 65 CE (also the year of Poppaea's murder). In the preface to the libretto published in *Delle hore ociose*, Busenello acknowledged his rather cavalier approach to the historical record:

> Nero, enamored of Poppaea, who was the wife of Otho, sent off the latter under the pretext of embassy to Lusitania so that he could take his pleasure with his beloved—so recounts Cornelius Tacitus. But here the matter is represented differently. Otho, desperate at seeing himself deprived of Poppaea, falls into deliriums and exclamations. Octavia, wife of Nero, orders Otho to kill Poppaea. Otho promises to do it; but lacking the spirit to deprive his adored Poppaea of life, he dresses in the clothes of Drusilla, who was in love with him. Thus disguised, he enters the garden of Poppaea. Amor disturbs and prevents that death. Nero repudiates Octavia, despite the counsel of Seneca, and takes Poppaea to wife. Seneca dies, and Octavia is expelled from Rome.

His account starts and ends with fact, but the bulk of his action is invention conceived with opera in mind: Ottone's "deliriums and exclamations," Ottavia plotting the murder of Poppea, the use of disguise, and the intervention of Amore. What Busenello does not tell us is still more interesting, however. "Seneca dies"—it is true—but by his own hand at the instigation of a petulant Nerone and a conniving Poppea. Busenello's plot summary also brushes over Poppea herself, whose manipulative scheming drives the action from the beginning to her triumphant end. But what else would one expect of an operatic diva?

Tacitus would not have approved of the historical distortions, but he might have understood Busenello's attempt to delve behind appearances and expose the corruptions of empire. He might also have appreciated the fact that Busenello's exploration of "historical" figures—however much they deviated from history—allowed for them separately and together to paint a broader and more nuanced dramatic and emotional canvas than mythological gods or even epic heroes. As for the obvious lessons to be drawn from *L'incoronazione*, they could be about the dangers posed by devious women—whether sexual predators or outraged wives—or about the abuses endemic to imperial regimes. The latter squares with the pro-republican propaganda that one would expect from Venice, always at odds with the Habsburg Empire—hence the soldiers' reference in Act I, scene 2 to Armenia in rebellion and Pannonia up in arms (this is, after all, the period of the Thirty Years' War)—and with Rome and the papacy. It also fits the various agendas of the Accademia degli Incogniti, a group that seems to have lain behind much operatic enterprise in Venice: Busenello was a member, as was Giacomo Badoaro, the librettist of Monteverdi's *Il ritorno d'Ulisse in patria*.

Like many such academies in northern Italy—although the term perhaps suggests a greater degree of formality than was often the case—the Incogniti debated, and wrote about, such burning issues of the day as "What color is most proper and appropriate for a lover's face?" and, perhaps more to the operatic point, "Which is most appropriate to beget affection: either a fair face weeping, or a fair one singing?" (these are titles of two of many discourses published by the academy's leader, Giovanni Francesco Loredano). This is not to dismiss the importance of the Incogniti for particular modes of Venetian political thought honed by long years of republican fervor: Loredano was, after all, a member of the senate. But it suggests a certain levity in at least some of these Incogniti texts, including opera librettos. For that matter, Emperor Nero was a typical subject—alongside madness, fleas, and syphilis—for the literary and rhetorical genre known as the paradoxical encomium: an exercise in praising that which cannot be praised. In short, Nerone and Poppea's triumph at the end of *L'incoronazione* may be undermined not so much by the historical record as by various levels of irony that can be discerned from the very start of the opera, at least within its text.

If we are not meant to admire—still less emulate—Nerone and Poppea, the search is on for any other character(s) who might rescue the opera for some kind of moral cause. Seneca has been one prime candidate, not least because of his "noble" suicide, though that comes less than halfway through the opera (II.3), and up to this point, he has not always been painted in a very sympathetic light: Seneca's attempts in Act I, scene 6 to convince Ottavia of the merits of stoically accepting what life might throw at her are dismissed by Valletto as the songs of an old windbag. One might feel sorry for Ottavia herself, but she then shamelessly blackmails the weak-willed Ottone to do her bidding. The one character to garner praise in the opera itself is Drusilla, whom Nerone proclaims in Act III, scene 4 to be a paragon of her sex as he grants her wish to join Ottone in exile; but she, too, connives in, and celebrates, the attempted murder of Poppea. At that point, one is more or less left just with the lower-class characters—the soldiers, Valletto, Damigella, and Ottavia and Poppea's nurses—as the carriers of worldly-wise messages commenting on the antics of their betters.

Busenello might well have resisted any such interrogation of *L'incoronazione*. He also sought to create a typical frame for it. His prologue is delivered by three allegorical characters: Fortuna, Virtù, and Amore. This, too, reads like an Incogniti debate in terms of which most governs human behavior: luck, virtuousness, or love. Fortuna and Virtù fight it out until they are forced to confront the reality that neither a human heart nor a celestial one dares contend with Amore (*Uman non è, non è celeste core / che contender ardisca con Amore*). Amore then announces that the single contest to be seen "today" will force Fortuna and Virtù, beaten by him, to admit that the world moves at his direction (*Oggi in un sol certame, / l'un'e l'altra di voi da me abbattuta, / dirà che 'l mondo a' cenni miei si muta*). That "today" (*oggi*) declares the opera's adherence to the Aristotelian unity of time: Act I begins at dawn (*al schiarir dell'alba*, according to the stage direction), and at the end of Act II, Busenello makes it clear that although Poppea falls asleep in her garden, this is in the manner of an afternoon nap. Thus Seneca dies, Ottavia is exiled from Rome, and Poppea is crowned empress, all in one action-packed day.

The prologue therefore sets up *L'incoronazione* as a classroom demon-
stration in the school of love. Fortuna as a character disappears from the
action—save that Poppea trusts herself to luck—and Virtù makes just a brief
further appearance in Busenello's printed libretto (1656), though not in any
known score; she appears in a scene after Seneca takes leave of his *famigliari*,
where he is welcomed into heaven by Virtù and a chorus of virtues. Amore,
on the other hand, intervenes to save Poppea from Ottone's attack in the
final scene of Act II, and he then returns with his mother, Venere (Venus), at
the end to celebrate his triumph.

Clearly Poppea has love on her side. In Act I, scene 4, she resists the warnings of her nurse, Arnalta: she has no fear of the future because Amore and
Fortuna are her comrades-in-arms (*No, no, non temo, no, di noia alcuna, /
per me guerreggia Amor e la Fortuna*), a rhyming couplet that Monteverdi
turns into a powerful refrain. In his printed libretto (1656), Busenello made
Poppea appeal still more strongly to the power of love at the end of Act I,
scene 10. She maneuvers Nerone into ordering Seneca's death, and he tells
her to be of good heart, because today (again!) she will see what love can
do (*Poppea, sta di buon core, / oggi vedrai ciò che sa far Amore*). The scene
ends here in the Venice score, but Busenello also provided a two-stanza text
(including another refrain) for Poppea after Nerone's exit:

	Se mi conduci, Amor,	7t	If, Amor, you lead me
	a regia maestà,	7t	to royal majesty,
	al tuo tempio il mio cor	7t	my heart at your temple
	voto si apprenderà.	7t	will offer up prayers.
5	Spirami tutto in sen,	7t	Inspire me in my breast,
	fonte d'ogni mio ben,	7t	fount of all my well-being,
	al trono innalza me,	7t	raise me to the throne:
	Amor, ogni mia speme io pongo in te.	11t	Amor, I place all my hope in you.
	Le meraviglie, Amor,	7t	All marvels, Amor,
10	son opre di tua man,	7t	are the work of your hand,
	trascende gli stupor	7t	transcending wonder
	il tuo poter sovran.	7t	is your sovereign power.
	Consola i miei sospir,	7t	Console my sighs,
	adempi i miei desir,	7t	fulfill my desires,
15	al trono innalza me,	7t	raise me to the throne:
	Amor, ogni mia speme io pongo in te.	11t	Amor, I place all my hope in you.

This soliloquy serves a purpose in terms of the staging: it allows time for Nerone to leave and Ottone to appear (for his argument with Poppea in I.11). Otherwise, it is not clear why Busenello should have felt it necessary to add this text (or Monteverdi to remove it), unless it serves somehow to excuse Poppea's behavior as Amore's pious acolyte.

As Dryden noted in his preface to *Albion and Albanus*, it was essential for at least some characters in any opera to fall under the power of love, "without somewhat of which Passion, no *Opera* can possibly subsist" (see chapter 1). One of his points was that this "passion" helped mitigate the problems of verisimilitude caused by singing on the stage. Busenello may have drawn a lesson from Monteverdi's *Arianna* (revived in Venice in the 1639–40 season): here, too, Amore appears at the outset (with Venere) to guide the action to its happy conclusion, and he and Venere return at the end (with other gods) to celebrate the outcome. In *L'incoronazione* (II.11), Busenello also has Amore quote the last line of Dante's *Paradiso*, where Love moves the sun and other planets (*Amor che move il sol e l'altre stelle*). But while love explains at least some of the sensuous music in *L'incoronazione di Poppea*—and Amore himself often sings in triple-time therein—it does not by any means solve all of the opera's musical problems.

"SPEAKING" AND "SINGING"

So far as we know, Monteverdi never set Poppea's "Se mi conduci, Amor" to music. But the poetry makes clear the manner in which he would have done it: the two stanzas of *versi tronchi* (with the accent on the final syllable of the line) with the same rhyme-scheme, plus the two-line refrain at the end of each stanza, would force some kind of aria, defined in the early seventeenth century as a strophic setting of a strophic text. The fact that the *versi tronchi* are still in seven- and eleven-syllable lines, however, reveals Busenello's evident reluctance in *L'incoronazione* to use other line lengths (four-, five-, six-, or eight-syllable lines) that would have stronger metrical implications in terms of prompting tuneful melodies in dance rhythms. The small number of texts in the libretto using such other lines also tend to be allocated to the characters of lower status; the exceptions are Nerone and Poppea's final duet, "Pur ti miro, pur ti godo" (mostly in eights), and the five-syllable lines in the scene for Seneca and Virtù that was never set to music, it seems.

Busenello's metrical shifts can still have musical consequences. In Act I, scene 5, Ottavia despairs over her ill treatment by Nerone: she is the scorned queen and afflicted wife of the ruler of Rome (*Disprezzata regina, / del monarca romano afflitta moglie*). Her nurse continues the *versi sciolti* until she decides to offer some commonsense advice:[3]

Ottavia, o tu dell'universe genti	11	Ottavia, you who of all peoples
unica imperatrice,	7	are the sole empress,
di tua fida nutrice odi gli accenti.	11	listen to the accents of your faithful nurse.
Se Neron perso ha l'ingegno	8	If Nerone has lost his mind
di Poppea ne' godimenti,	8	in taking his pleasures with Poppea,
scegli alcun, che di te degno,	8	choose someone who, worthy of you,
d'abbracciarti si contenti.	8	would be happy to embrace you.
Se l'ingiuria a Neron tanto diletta,	11	If Nerone so much delights in injuring you,
abbi piacer tu ancor nel far vendetta.	11	then take your own pleasure in revenge.

Nutrice's shift to from *versi sciolti* to eight-syllable lines (beginning at *Se Neron perso ha l'ingegno*) prompts Monteverdi to move to triple-time, as is enabled by the stresses within the new poetic meter, and also by the notion that her homily is in the manner of a song: she asks Ottavia to listen to her *accenti* (a musical term). *Se Neron perso ha l'ingegno* also initiates the first of two six-line stanzas ($a^8b^8a^8b^8CC$) separated by a six-measure instrumental ritornello. The second stanza begins with the music of the first, as one would expect, although Monteverdi has Ottavia interrupt it; he also gives special emphasis to the third and fourth lines of this second stanza, where Nutrice tells her to reflect on what she says, for all suffering can thereby turn to joy (*Fa riflesso al mio discorso, / ch'ogni duol ti sarà gioia*). This becomes a refrain that Monteverdi (not Busenello) brings back later in the scene.

Nurses can reasonably sing to their charges, and good or bad advice can plausibly be set within a formal frame. But this is the exception rather than the rule in *L'incoronazione*, and elsewhere one has a harder time to rationalize its lyrical turns. Act I, scene 1 begins at dawn: Ottone has returned to Rome; and he stands before Poppea's palace in anticipation of seeing his beloved again. However, his hopes are soon shattered:

---

3. Here I follow the layout in the 1656 libretto; the score has Nutrice's first two lines come before Ottavia finishes her prior speech.

[Ritornello 1]

E pur io torno qui, qual linea al centro,	11
qual foco a sfera, e qual ruscello al mare,	11
e se ben luce alcuna non m'appare,	11
ah! so ben io, che sta 'l mio sol qui dentro.	11

And so I return here, like a line to its center,
like fire to the sphere, and like a stream to the sea,
and although no light appears to me,
ah! I well know that my sun stands here within.

[Ritornello 1]

5 Caro tetto amoroso,   7   Dear roof of love,
albergo di mia vita e del mio bene,   11   shelter of my life and of my well-being,
il passo e 'l core ad inchinarti viene.   11   my step and my heart come to bow before you.

[Ritornello 2]

Apri un balcon, Poppea;   7   Open a balcony, Poppea;
col bel viso in cui son le sorti mie,   11   with your fair face in which lies my fate,
10 previeni, anima mia, precorri il die.   11   foretell, my soul, and precede the day.

[Ritornello 2]

Sorgi, e disgombra omai   7   Rise and chase now away
da questo ciel caligini e tenebre   11   the shadows and darkness from this sky
con il beato aprir di tue palpebre.   11   with the blessed opening of your eyelids.

[Ritornello 2]

Sogni, portate a volo,   7   Dreams, carry off in flight,
15 fate sentire in dolce fantasia   11   make heard in sweet fantasy
questi sospir alla diletta mia.   11   these sighs to her who is my delight.

Ma che veggio, infelice?   7   But what do I, unhappy, see?
Non già fantasmi o pur notturne larve,   11   No phantasms or nocturnal spirits these,
son questi i servi di Nerone . . .   . but Nerone's servants . . .

The text starts with a four-line grouping (rhyming *ABBA*), then four three-line stanzas (each *aBB*), prior to the shift at line 17 (*Ma che veggio, infelice?*) prompted by a typical "But . . ." and a rhetorical question ("what do I, unhappy, see?"), where the text moves into *versi sciolti*.

The rather stilted language, with its images both convoluted (a line returning to the center or fire to the sphere) and extravagant (Poppea chasing off the darkness by the blessed opening of her eyelids), is typical of Busenello and his contemporaries under the influence of the mannerist poet Giambattista Marino. But it poses various dilemmas for the music. The first four lines are treated as a single unit preceded and followed by an eight-measure instrumental ritornello. Ottone begins in a declamatory style to establish his presence while also giving the impression of starting in midstream: *E pur io torno* (*And so* I return). He then quickly shifts into a more lyrical triple-time—perhaps because the words matter less—ending with an indulgent setting of *ah!* (stated four times). He moves back to declamation for the next segment of the text (line 4) to convey the important information that his "sun"—a conventional metaphor for the beloved—lies within the palace before which he stands. The first line of the quatrain is then repeated at the end, as a refrain (so Ottone keeps returning, an image reinforced by the rather circular triple-time melody). This starts to give us some sense of the opera's modus operandi: key phrases that an audience needs to hear so as to understand the character or situation are set in a declamatory style, whereas less important ones can be an excuse for greater lyricism.

All four of the subsequent three-line stanzas (lines 5–7, 8–10, 11–13, 14–16) should in principle be set to the same or similar music. The score follows for the last three, each in a lyrical triple-time and preceded by a new six-measure ritornello: the trigger seems to be the fact that the second and third stanzas both begin with an imperative (*Apri* and *Sorgi*) and the fourth, beginning with a vocative, can easily follow (*Sogni*; though it needs to be set differently from *Sorgi* to avoid confusion). But in these three stanzas, too, the text is not particularly important for understanding the action. The first stanza (*Caro tetto amoroso*), in contrast, does need to be presented more clearly so as to fix our understanding of the place where the action takes place (the "dear roof" to which Ottone's step and heart are drawn): the music again adopts a declamatory style and emphasizes the point by repetition (*Caro tetto, caro tetto amoroso . . . il passo e 'l core ad inchinarti viene, il passo e 'l core ad inchinarti viene*). Again we see the score parsing the text according to what we need to hear. For the rest, Ottone's song, rather than speech, matches the sighs that he hopes Poppea will hear (lines 14–16). The most important dramatic point of this passage, however, is that rhetorical shift at line 17, where Ottone is forced to cease his amorous musings by way of a "But" (*Ma*) following the abrupt realization that he is not alone on the stage. The presence of Nerone's servants (two soldiers asleep) changes his situation for the worse, and the rest of the scene plays out in recitative as Ottone inveighs against Poppea's evident infidelity.

These lyrical triple-times—and the use of instrumental ritornellos to set off "songful" passages from speechlike ones—create various distinctions between the rhapsodic and the mundane, or wishful thinking and reality. They also tend to weaken Ottone as a character: a "real man" should be less inclined to sing soppy love-songs at dawn. For all that he is the character moving across the widest dramatic and emotional range in the opera, the tendency to have him sing, rather than just musically speak, does not always serve him well. His lowest point comes in Act I, scene 11, where we see him and Poppea together onstage for the first time. Ottone enters lamenting his fate: others drink the wine while he looks only at an empty glass (*Ad altri tocca in sorte / bere il licor, e a me guardar il vaso*); Poppea responds that he who is born unlucky should blame himself and not others (*Chi nasce sfortunato / di sé stesso si dolga, e non d'altrui*). Busenello constructs the scene by way of seven six-line stanzas (*aBaBCC*): the first six stanzas are allocated alternately to Ottone and Poppea, with the seventh divided between them (the 1656 libretto then adds four lines for Ottone and eight for Arnalta—who has been watching from the side—which are also included in the Naples score). Monteverdi sets the six stanzas strophically (each has more or less the same music), separating them by two ritornellos—one associated with each character—then moves to declamatory recitative for the seventh. Only in that recitative, however, do Poppea and Ottone seem to be speaking directly to, not just at, each other: for the strophic aria, she seems, rather, to be parroting, and therefore mocking, his outpouring of self-pity. Ottone is also at a disadvantage by way of his vocal range: he is an alto whereas Poppea is a soprano, so her music is set in a higher key than his, and accordingly, she has the upper hand.

Creating a distinction between (lyrical) "singing" and (declamatory) "speaking" might seem odd for an opera set to music throughout (because in fact the characters always sing). Nor does this distinction operate in the clearer-cut way (we shall see) typical of later Baroque *opera seria*, where it maps onto aria and recitative. Yet the further Monteverdi moves away from musical declamation—whether or not in connection with strophic texts—the more he raises some of the fundamental dilemmas facing opera of all periods: first, issues of verisimilitude; and second, the receptivity of characters to one another's music and not just their words. The more a character "sings" rather than "speaks," the more that character seems detached from the world represented on the stage, in effect calling time out on the dramatic action. This is one reason the confrontation between Ottone and Poppea in Act I, scene 11 seems to take place on separate planes until the two characters interact more normally in the final recitative. The question for any director is whether and how to establish any such interaction earlier in the scene despite the music's apparent resistance to it.

SEDUCTIVE POPPEA

It is clear from the examples discussed thus far that Busenello's libretto for *L'incoronazione* is not always strongly articulated in poetic terms, at least by way of meter, and that Monteverdi can take significant liberties with it. He does so both on a small scale such as by way of text repetition, and on a larger one by, say, treating different stanzas of a strophic text in different ways. In other words, the libretto does not direct the composer in the manner typical for later opera, and as a corollary, Monteverdi feels freer—or is given less guidance—in terms of what to do with it. Many of his musical decisions therefore seem to hinge on matters of rhetoric, where a change of style is triggered by some immediate textual cue—or flash of inspiration—that rarely has longer-term implications. *L'incoronazione* moves from moment to moment in a somewhat febrile manner that befits the hothouse world in which it is set, but which also seems to reflect early opera in a state of flux.

A good example is provided by the first time we see Nerone and Poppea, as they take their farewells after a night of passion. Here is the beginning of Act I, scene 3 as Busenello laid it out in the 1656 edition of his libretto:

POPPEA

	Signor, deh non partire,	7	Sire, ah do not leave,
	sostien che queste braccia	7	let these arms
	ti circondino il collo,	7	surround your neck,
	come le tue bellezze	7	just as your beauties
5	circondano il cor mio.	7	surround my heart.
	Appena spunta l'alba, e tu che sei	11	Dawn has scarce broken, and you who are

l'incarnato mio sole,	7	my sun incarnate,
la mia palpabil luce,	7	my palpable light,
e l'amoroso dì della mia vita,	7	and the loving day of my life,
10 vuoi sì repente far da me partita?	11	wish so suddenly from me to depart?
Deh non dir	4t	Ah, say not
di partir,	4t	"depart,"
che di voce sì amara a un solo accento,	11	for at the single sound of so bitter a word,
ahi perir, ahi spirar quest'alma io sento.	11	I feel my soul, ah, languish and, ah, die.

NERONE

15 Poppea, lascia ch'io parta.	7	Poppea, let me leave.
La nobiltà de' nascimenti tuoi	11	Your noble birth
non permette che Roma	7	does not permit that Rome
sappia che siamo uniti	7	should know that we are united
in sin ch'Ottavia non rimane esclusa	11	until Ottavia remains exiled
20 col repudio da me. Vanne, ben mio.	11	with my repudiation. Go, my love.
In un sospir che vien	7t	In a sigh that comes
dal profondo del sen,	7t	from the bottom of my heart,
includo un bacio, o cara, et un'à dio;	11	I include a kiss, my dearest, and a farewell;
si [= ci] rivedrem ben tosto, idolo mio.	11	we will see each other again very soon, my idol.

This text is mostly in *versi sciolti*, with occasional *versi tronchi* (lines 11–12, 21–22), and strong rhymes tend to be reserved for the punctuation and conclusion of individual statements. Four lines (11–14) will be repeated later in the scene, which may suggest some kind of refrain, although it does not seem to have a strong structural force. The characters tend to speak at length rather than interact; however, the pace speeds up toward the end of the scene (not given here) as lines become divided between the two characters. This is as natural a dialogue as Busenello is apt to produce, even if the opening speeches are too drawn out, and (again typically) some of the conceits seem overly artificial and mannered ("and you who are my sun incarnate, my palpable light, and the loving day of my life, wish so suddenly from me to depart?").

Monteverdi, however, moves the text around, breaking up the long opening speeches for each character and using repetition for rhetorical effect. In the libretto, Poppea has fourteen lines before Nerone can get a word in edgeways; in the score, she has five before he asks her to let him leave (*Poppea, lascia ch'io parta*; line 15), only to have her renew her entreaties with a different, nonmetrical version of line 1 and then lines 6–14. Monteverdi then heats up the rhetoric by shifting between two quite distinct musical styles: declamatory recitative over a slow-moving bass line, and a more lyrical triple-time (setting the words given in italic, below) with an active bass.

NERONE

16	La nobiltà de nascimenti tuoi	Your noble birth
17	non permette che Roma	does not permit that Rome
18	sappia che siamo uniti	should know that we are united
19	in sin ch'Ottavia . . .	until Ottavia . . .

POPPEA

(19)	In sin che, in sin che . . .	Until what, until what . . .

NERONE

19	. . . in sin ch'Ottavia non rimane esclusa . . .	. . . until Ottavia remains exiled . . .

POPPEA

(19)	Non rimane, non rimane . . .	Remains, remains . . .

NERONE

19	. . . in sin ch'Ottavia non rimane esclusa	. . . until Ottavia remains exiled
20a	col repudio da me.	with my repudiation.

POPPEA

20b	*Vanne, vanne, ben mio, ben mio; vanne, vanne, ben mio, ben mio; vanne, ben mio.*	*Go, go, my love, my love; go, go, my love, my love; go, my love.*

[Sinfonia]

NERONE

21	*In un sospir, sospir che vien*	*In a sigh, a sigh that comes*
22	*dal profondo del sen,*	*from the bottom of my heart,*
21	*in un sospir, sospir che vien, sospir che vien*	*In a sigh, a sigh that comes, a sigh that comes*
22	*dal profondo del sen,*	*from the bottom of my heart,*
23	*includo un bacio, o cara, o cara, et un'à dio;*	*I include a kiss, my dearest, my dearest, and a farewell;*

24 *ci rivedrem ben tosto, sì, sì, ci*	*we will see each other again very soon,*
rivedrem, ci rivedrem ben tosto,	*yes, yes, we will see each other again,*
idolo mio; ci rivedrem ben tosto,	*we will see each other again very*
idolo mio.	*soon, my idol; we will see each other*
	again very soon, my idol.

The benefit of shifting lines around is clear, as is that of having Poppea eagerly interrupt Nerone's declaration of his intention to repudiate Ottavia (lines 19–20). Monteverdi also allocates *Vanne, ben mio* (Go, my love; line 20) to Poppea rather than Nerone, which makes dramatic sense (and giving it to Nerone in the 1656 edition may have been a mistake): once Poppea has heard Nerone's intention, she is eager for him to leave to carry it out.[4] As for the triple-times, Poppea's (at *Vanne, ben mio*) is linked to an imperative ("Go . . ."), whereas Nerone's seems more to do with the sigh coming from the bottom of his heart. However, his *ci rivedrem ben tosto* (we will see each other again very soon) has greater grammatical force, and Monteverdi shifts to a more active duple-time in response.

Nerone's "we will see each other again very soon" leads Poppea to develop an even more extravagant argument:

Signor, sempre mi vedi,	7	Sire, you always see me,
anzi mai non mi vedi:	7	or rather, you do not see me:
perché s'è ver che nel tuo core io sia,	11	for if it is true that I am in your heart,
entro al tuo sen celata,	7	and hidden in your breast,
non posso da tuoi lumi esser mirata.	11	then I cannot by your eyes be seen.

The music, too, has greater drive: it is preceded by a four-measure sinfonia that establishes a yet more forceful duple-time that also animates Poppea's line over a marchlike "walking bass." The immediate textual cue for this change is the vocative *Signor* (Sire), although the music also tells us something about the character.

None of these more focused musical passages is cued directly by metrical shifts in the poetry: these are not the "real" songs with stanzaic texts found in Monteverdi's *Orfeo*; nor are they the formal arias of later Baroque opera. Monteverdi uses them to make rhetorical points, to reinforce grammatical structures, or to mark some kind of

---

4. It is clear in the Venice score that *Vanne, ben mio* is to be sung by Poppea, although Alan Curtis's edition of the opera allocates it to Nerone.

emotional moment, but he does so in the context of a musical recitative that moves—as one would expect from the predominant *versi
sciolti*—across a spectrum from declamation to lyricism: there is no
contemporary or modern term that one can apply to it. The difficulty
for Monteverdi is that seven- and eleven-syllable lines are less well
suited to lyrical moments than other line lengths, in part because of
the number of syllables but also because of the multiple positions of
their internal accents: this explains why he breaks these lines down into
smaller segments and also engages in an unusual amount of text repetition. But while his musical rhetoric certainly presents the text in an
effective way, it also contributes to the characterization. Just as Poppea
takes the lead in the declamatory passages, so does she in the more lyrical ones, not least in terms of the contrast between Nerone's somewhat
indulgent triple-times and her sturdy duple-time (at *Signor, sempre mi
vedi*). Poppea is the consummate seductress, leading her lover by the
nose just as she does the audience.

SENECA'S DEATH

Given the lack of strong metrical cues in the libretto and Monteverdi's
evident tendency to treat it flexibly both line by line and in terms of reor-
dering the verses—as well as repeating phrases at various distances from
their first utterances—it is hard to predict his response to the text at any
given moment. These fluid musical shifts also mean that the music of
L'incoronazione can sometimes present mixed, even confusing, messages.
The 1643 *scenario* works quite hard to paint Seneca in a positive light,
and more so, in fact, than the opera itself, where he has already been
undermined by the soldiers (in I.2) as a pedant, a panderer, and a fortune
hunter. He then offers cold comfort to Ottavia in Act I, scene 6: according
to Valletto, what the "old windbag" sells as philosophical mysteries are
mere songs (*le vende per misteri, e son canzoni*), an image that Monteverdi
underscores by having Valletto literally sing a brief but jolly triple-time
"song" over a repeating ground-bass pattern drawn from contemporary
dance music (the *ciaccona*).

But if triple-time and some kind of song go hand in hand, how might we
best read Act II, scene 3, where Seneca says farewell to his *famigliari* prior
to committing suicide?

Amici, è giunta l'ora	7	Friends, the hour has come
di praticare in fatti	7	to practice in deed
quella virtù che tanto celebrai.	11	that virtue which I so much celebrated.
Breve angoscia è la morte,	7	Death is brief anguish,
5 un sospir peregrino esce dal core,	11	a wandering sigh leaves the heart,
ov'è stato molt'anni,	7	where it has stayed for many years
quasi in ospizio, come forestiero,	11	like a guest, as a stranger,
e sen vola all'Olimpo,	7	and flies towards Olympus,
della felicità soggiorno vero.	11	the true resting-place of happiness.

Famigliari

10 Non morir, Seneca, nò.	8t	Do not die, Seneca, no.

Uno [de' famigliari]

Questa vita è dolce troppo,	8	This life is too sweet,
questo ciel troppo sereno,	8	this sky too serene,
ogni amaro, ogni veleno	8	all bitterness and poison
finalmente è lieve intoppo.	8	finally is a light burden.

Famigliari

15 Io per me morir non vuò.	8t	For myself, I would not die.
Non morir, Seneca, nò.	8t	Do not die, Seneca, no.

Uno [de' famigliari]

Se mi corco al sonno lieve	8	If I lie down to light sleep
mi risveglia in sul mattino,	8	I wake up in the morning,
ma un avel di marmo fino	8	but a tomb of fine marble
20 mai non dà quel che riceve.	8	never yields up what it receives.

Famigliari

Io per me morir non vuò.	8t	For myself, I would not die.
Non morir, Seneca, nò.	8t	Do not die, Seneca, no.

Seneca

Itene tutti a prepararmi il bagno,	11	Go, all of you, to prepare the bath for me,
che se la vita corre	7	for if life runs by
25 come il rivo fluente,	7	like the flowing river,
in un tepido rivo	7	in a warm river
questo sangue innocente io vò che vada	11	I wish this innocent blood to run
a imporporarmi del morir la strada.	11	so as to empurple for me the path to death.

One has to assume that Seneca's preparations for his death are a serious matter, and as a low bass voice, he has an appropriate gravitas. Pallade (Pallas Athene) has already taken his side in Act I, scene 8, and as the goddess promises there, her messenger, Mercurio (Mercury), tells him in Act II, scene 1 that he is to die, such that when the actual order from Nerone is delivered by Liberto in the next scene, Seneca is well prepared, much to Liberto's surprise. In keeping with his stoic position, Seneca welcomes Mercurio's news, singing twice in triple-time, first to declare how happy he is (O *me felice*) and second to pronounce that death is a blessed fate (*L'uscir di vita è una beata sorte*); Mercurio responds in like manner as he tells Seneca to prepare himself joyfully for his journey to the heavens (*Lieto dunque t'accingi / al celeste viaggio*), and then Liberto establishes a triple-time refrain inviting the philosopher to die happy (*Mori felice*). Seneca's tendency to sing in triple-time at key moments continues through scene 2 to scene 3, which begins, precisely, in lyrical mode as he tells his friends that the hour has come for him to die (*Amici, amici, è giunta, è giunta l'ora*). Again, Monteverdi seems to be responding to rhetorical cues within *versi sciolti*—the opening vocative (*Amici*)—as well as engaging in what one might call word painting (an upward roulade on *vola* as Seneca speaks of how the soul "flies" toward Olympus). Or perhaps the triple-time just signifies a calm acceptance as Seneca, true to his philosophical principles, welcomes death.

The *famigliari*, however, present a somewhat different case. Monteverdi reorders the libretto slightly and also maintains the trio texture throughout:

> line 10: *Non morir, Seneca, nò.*
> line 15: *Io per me morir non vuò*
> Ritornello
> lines 11–14: *Questa vita è dolce troppo* (set for all three Famigliari)
> Ritornello
> lines 17–20: *Se mi corco al sonno lieve* (same music as for lines 11–14)
> line 21 (= 15): *Io per me morir non vuò* (same music as for line 15)
> line 22 (= 10): *Non morir, Seneca, nò* (same music as for line 10)
> Ritornello
> line 23 (Seneca): *Itene tutti . . .*

The palindromic structure (lines 10, 15 . . . 15, 10) works nicely, meaning that the *famigliari* begin and end with their plea for Seneca not to die (*Non morir, Seneca, nò*). Monteverdi sets this as the contrapuntal elaboration of a rising chromatic line in a manner that he had associated with the Holy Cross in a five-voice motet, "Christe adoramus te," that he published in 1620. To make an association here between Seneca and Christ is obvious enough, and it is only slightly undermined by Monteverdi's use of more or less the same music (this time for three voices, as with the *famigliari*) in a clearly parodic madrigal, "Non partir, ritrosetta," in his Eighth Book of madrigals of 1638 (the *Madrigali guerrieri, et amorosi*). "Non partir, ritrosetta" draws on the Venetian tradition of the *giustiniana*, where three lascivious old men complain about the reluctance of a pretty young girl to yield to their sexual advances: the chromaticism comes where the men complain that she does not hear their laments.

So far, so (almost) good. However, the eight-syllable lines in the *famigliari*'s subsequent two stanzas (*Questa vita è dolce troppo*) create difficulties. This meter's typical accents (on the third, fifth, and seventh syllables) more or less force Monteverdi to adopt a triple-time dance pattern that also appears in the ritornello prior to each stanza; we find it also in the eight-syllable lines of Nutrice's *Se Neron perso ha l'ingegno* in Act I, scene 5 (see above). But while the dance rhythms, and the fast(er) tempo inevitably associated with them, fit the immediate sentiments expressed by the *famigliari*'s extolling of the pleasures of life, contrary to Seneca's teaching, they seem less appropriate for the overall mood of this somber scene. The incongruity is still more striking when the same ritornello returns (after the final *Non morir, Seneca, nò*) before Seneca's closing recitative: it is difficult to know what is meant to happen onstage during this ritornello, and Seneca's final remarks need to work quite hard to restore gravity to the situation. Not for nothing do the 1656 libretto and the Naples score add ten lines of additional text (in *versi sciolti*) for Seneca immediately prior to his ordering the *famigliari* to leave (*Itene tutti*).

It is not surprising that some of the sources for *L'incoronazione* mark this whole scene to be cut—although that may also have been for religious reasons—despite the fact that removing it leaves Seneca without an ending. There are two separate problems here. The first is that Busenello's eight-syllable lines for the *famigliari* have painted Monteverdi into a tight rhythmic corner; the second and more general one is that members of the same class of musical signs (in triple-time) can appear to mean quite different things—by virtue of the metric, syntactical, semantic, or rhetorical cues that prompt them—in ways that cannot always be clearly distinguished in, or by way of, performance. Although the ears of listeners at the time may have been more sensitively attuned to nuances now lost to us today, it is not clear that musical meaning was any more transparent. This is one reason why *L'incoronazione* is so slippery—not just because of its plot, but also because of its music.

Clearly Seneca's death is a climactic moment in *L'incoronazione*, although Busenello appears to have been somewhat confused about how best to respond to it. His additional scene (in the 1656 libretto) for Seneca and Virtù suggests some attempt to affirm the nobility of his final act. But his death is immediately undercut—and still more so absent an apotheosis—by a wholly inconsequential love-scene for Valletto and Damigella. There may be a technical reason for this: if that scene for Valletto and Damigella is done "in one"—that is, before a drop at the front of the stage—it makes it easier to change the main stage set back from Seneca's villa to the city of Rome. But whether this scene seeks to dissipate the tension of the prior one or to emphasize the degeneracy that surrounds it, it creates an awkward disjunction that is emphasized still more by the next, for Nerone and Lucano (discussed further, below). From this point on, as many have noted, *L'incoronazione* seems to lose whatever moral compass it might have had, posing some difficult questions about what the final point of the opera might be.

OTTAVIA IN EXILE

Matters would appear more straightforward in the case of Empress Ottavia, who seems to be one of countless wronged women left to lament their fate on the operatic stage. In terms of casting the role, we should probably remember that the "real" Octavia was some twenty-two years old at her exile and death—Nero was twenty-four and Poppaea thirty-two—and the singer who played her, Anna Renzi, was about the same age. One model was the protagonist of Monteverdi's *Arianna*: *Lasciatemi morire* (Let me die), she cries on discovering that she has been abandoned on the island of Naxos by perfidious Teseo. Just as Virginia Andreini moved her audience to tears as Arianna, so did Anna Renzi as Ottavia, it seems. But while Arianna's story at least had a happy ending steered by Amore—the god Bacchus is moved by her weeping and leads her to a celestial marriage—Ottavia's does not.

She appears just three times in the opera—less often than one would expect for a role allocated to so prominent a singer, but Renzi may have had more to do in the other opera of the season at the Teatro SS. Giovanni e Paolo, as Aretusa in *La finta savia*. In Act I, scenes 5–6, Ottavia laments her situation as a scorned queen (*Disprezzata regina*) and as one of the miserable sex of women who, although born free by nature and the heavens, end up in marital chains (*O delle donne miserabil sesso: / se la natura e 'l cielo / libere ci produce, / il matrimonio c'incatena serve*). The more misogynist members of the Incogniti may not have been sympathetic to so feminist a plea, but clearly the opera's audiences were meant to be. Ottavia is humiliated by Nerone's behavior with Poppea; she refuses the pragmatic advice of her nurse to take a lover; and she finds little comfort in Seneca's attempt to persuade her that a stoic acceptance of fate is the best option.

By Ottavia's third appearance—in Act III, scene 6 (or scene 7, depending on where Arnalta's scene comes)—she is at the lowest of ebbs, alone on stage bidding a sad farewell:

	Addio Roma, addio patria, amici addio.	11	Farewell Rome, farewell fatherland, friends, farewell.
	Innocente da voi partir convengo.	11	Innocent, I am required to leave you.
	Vado a patir l'esilio in pianti amari,	11	I go to suffer exile in bitter tears,
	navigo disperata i sordi mari.	11	I sail, desperate, the deaf seas.
5	L'aria, che d'ora in ora	7	The air which from time to time
	riceverà i miei fiati,	7	will receive my breaths,
	li porterà, per nome del cor mio,	11	will carry them in the name of my heart
	a veder, a baciar le patrie mura,	11	to see, to kiss, my native walls,
	ed io starò solinga,	7	and I will stand alone,
10	alternando le mosse ai pianti, ai passi,	11	alternating my movements between tears and footsteps,
	insegnando pietade ai tronchi, e ai sassi.	11	teaching pity to tree trunks and to rocks.
	. . .		. . .

Monteverdi's setting captures perfectly her painful hesitations (*A-a-a-addio Roma, a-a-addio patria, a-amici, amici addio*) and her poignant resignation at desolate exile. There are no rhetorical triple-time passages here or most anywhere else in Ottavia's music in the opera: like the noble Penelope for the bulk of *Il ritorno d'Ulisse in patria*, she has nothing much to sing about.

Ottavia's laments in Act I, scene 5 and Act III, scene 6 follow a typical pattern already established in the *Lamento d'Arianna*: a benighted noblewoman bemoans her state, rails against the cause of her misfortunes (be it a man or the gods), but then regrets her outburst, recanting such strong feelings and turning to a more appropriately submissive form of womanly voice. The musical recitative responds in typical ways, moving from plaintiveness to more energetic gestures to resignation. The problem with Ottavia, however, is that despite her claims in "Addio Roma, addio patria, amici addio," she is hardly "innocent." Her second appearance in *L'incoronazione*, in Act II, scene 7, is the most problematic, for here she blackmails Ottone into assassinating Poppea (if he refuses, she will denounce him to Nerone for attempted seduction). Given that the last time we saw Ottavia she was asking Seneca to plead her case in the senate while she would go to offer prayers at the temple, it is a strange change of tack, and one scarcely calculated to gain our sympathy.

Clearly the issue caused concerns for Busenello in his 1656 libretto, as it did also for the creator(s) of the Naples score. Both contain additional material for Ottavia around here. Act II, scene 7 ends with a further speech for her after Ottone has left to prepare himself to carry out the dastardly deed:

Vattene pure: la vendetta è un cibo	11	Go then: vengeance is a dish
che col sangue inimico si condisce.	11	flavored with an enemy's blood.
Della spenta Poppea su 'l monumento,	11	On the tomb of the dead Poppea,
quasi a felice mensa,	7	as at a happy banquet,
prenderò così nobile alimento.	11	shall I take such noble nourishment.

(The Naples score, but not the 1656 libretto, continues in similarly vindictive vein, leading to a two-stanza text that is, however, not set strophically.) While still not gaining our compassion, this addition has the virtue, at least, of emphasizing Ottavia's vengeful bloodlust.

The Naples score also includes a soliloquy for Ottavia preceding Ottone's entrance in Act II, scene 6 (his own soliloquy moment). This paints her in a much more sympathetic light, with a text that includes a passage that becomes a varied refrain throughout the scene (in italic, below):

Eccomi quasi priva	7	Here am I almost deprived
dell'impero e 'l consorte,	7	of empire and of my consort,
ma, lasso me, non priva	7	but, alas, not deprived
del ripudio, e di morte.	7	of repudiation and of death.
Martiri, o m'uccidete,	7	*Suffering, oh kill me,*
o speranze alla fin, non m'affliggete.	11	*o hopes at an end, do not afflict me.*
Neron, Nerone mio,	7	Nerone, my Nerone,

chi mi ti toglie, oh dio,	7	who takes you away from me, oh god,
come ti perdo, ohimè,	7t	how do I lose you, alas,
cadde l'affetto tuo, mancò la fè?	11t	how did your affection decline, your faith fall lacking?
. . .		. . .

This text is unlikely to be by Busenello, and the music is almost certainly not by Monteverdi, though it plays well enough with mid seventeenth-century conventions. Most striking is the treatment of the *Martiri, o m'uccidete* couplet (the words change at its two subsequent appearances, although the music remains the same). This is in a lyrical triple-time—a style hardly ever associated with Ottavia elsewhere in the opera—and is based on a recurring bass pattern treated almost as a ground or ostinato, being repeated over and over again. The pattern is a version of the descending (minor) tetrachord, moving stepwise down the four notes from tonic to dominant (*do–sol*), that Monteverdi and others were associating with lament from the 1630s on: one classic example is Monteverdi's own *Lamento della ninfa* in his Eighth Book of madrigals (1638). This pattern is often treated as emblematic in the rest of the seventeenth century and beyond, whether in its diatonic form (four notes) or filled in chromatically (six notes within the same tonic–dominant span): Dido's lament from Purcell's *Dido and Aeneas* ("When I am laid in earth") uses as a strict ground bass the chromatic form with a cadential extension.

This is a lyrical mode of lament quite different from the heightened oratorical "speech" of the *Lamento d'Arianna* and of much of Ottavia's music in *L'incoronazione*. It also poses problems, being arguably more powerful musically, but moving still further beyond the bounds of verisimilitude. Moreover, of all the higher-class characters in *L'incoronazione*, Ottavia is the one least likely to "sing": Poppea and Nerone do so because they are in love; Seneca because (we hope) he has his eyes on higher things; and Ottone because, well, he is feeble. A Roman empress should be made of sterner stuff, and for the most part in *L'incoronazione* she is. We do not know who added that scene for Ottavia in the Naples score, or why: perhaps it was to fill out the character (as it does); perhaps it was to give the singer a chance to display a greater vocal and dramatic range (as it also does). But it serves to point up a typical paradox: stern, and therefore musically restricted, characters still need to generate audience sympathy, for which one needs musical expansiveness.

The printed libretto associated with the Naples performance (1651) also includes a two-stanza text for Ottavia inserted in Act I, scene 5—"Lingua mia, non tanto ardire" ($a^8b^8b^8a^8a^8a^8$)—which suggests a similar lyric impulse, though no music survives. This production clearly sought to rethink the role of Ottavia (we do not know who sang it there). Indeed the argument made in the dedication of that libretto almost turns her into a would-be title role for the opera: Empress Ottavia, abandoned at the peak of her felicity and repudiated by Nerone, has left the Adriatic (Venice) to reach the shores of the Tyrrhenian Sea (Naples) so that she might recuperate from her misadventures. However, the expansion of the character helps make a broader point: we might reasonably follow Valletto's accusation against Seneca, that the purported mysteries of opera are mere "songs" (e son canzoni), but those songs are, of course, what makes opera work. The question is what one should do with them.

ECSTASIES OF LOVE

All these various additions and alterations to Act II in the Naples score and in the 1656 libretto—and also cuts marked in the Venice score—suggest that L'incoronazione somewhat loses its way in the middle of the opera. That libretto also includes another additional scene immediately after the one for Nerone and Lucano: this time for Nerone and Poppea, where he praises her eyes brighter than the day and then says that he wishes himself to be a breath of air that might therefore pass through her beloved mouth (in quella bocca amata) so that he might kiss her heart. This scene appears to have been intended for the first performance (it is present in the 1643 scenario), though no music survives; it would seem to add nothing to the drama save keeping the two characters present in the eyes of the audience, given that they do not otherwise appear together in the act. Yet this juxtaposition of eyes and mouth plays into another Incogniti debate about how true beauty might best be perceived in another, whether by sight (which might in fact be deceptive) or by sound. Given that the mouth, and the breath that passes through it, are also what give life to song, L'incoronazione starts to become fixated, it seems, on the power of various types of song liberated, it also seems, by Seneca's death.

Poppea makes the point in her exchange with Arnalta in Act II, scene 10:

Hor che Seneca è morto,	7	Now that Seneca is dead,
Amor, ricorro a te:	7t	Amor, I turn to you:
guida mie spemi in porto,	7	steer my hopes to harbor,
fammi sposa al mio re.	7t	make me the bride of my king.

Monteverdi sets this in a languid triple-time, perhaps encouraged by the *versi tronchi*. The potential lapse in verisimilitude is quickly excused by Arnalta's following remark, that Poppea spends all her time making up songs about her wedding: *Pur sempre su le nozze / canzoneggiando vai.* That *canzoneggiando* is important, because it is precisely what Poppea is doing—singing, not speaking.

It is common enough for operatic characters to use such verbs associated with speech as *dire, parlare,* or the like. Words that draw attention to the fact of their singing are more revealing, however, in terms both of particular dramatic moments and of broader anxieties underlying the genre. We have already seen the trick in Nutrice's *accenti* that Ottavia should heed in Act I, scene 5. Busenello repeats it in Act II, scene 5 as Nerone celebrates with Lucano (the poet Lucan) Seneca's demise, an extravagant episode subjected to various cuts in the Venice score and then marked for deletion. It begins with the same line that Poppea will repeat later:

Hor che Seneca è morto,	7	Now that Seneca is dead,
cantiam, cantiam Lucano,	7	let us sing, let us sing, Lucano,
amorose canzoni	7	amorous songs
in lode d'un bel viso,	7	in praise of a fair face,
che di sua mano Amor nel cor, m'ha inciso.	11	which Amor with his hand has engraved upon my heart.

LUCANO

Cantiam, Signor, cantiamo	7	Let us sing, Sire, let us sing
di quel viso ridente,	7	of that smiling face
che spira glorie, ed influisce amori.	11	which breathes glories and influences cupids.

Again the references to characters actually singing mitigate any problems of verisimilitude, and Monteverdi takes advantage of it. Although the libretto allocates lines separately to the two characters, he treats them first as a sequence of duets as Nerone and Lucano—both poets according to the historical record—vie with each other to produce the most virtuosic display in ways that take on the air of a musical orgy. Some directors have taken this as a cue for a homoerotic one as well, but that is another matter altogether.

While this scene cues song, the libretto does not provide sufficient strophic texts to support it. Once more, Monteverdi is left to his own initiative based on whatever cues he can find in the poetry. And he, too, seems sensitive to the sight/sound issue. Nerone and Lucano begin with "amorous songs in praise of a fair face" but soon graduate to that face's most important feature:

Cantiam, di quella bocca	7	Let us sing of that mouth
a cui l'India e l'Arabia	7	to which India and Arabia
e perle consacrò, donò gli odori.	11	both consecrated pearls and gifted perfumes.
Bocca, ahi destin, che se ragiona o ride,	11	Mouth, ah destiny, which whether it speaks or smiles,
con invisibil arme punge, e all'alma	11	strikes with invisible weapons, and to the soul
dona felicità mentre l'uccide.	11	gives happiness while it kills it.
Bocca, che se mi porge	7	Mouth that, if it offers me
lasciveggiando il tenero rubino,	11	sensuously the tender ribbon,
m'inebria il cor di nettare divino.	11	makes my heart drunk on divine nectar.

Again, the 1656 libretto allocates these words to Nerone, but Monteverdi starts by setting them for him and Lucano, treating the fourth line (*Bocca, ahi destin, che se ragiona o ride*) as the cue to shift to a sensuous triple-time. There is not much within the structure of these *versi sciolti* to prompt the move save perhaps for a loosely organized rhyme-scheme from line 4 (*ABAcDD*), and the subdivision of that text into two three-line groupings each beginning *Bocca*. Yet clearly the music is designed to have an effect: Nerone is reduced to a spluttering incoherence (with repeated ejaculations of *ahi, ahi, ahi, ahi destin!*) that Lucano then identifies as his reveling in the ecstasies of love (*Tu vai, Signor, tu vai / nell'estasi d'amor deliciando*). But Nerone needs just a moment of recuperation (helped by a ritornello) before returning to songful praise—this time on his own—of Poppea's "precious ribbons," her loving lips (*Son rubin preziosi / i tuoi labbri amorosi*). Here, at last, Busenello provides two stanzas of text in the 1656 libretto, although only the first is set to music in the Venice score (the second is included in the Naples one), presumably because we have already had enough "singing" in the scene.

The absence of a strongly defined poetic structure at *Bocca, ahi destin, che se ragiona o ride* clashes with Monteverdi's evident intent to produce an extended musical section here. Thus he adopts a technique also found in his chamber madrigals as well as elsewhere in *L'incoronazione*, such as in the songful portions of Nerone's and Poppea's exchanges in Act I, scene 10 and Act III, scene 5. In cases where a loosely defined text or portion thereof requires a greater degree of musical focus, he quite often establishes a bass pattern to be repeated as an ostinato, either exactly or with some manner of variation. As with the Naples setting of Ottavia's refrain in her added scene in Act II noted above, this particular passage for Nerone in Act II, scene 5 is based on four notes slowly descending stepwise in equal measure from tonic to dominant, but this time in a major key rather than a minor one (so, *do–ti–la–sol*). That pattern is heard nine times in this passage—ten if one counts a slightly different version of it at the beginning—and has a definite hypnotic effect, the regular repetitions giving the feeling of time standing still.

The same ostinato recurs in *L'incoronazione*, most obviously in Nerone and Poppea's final duet of the opera, once more in a sensuous triple-time:

Pur ti miro, pur ti godo,	8	Now I gaze upon you, now I enjoy you,
pur ti stringo, pur t'annodo,	8	now I embrace you, now I entwine you,
più non peno, più non moro,	8	no longer do I suffer, no longer do I die,
o mia vita, o mi tesoro.	8	o my life, o my treasure.

POPPEA

Io son tua . . .	→	I am yours . . .

NERONE

Tuo son io . . .	8	Yours am I . . .

POPPEA, NERONE

speme mia, dillo, dì.	8t	my hope, say it, say.
Tu sei pur[e] l'idol mio,	8	You are my idol,
sì, mio ben, sì, mio cor, mia vita, sì.	11t	yes, my love, yes, my heart, my life, yes.

The text is a bit of a mishmash—it is most unlikely to be by Busenello—but the music tries to even it out, dividing lines between the characters and repeating the first four lines at the end to produce an ABA form. As for the

A section, it has eight statements of that descending four-note bass (one is slightly varied). In Baroque music, a ground bass can just be a constructivist technique without any semiotic implications: the minor-key descending four-note pattern seen in Ottavia's refrain—seemingly associated there with lament—also appears in Arnalta's lullaby, sung to Poppea in Act II, scene 10. The major key version heard in Act II, scene 5 and at the end of Act III may be equally neutral: it is just a way of building up an extended piece of music. Yet whether the bass line is structural or meaningful, the musical cross-reference seems significant: what was first associated with the praise of Poppea's mouth—her *bocca*—now emerges straight from it. Much of *L'incoronazione* seems concerned with singing and speaking, but it is clear what must win out in the end.

This is not how Busenello chose to end his libretto, at least when he presented it for literary consumption in 1656. There—as also seems to have occurred at the first performance(s) of the opera in 1643—Nerone leads Poppea to her coronation, the consuls and tribunes proclaim the empire's loyalty to her, Amore descends with a chorus of cupids (adding his own crown to the one already given to her), and he asks his mother, Venere (Venus), to agree that Poppea be proclaimed a goddess. Amore (in the Naples score, a chorus of cupids) then has the final word:

Hor cantiamo giocondi,	7	Now let us sing happily,
festeggiamo ridenti in terra e in cielo,	11	let us celebrate with smiles on earth and in heaven,
il gaudio sovrabbondi,	7	may joy abound,
e in ogni clima, in ogni regione	11	and in every zone, in every region
si senta rimbombar "Poppea e Nerone."	11	let there resound "Poppea and Nerone."

The scene is expanded still further in the Naples score by way of a central duet for Nerone and Poppea ("Su, su, Venere ed Amore"). For Busenello to have a final celebration in the heavens was by no means unusual in opera of the period. It also brings things full circle from the prologue: Amore's object lesson has run its course and has ended, inevitably, with his triumph. But the final love-duet—present in both surviving scores of *L'incoronazione*—brings things back down to earth, perhaps in a musically satisfying way (that duet is truly ravishing) but certainly not in any moral one.

The changes evidently made to *L'incoronazione* in its various textual and musical sources suggest that different aspects of it raised sufficient concerns to warrant revision, and sometimes several times over. What is not clear is the extent to which these concerns might have hinged on issues of morality. Whether *L'incoronazione* is an immoral opera may well be a foolish question, and one wonders just how many, if any, members of its first audiences would have been troubled by it. Modern critics necessarily have a harder time given the sterner values invested in "great" musical works, at which point they will often resort to claims that *L'incoronazione* engages with some form of dramatic irony, where nothing is quite what it seems. The difficulty with this reading, however, is that music in general tends to resist ironic interpretation: its power draws us in, suspending rational judgment to the point where we must accept that even the devil can sometimes have the best tunes. The easy excuse for *L'incoronazione* is that it comes so near the beginnings of opera that one should forgive its apparent problems. Probably the better argument, however, is that these problems are endemic to opera as a genre, at which point we should not be surprised that they were raised so early in its history. Certainly, later operas were forced to tackle them head on.

FURTHER READING

The most thorough discussion of *L'incoronazione di Poppea* and its complex sources is in Ellen Rosand, *Monteverdi's Last Operas: A Venetian Trilogy* (Berkeley and Los Angeles: University of California Press, 2007); a gentler introduction, also covering Monteverdi's other dramatic works across his career, is offered by Tim Carter, *Monteverdi's Musical Theatre* (New Haven, CT: Yale University Press, 2002). Ellen Rosand, *Opera in Seventeenth-Century Venice: The Creation of a Genre* (Berkeley and Los Angeles: University of California Press, 1991) offers an overview of the period, while Jonathan E. Glixon and Beth L. Glixon, *Inventing the Business of Opera: The Impresario and His World in Seventeenth-Century Venice* (Oxford and New York: Oxford University Press, 2006) covers the opera industry, albeit for a slightly later period than Monteverdi's. My comments on gender owe an obvious debt to Wendy Heller, *Emblems of Eloquence: Opera and Women's Voices in Seventeenth-Century Venice* (Berkeley and Los Angeles: University of California Press, 2003). For the singers at the Teatro SS. Giovanni e Paolo in the 1642–43 season, see Roberta Ziosi, "I libretti di Ascanio Pio di Savoia: un esempio di teatro musicale a Ferrara nella prima metà del Seicento," in *Musica in torneo nell'Italia del Seicento*, edited by Paolo Fabbri (Lucca: Libreria Musicale Italiana, 1999), 135–65. The standard edition of *L'incoronazione di Poppea* is the one edited by Alan Curtis (London: Novello, 1989).

CHAPTER 3

Nicola Francesco Haym and George Frideric Handel, *Giulio Cesare in Egitto* (London, 1724)

GEORGE FRIDERIC HANDEL (MEZZOTINT BY CHARLES TURNER, AFTER HOGARTH)

William Hogarth's portrait of Handel (1725) shows the composer at the time of his first run of successful operas in London at the King's Theatre, Haymarket.
AKG-IMAGES.

Giulio Cesare [Julius Caesar], Roman emperor: Francesco Bernardi ("Senesino"; alto castrato)
Cleopatra, Queen of Egypt, sister of Tolomeo: Francesca Cuzzoni (soprano)

Cornelia, wife of Pompey: Anastasia Robinson (alto)

Sesto, son of Pompey and Cornelia: Margherita Durastanti (soprano)

Tolomeo [Ptolemy], King of Egypt, brother of Cleopatra: Gaetano Berenstadt (alto castrato)

Achilla, head of the Egyptian army and Tolomeo's counsellor: Giuseppe Maria Boschi (bass)

Nireno, confidant of Cleopatra: Giuseppe Bigonzi (alto castrato)

Curio, Roman tribune: Mr. Lagarde (= John Laguerre; bass)

Caesar's soldiers, Egyptians

SETTING: Egypt, 48–47 BCE.

SOURCE: Giacomo Francesco Bussani (*fl* 1673–1680), *Giulio Cesare in Egitto*, libretto (1676) for Antonio Sartorio, revised 1685.

First performed: London, King's Theatre, 20 February 1724. The opera had twelve or so performances from then to 11 April. Handel revived it in January 1725 for ten performances, making various cuts and revisions (including the omission of Curio and rewriting Sesto—originally a trouser role, i.e., a male character played by a female singer—for the tenor Francesco Borosini), and then in January 1730 (eleven performances) and February 1732 (four).

ACT I. (Scenes 1–4: *A plain in Egypt with an old bridge over a branch of the Nile.*) A chorus welcomes Cesare ("Viva, viva il nostro Alcide"), who enters with the Roman tribune, Curio, to celebrate his victory over Pompey ("Presti omai l'Egizia terra"). Pompey's wife and son, Cornelia and Sesto, sue for peace, which Cesare grants. However, Tolomeo, joint ruler of Egypt with his sister, Cleopatra, has preempted matters by seeking to ingratiate himself with Cesare: his henchman Achilla delivers Pompey's head on a platter, and Cesare is outraged ("Empio, dirò tu sei"). Curio, who has long been in love with Cornelia, offers her his hand, but she is far too distraught ("Priva son d'ogni conforto"), while Sesto vows revenge ("Svegliatevi nel core"). (Scenes 5–6: *A small room [Gabinetto].*) Cleopatra deplores the news (from her servant, Nireno) of Tolomeo's actions, and when her brother enters, she taunts him as an "effeminate lover" ("Non disperar, chi sa"). Achilla reports on Cesare's cold reception of Tolomeo's "gift" and promises to assassinate the Roman emperor if he can have Cornelia as a reward; Tolomeo vows revenge, also fearing that Cesare wants to steal Egypt from him ("L'empio, sleale, indegno"). (Scenes 7–8: *Cesare's camp.*) Cesare, alongside Curio, pays homage to Pompey's remains in an urn atop a mound of war trophies. Cleopatra enters with Nireno and pretends to be the queen's servant, Lidia, who has been mistreated by Tolomeo; Cesare and Curio are entranced (Cesare, "Non è si vago e bello"), while Cleopatra sees the advantage in having Cesare aid her cause against her brother ("Tutto può donna vezzosa"). Cornelia (observed from the side by Cleopatra and Nireno) approaches the urn and laments ("Nel tuo seno, amico sasso"), then seeks to kill herself. She is prevented by Sesto, who promises revenge, much to his mother's pride and delight. Cleopatra (as Lidia) offers to help, and Sesto takes heart ("Cara speme, questo core"); the queen is left alone to contemplate the thickening plot ("Tu la mia stella sei"). (Scenes 9–11: *An atrium in Tolomeo's palace.*) Tolomeo and Cesare exchange diplomatic niceties while cursing each other in asides; the king invites Cesare to stay in the royal palace, but the emperor is wary ("Va tacito e nascosto"). Achilla leads in Cornelia and Sesto, and the latter challenges Tolomeo, who orders him imprisoned, while Cornelia should be forced to work in the garden of the seraglio; Tolomeo leaves, hinting in an aside that he has his own plans for Cornelia. Achilla offers to aid Cornelia and Sesto's escape if she will wed him, but they are outraged at the idea of a Roman marrying a "vile Egyptian," despite Achilla's admission of love ("Tu sei il cor di questo core"). Cornelia and Sesto are left in despair (duet, "Son nata a lagrimar").

Act II. (Scenes 1–2: *A garden of cedars with a prospect of Mount Parnassus, on which is seated the Palace of Virtue.*) Cleopatra and Nireno prepare a set-piece performance to seduce Cesare. He enters, captivated by the sound of instruments; the set opens to reveal Mount Parnassus, with "Lidia" as Virtue surrounded by the nine Muses ("V'adoro, pupille"); and Cesare is enraptured ("Se in fiorito ameno prato"). (Scenes 3–6: *A garden of the seraglio, next door to that of the wild beasts.*) Cornelia laments her fate ("Deh piangete, o mesti lumi") and is wooed unsuccessfully first by Achilla ("Se a me non sei crudele") and then by Tolomeo, who threatens her when she resists ("Sì, spietata, il tuo rigore"). Cornelia decides to climb the wall into the menagerie so that she might be devoured by the beasts therein, but Sesto enters and prevents her, once more promising to kill Tolomeo. Nireno arrives with orders to lead Cornelia to Tolomeo but offers to conceal Sesto so that the boy might take his revenge, which gives Cornelia some hope ("Cessa omai di sospirare"). Sesto, left alone, summons up his courage ("L'angue offeso mai riposa"). (Scenes 7–8: *A pleasant spot* [*Luogo di delizie*].) Cleopatra (as "Lidia") prays to Venus to make her irresistible ("Venere bella") and decides to feign sleep for Cesare's arrival. He is still entranced by her, but is also shocked by her boldness in admitting her love for him as she "wakes." Curio enters to reveal that Cesare is betrayed and that assassins are pursuing him; Cleopatra urges him to flee, admitting her real identity, but this only emboldens him to fight ("Al lampo dell'armi") even as the conspirators are heard offstage clamoring for his death. Cleopatra is left alone fearing for the future ("Se pietà di me non senti"). (Scenes 9–11: *A room in the seraglio.*) Tolomeo is fascinated by Cornelia ("Belle dee di questo core") and decides to take her to his bed. Sesto snatches Tolomeo's sword to prevent it, but he is caught by Achilla, who then reports that Cesare and Curio have been forced to jump off a high balcony in the palace into the sea, where they are presumed drowned, and that Cleopatra has fled to the Roman camp to pursue her revenge against her brother. Achilla then asks for his reward, Cornelia, but Tolomeo refuses and leaves, as Achilla realizes he has been betrayed. In despair at the news about Cesare, Sesto tries to kill himself but is prevented by Cornelia, and he recovers his courage ("L'aure che spira").

ACT III. (Scenes 1–3: *A wood near the city of Alexandria.*) Achilla decides to side with Cleopatra ("Dal fulgor di questa spada"). To the sound of a warlike "sinfonia" Cleopatra's and Tolomeo's soldiers fight. Tolomeo proclaims his victory over his sister ("Domerò la tua fierezza") and she is led off in chains, lamenting her fate but also resolving to pursue her brother beyond the grave ("Piangerò la sorte mia"). (Scenes 4–6: [*The same wood*] *with a view of the port.*) Cesare enters and blesses his fate for having been able to swim ashore, even as he wonders about the future and is dismayed at the sight of dead soldiers around him ("Aure, deh per pietà"). Sesto and Nireno, observed by Cesare, come across Achilla, who is lying near the port, mortally wounded. Achilla gives them a seal that will be recognized by a hundred soldiers, who will also show them a secret passage to Tolomeo's palace. He dies, and Sesto has his body thrown into the sea. Cesare reveals himself, takes the seal, and resolves to save Cornelia and Cleopatra or die in the attempt ("Quel torrente che cade dal monte"). Sesto is delighted that justice at last seems to prevail ("La giustizia ha già sull'arco"). (Scene 7: *Cleopatra's apartment.*) Cleopatra, under guard and surrounded by her handmaidens, is in despair, but her spirits start to lift at the sound of clashing arms, and still more as Cesare enters triumphant. After a brief reunion he leaves to complete his task, while Cleopatra celebrates having survived the storm ("Da tempeste il legno infranto"). (Scene 8: *A royal hall.*) Tolomeo forces himself on Cornelia, who draws a dagger as she resists. Sesto enters sword in hand, fights Tolomeo, and kills him, and Cornelia rejoices in their revenge ("Non ha più che temere"). (*Scena ultima* [9]: *The port of Alexandria.*) Cesare and Cleopatra enter in triumphal procession with their followers. Nireno and (a silent) Curio pay homage, and Sesto and Cornelia kneel before Cesare, who declares them to be his friends. Cornelia hands Cesare Tolomeo's crown and scepter, and he in turn passes them to Cleopatra, who proclaims her fealty to Rome. Cesare and Cleopatra vaunt their love ("Caro! Più amabile beltà"), and the chorus celebrates the return of joy and pleasure ("Ritorni omai nel nostro core").

IT IS HARD NOWADAYS to conceive of the sheer scale of the operatic enterprise in the seventeenth and eighteenth centuries, especially given the highly limited repertoire of most modern opera houses. Claudio Sartori's catalog of printed Italian librettos (operas, oratorios, serenatas, cantatas, and *balli*) up to 1800 lists well over 25,000 separate editions; the Albert Schatz Collection of opera librettos printed before 1800 at the Library of Congress, Washington, D.C., contains around 12,000, not counting duplicates. The burgeoning opera industry also created complex infrastructures of supply and demand that prompted a certain standardization of operatic subjects and the conventions by which they might be represented, both for ease of

production and to meet audience expectations. This also meant that composers working in the field of Italian opera could be relatively mobile across Europe—excluding France, which tended to adhere strongly to its own operatic traditions—and, if they were lucky, could find fame and fortune in the opera house without (albeit preferably with) the support of a patron.

George Frideric Handel's career, for example, took him from Germany (he was born in Halle on 23 February 1685) through Italy (with extended stays there from 1706 to early 1710) to England from autumn 1710 until his death on 14 April 1759: he resided there permanently from 1712 on and took British nationality in 1727. The move to London was not as strange as it might seem given his connections with the electoral court of Hanover, whence came King George I in 1714, then George II in 1727. Although Handel attracted royal and noble patrons, he also became intimately involved with Italian opera in London, dominating the field first at the King's Theatre, Haymarket, then at Covent Garden until, given financial pressures and also increasing competition from Italian rivals, he turned his attention to oratorio instead. He wrote some thirty-five operas for London, from *Rinaldo* (1711) to *Deidamia* (1741), as well as contributing to others and arranging so-called pasticcios, that is, operas concocted around a new libretto by cobbling together favorite arias drawn from other works.

The relative standardization of opera also meant that librettos that had established some kind of reputation, for whatever reason, could often be taken and set to new music to suit particular local circumstances defined in terms of audiences on the one hand, and of the singers contracted to put the work onstage, on the other. *Giulio Cesare in Egitto* is a case in point. For the libretto, Nicola Francesco Haym revised a text by Giacomo Francesco Bussani (*fl* 1673–1680) first set by Antonio Sartorio (Venice, 1676), incorporating changes made to it for a performance in Milan in 1685 (to unknown music). These revisions for Milan included the Parnassus scene at the beginning of Act II (in the original, Cleopatra is just in a music room, playing the spinet). Haym and Handel also made further changes to the text as the composition of the opera proceeded the year before the premiere. In particular, the early version of Act I drafted in the summer of 1723 has some significant differences, not least because the casting would later change: it seems that the soprano Margherita Durastanti (Sesto) was originally to be Cornelia; Tolomeo was to be played by the tenor Alexander Gordon, but he abandoned his operatic career in August, forcing a reallocation of the role to the castrato Gaetano Berenstadt (originally planned for Sesto); and Anastasia Robinson (Cornelia) was to be Cleopatra's cousin and confidante, Berenice (replaced by the character Nireno in the final version).

Giulio Cesare in Egitto was Handel's sixth opera for the so-called first Royal Academy. By now, he was working with a well-known team of singers. The star castrato Senesino (Francesco Bernardi), who performed Giulio Cesare, had taken the lead role in every Handel opera since *Radamisto* (1720); Francesca Cuzzoni (Cleopatra) joined the troupe at the King's Theatre, Haymarket, in 1723; and Anastasia Robinson, Margherita Durastanti, Giuseppe Maria Boschi, and John Laguerre were regulars on Handel's stage (Durastanti had sung for him much earlier in Rome, and Robinson's appearance in Handelian roles dated back to 1715, including creating that of Oriana in *Amadigi di Gaula*). The original cast of *Giulio Cesare in Egitto* is particularly close to that of *Ottone* (12 January 1723) and *Flavio, re de' Longobardi* (14 May 1723); the former included the first London role that Handel wrote for Gaetano Berenstadt, and it was also the cause of a famous argument between the composer and the star soprano Francesca Cuzzoni when he threatened to throw her out of the window for refusing to sing one of his arias. Senesino, Cuzzoni, and Boschi continued to perform in Handel's next operas, including *Tamerlano* (31 October 1724), *Rodelinda* (13 February 1725), *Scipione* (12 March 1726), and beyond.

The subjects of those operas, as with *Giulio Cesare in Egitto*, dealt with ancient history, whether of the Tartars, the Lombards, or the Romans, although in the 1730s Handel turned more to subjects drawn from romance epic, in particular Lodovico Ariosto's *Orlando furioso*. Thus the "real" Julius Caesar did indeed pursue the rebel Pompey to Egypt, only to find his head on a platter, and he then joined with Cleopatra in her campaign against her brother and co-regent (Ptolemy XIII) in the Siege of Alexandria and then the Battle of the Nile (47 BCE). Haym needed to rewrite history just slightly, not least as regards the manner of Ptolemy's actual death (Bussani has Tolomeo end up in chains). However, he took a freer hand in inventing and exploring what motivated these historical figures, and in particular—if inevitably—how Cleopatra made Caesar fall in love with her.

ARCADIAN REFORMS

The relatively free market for opera in the Baroque period inevitably prompted periodic attempts to control its abuses, particularly on the part of those who saw themselves as falling victim to them. The "Arcadian Academy," for example, was founded in Rome in 1690 for the reform and "purification" of Italian poetry, not least the opera libretto. It emerged like many such Roman gatherings from the circles of specific patrons, in this case Cardinal Pietro Ottoboni (also one of Handel's patrons when the composer was in Rome), although its influence spread widely through Italy and abroad. Among the librettists associated with the Arcadians were Ottoboni himself, Apostolo Zeno, Gian Vincenzo Gravina, Silvio Stampiglia, and Pietro Metastasio. Their spokesmen included Giovanni Maria Crescimbeni and Ludovico Muratori, who ranged widely in their attacks on the abuses of contemporary poetry, advocating a return to classical simplicity, in part via French models drawn from Corneille and Racine. In his *La bellezza della volgar poesia* (The Beauty of Vernacular Poetry; 1700), Crescimbeni reserved particularly harsh criticism for Giacinto Andrea Cicognini and his libretto for Francesco Cavalli's *Giasone* (Venice, 1649):

> with it he brought the end of acting, and consequently, of true and good comedy as well as tragedy. Since to stimulate to a greater degree with novelty the jaded taste of the spectators, equally nauseated by the vileness of comic things and the seriousness of tragic ones . . . [he] united them, mixing kings and heroes and other illustrious personages with buffoons and servants and the lowest men with unheard-of monstrousness. This farrago of characters was the reason for the complete ruin of the rules of poetry, which thus went into disuse such that not even locution was considered, which, forced to serve music, lost its purity, and became filled with idiocies. The careful deployment

of figures that ennoble oratory was neglected, and was for the most part restricted to terms of common, familiar speech, which is more appropriate for music; and finally the series of those short meters, commonly called *ariette*, which were sprinkled with a generous hand over the scenes, and the overwhelming impropriety of having characters speak in song completely removed from the compositions the power of the affections, and the means of moving them in the listeners.[1]

Save for the reference to an abundance of *ariette* in short meters, Crescimbeni could also have been talking about Busenello's *L'incoronazione di Poppea*, and one doubts that he would have approved of its questionable morality and other problems any more than in the case of *Giasone*.

Much of Crescimbeni's argument was a classic case of shutting the stable door after the horse had bolted: after all, not much could now be done about the impropriety of having characters "speak in song." However, the Arcadians could plausibly argue in favor of a more "moral" form of operatic art, and one adhering more closely to generic proprieties and stylistic decorum. As for all those *ariette*, however, the Arcadian solution—sensibly enough—was not banishment but regulation. The strophic and other structures adopted for "aria" poetry through the seventeenth century were strikingly varied. However, the Arcadians established a relatively standard pattern: aria texts would consist of two isometric strophes, usually of four or three lines each (seven- or eight-syllable lines tend to be preferred) with regular (and generally parallel) rhyme-schemes and each often ending with a *verso tronco* rhyming with its counterpart: we shall see multiple examples below. This meshes with the musical structure that was emerging to dominate opera in the early eighteenth century, the *da capo* aria, with one strophe each for the A and B sections.

Late Baroque and early Classical *opera seria* ("serious" opera), the genre normally considered to represent best the Arcadian reforms, has tended to gain a bad reputation, with its long sequences of arias decried as static and artificial. Critics often feel more comfortable with the *opera buffa* ("comic" opera) that emerged in the second quarter of the eighteenth century and seemed to present a more naturalistic, and also human, form of musical drama. It is true that the two genres are often distinct

---

1. Given in Ellen Rosand, *Opera in Seventeenth-Century Venice: The Creation of a Genre* (Berkeley and Los Angeles: University of California Press, 1991), 434 (my translation).

in terms of subject matter and didactic purpose: *opere serie* tend to be based on historical or pseudo-historical subject matter located in some ancient time, with noble characters invoking grand themes concerning honor and love. But they can contain comic elements—just as *opere buffe* can have serious ones—and they are not always as earnest as they might seem: like many operas, they often have an element of tongue-in-cheek self-awareness. Moreover, while the dramatic and musical conventions of *opera seria* might appear strict, they do not always turn out to be so in practice, and their formality allows deviations from them to make a strong effect by subverting audience expectations. This type of opera may not be the most natural in dramatic terms—for all its virtues and delights, opera can never be described as "natural"—but it can be very powerful indeed.

Adapting Bussani

Given that *Giulio Cesare in Egitto* adapts an earlier libretto from 1676, it reveals how *opera seria* of the second quarter of the eighteenth century transformed and codified forms and conventions that were more loosely defined earlier in the Baroque era. Handel's poet, Nicola Francesco Haym (1678–1729), moved from his native Rome to London in 1701, where he first became master of the chamber music to Wriothesley Russell, the second Duke of Bedford. He was a cellist and sometime composer but became better known as an adapter of Italian operas for the London stage, often in the form of pasticcios.

He was also associated with the first Royal Academy of Music, founded in 1719 to set Italian opera on a more permanent footing in London, with Handel as in effect its musical director, selecting repertoire, recruiting singers, and leading the orchestra. Productions included operas by Giovanni Bononcini, Attilio Ariosti, and Handel himself. Haym was to be the continuo cellist, but he became secretary of the Academy in 1722, which gave him primary responsibility for adapting librettos for Handel and other composers and for staging the operas each season.

Haym had moved on the periphery of the Arcadians during his time in Rome, but his work in London did not gain much approval from them: his critics accused him of being ignorant of belles-lettres and of sacrificing poetic artifice to the prevalent British taste—and the demands of the singers—for virtuoso arias as opposed to recitative. The criticism is unfair and also does an injustice to Haym's other interests as an editor, bibliographer, and historian. He managed to find a formula that worked well for London, and that seems to have suited Handel: they collaborated on at least six operas in the 1720s (as well as the earlier *Teseo* of 1713 and perhaps others).

While Haym's libretto for *Giulio Cesare in Egitto* might not be viewed as a model of the Arcadian reforms, the comparison with Giacomo Francesco Bussani's text, written for Antonio Sartorio just under fifty years before, still reveals some typical trends. In Bussani's Act I, scene 14, Cornelia approaches the temporary monument erected by Giulio Cesare in honor of her husband, Pompey (whose head Tolomeo has recently delivered on a platter). She is observed by Cleopatra and the queen's two servants, Rodisbe (her nurse) and Nireno, but is unaware of them. Cornelia vows revenge and takes up a sword to enter Tolomeo's palace but is abruptly halted by the arrival of her son, Sesto. However, the scene begins with her moving monologue:

	Nel tuo seno, amico sasso,	a^8	In your bosom, dear rock,
	sta sepolto il mio tesoro.	b^8	lies buried my beloved.
	Calamita del mio passo	a^8	A magnet to my footsteps
	è quel cenere, ch'adoro.	b^8	are those ashes, which I adore.
5	Solo brama il mio cor, che a te si volve,	C	My heart which turns to you seeks only
	misurar l'ore sue con quella polve.	C	to measure out its hours with this dust.
	Ma che! Vile, e negletta	7	But what! Abject and neglected
	sempre starai Cornelia?	7	shall Cornelia always be?

CLEOPATRA

	È Cornelia costei?	7	Is that Cornelia?

RODISBE

10	La moglie di Pompeo?	→	The wife of Pompey?

NIRENO

	Strano accidente!	11	Strange goings-on!

CORNELIA (*si porta a sceglier armi tra cumuli di arnesi guerrieri*) — (*moves to choose arms from the mound of military weapons*)

	Ah no! Tra questi arnesi	7	Ah no! From these weapons
	mi sceglierò l'usbergo.	7	shall I choose for myself the cuirass.

Vestirò di lorica il molle seno.	11	I will clothe my soft breast with a breastplate.
E con vindice ferro	7	And with vengeful sword
15 contro di Tolomeo dentro la reggia . . .	11	will I [fight] against Tolomeo within the palace . . .
SESTO (*che sopraviene*)		(*who arrives*)
Madre. Ferma, che fai?	→	Mother. Stop, what are you doing?

Cornelia's opening monologue consists of four eight-syllable lines and a closing rhyming couplet (two eleven-syllable lines): the regular rhyme with mixed meter is not unusual for "closed" sections in opera librettos around the third quarter of the seventeenth century. The text then moves into flexible *versi sciolti* (seven- and eleven-syllable lines) as Cornelia stirs herself from mourning, with a typical *Ma che!* (But what!). Cleopatra and her companions comment on the scene, also reminding the audience of who is who on the stage. Cornelia then decides to take action, although Sesto intervenes, again with a typical vocative–imperative–question formulation: *Madre. Ferma, che fai?* (Mother. Stop, what are you doing?).

For Act I, scene 8 of Handel's *Giulio Cesare in Egitto*, Haym cuts these sixteen lines down to ten. The poetic structure is simplified, moving (after the opening) mostly in clear-cut seven-syllable lines, and Haym also avoids such unusual words as *usbergo* (cuirass) and *lorica* (breastplate):

1	Nel tuo seno, amico sasso,	a^8	In your bosom, dear rock,
2	sta sepolto il mio tesoro.	b^8	lies buried my beloved.
7	Ma che! Vile, e negletta	7	But what! Abject and neglected
8	sempre starai Cornelia?	7	shall Cornelia always be?
	CLEOPATRA		
9	È Cornelia, costei,	7	Is that Cornelia,
(10a)	la moglie di Pompeo?	7	the wife of Pompey?
	CORNELIA		
11	Ah no! Tra questi arnesi	7	Ah no! From these weapons
	un ferro sceglierò, con mano ardita	7	shall I choose a sword, with bold hand

15	contro di Tolomeo dentro la reggia . . .	11	will I [fight] against Tolomeo within the palace . . .
	(*Non si tosto Cornelia ha preso una spada fuori degli arnesi di guerra, che Sesto sopraggiunge.*)		(*No sooner has Cornelia taken a sword from the weapons of war than Sesto arrives.*)

SESTO

16	Madre, ferma; che fai?	→	Mother, stop—what are you doing?

Cornelia loses six lines, and only Cleopatra comments from the side (Nireno is with her, but Rodisbe has been dropped from the cast), turning her question about whom we are seeing onstage into a rather awkward rhetorical one that also gets answered in the negative by Cornelia herself. This is an editorial error, as it were. But the fact that Cornelia now moves "with bold hand" (*con mano ardita*) makes her transgress the norms of female behavior, raising questions about whether and how she might subsequently be constrained within the bounds of feminine decorum: Bussani has her marry Curio in the end, but Haym leaves her future unclear.

More striking, however, is the cut to Cornelia's opening monologue to only her first two eight-syllable lines. She has already had a chance to mourn (with her aria "Priva son d'ogni conforto" in Act I, scene 4), so Haym now seems to want to pick up the pace. However, giving her another aria at the beginning of a scene (as does Bussani) would contravene what were now becoming standard conventions in terms of who is allowed to sing what, and when. In the Haym-Handel *Giulio Cesare in Egitto*, Cornelia has one aria in each act, plus a duet in Act I and two *arioso* movements (but I shall refine the terminology, below), one each in Acts I and II—this is typical for a *seconda donna* (Cleopatra, in contrast, has eight arias and one duet). Still more to the present point, the arias come at the ends of scenes and not their beginnings. Cornelia's "Nel tuo seno, amico sasso" is cut to two lines not just for dramatic reasons, but also, we shall see, as a matter of genre.

RECITATIVES AND ARIAS

Although *L'incoronazione di Poppea* included a few strophic songs (so, arias in the early seventeenth-century sense of the term), its predominant musical language was a flexible form of recitative moving between declamation and lyricism according to syntactic, semantic, or rhetorical cues. Thus, while

Monteverdi's musical choices can usually be explained, they cannot always be predicted with any accuracy on the basis just of a reading of the libretto. Distinctions became more formalized, however, in the course of the seventeenth century and into the eighteenth, such that there emerged a much clearer separation of recitative and aria in poetic, musical, and dramatic terms. Aria texts continued to be distinguished by their strophic organization and poetic meters, but their musical treatment set them still more apart from the prevailing context.

Moreover, the arias could serve without needing some external justification as "real" songs: they are a personal statement on the part of the character, they mark a rhetorical shift in the discourse, and they articulate some kind of dramatic and/or emotional point. While they inevitably respond to a situation that has already been established through the recitative, it is probably a mistake to argue—as it often is—that they represent merely a reaction to the recitative's action. This is too simplistic a view of a much more dynamic and fluid set of possibilities. It also does a grave injustice to the genre of Baroque *opera seria*.

For example, in Act I, scene 6 of Handel's *Giulio Cesare*, Achilla, henchman of the wicked Tolomeo, reports how Giulio Cesare had received the gift of Pompey's head and makes his own claim for the hand of Cornelia if, in return, he kills Cesare. Tolomeo appears to agree to the proposal (although he will renege on it later) and is left alone onstage to contemplate his enemy:

ACHILLA (*entra*)			(*enters*)
Sire, signor!		→	Sire, my lord!
TOLOMEO			
Come fu il capo tronco	11		How was the cut-off head
da Cesare gradito?	7		received by Cesare?
ACHILLA			
Sdegnò l'opra.		→	He scorned the deed.
TOLOMEO			
Che sento?	7		What do I hear?
ACHILLA			
T'accusò d'inesperto e troppo ardito.	11		He accused you of being inexperienced and too brash.

TOLOMEO

5   Tant'osa un vil romano?   →   Does a vile Roman dare so
                                                                much?

ACHILLA

        Il mio consiglio   11   Take my advice,
apprendi, o Tolomeo!   7   o Tolomeo!
Verrà Cesare in corte; in tua vendetta   11   Cesare will come to court; for
                                                           your revenge

cada costui, come cadde Pompeo.   11   let him fall as Pompey fell.

TOLOMEO

Chi condurrà l'impresa?   →   Who will carry out the deed?

ACHILLA

        Io ti prometto   11   I promise you
10 darti estinto il superbo al regio piede,   11   to place the proud one dead at
                                                           your royal feet,

se di Pompeo la moglie   7   if Pompey's wife
in premio a me il tuo voler concede.   11   your will gives to me as
                                                           a reward.

TOLOMEO

È costei tanto vaga?   7   Is she so beautiful?

ACHILLA

Lega col crine, e col bel volto impiaga.   11   She binds [the heart] with her
                                                           hair, and she wounds with
                                                           her fair face.

TOLOMEO

15 Amico, il tuo consiglio è la mia stella: 11   Friend, your advice is my
                                                           guiding star:

vanne, pensa e poi torna.   7   go, think on it, and then return.

(Parte Achilla.)   (Achilla leaves.)

Muora Cesare, muora, e il capo altero   11   Let Cesare die, die, and may his
                                                           proud head

sia del mio piè sostegno.   7   be my footstool.
Roma, oppressa da lui, libera vada,   11   Let Rome, oppressed by him,
                                                           go free,

20 e fermezza al mio regno   7   and let support for my
                                                           kingdom

sia la morte di lui più che la spada.	11	be given by his death more than by the sword.
L'empio, sleale, indegno	7	The wicked, disloyal, unworthy one
vorria rapirmi il regno,	7	would wish to seize my kingdom from me,
e disturbar così la pace mia.	11	and disturb thus my peace.
25 Ma perda pur la vita,	7	But let him lose his life,
prima che in me tradita	7	before there be betrayed for me
dall'avido suo cor la fede sia!	11	my confidence by his greedy heart!

The structure of the scene is typical enough. The dialogue between Achilla and Tolomeo is in *versi sciolti*, cueing recitative, with lines divided between the characters so as to increase the pace and flow. As is typical, the poetic meter is not strongly established, and indeed, sometimes can be read in different ways: the tendency of *endecasillabi* to fall into two halves (for example, 7 + 5 or 5 + 7 syllables, with an elision at the split) allows for merging with prior or subsequent *settenari*, as is the case with (ll. 5–6) *Tant'osa un vil romano? Il mio consiglio / apprendi, o Tolomeo!* (or *Tant'osa un vil romano? / Il mio consiglio apprendi, o Tolomeo!*). Achilla exits within the recitative and has no aria: Bussani and Sartorio gave him one here, but as a minor character in Haym and Handel's opera, he gets only a single aria in each act, and we have not yet reached the point where the dramatic pace can slow enough to allow him to sing. Bussani also had Tolomeo, left alone, speculate on the delights of seizing Cornelia for himself. But Haym has a different strategy, settling on Tolomeo's fierce hatred of Cesare: this comes somewhat abruptly and almost out of the blue, but it sets up one of the situations that the drama will seek to resolve. Tolomeo's speech gains greater gravitas by way of more forceful rhymes: the five lines beginning *Muora Cesare, muora* rhyme AbCbC, which prepares the way for the even more regular structure of the two-stanza text beginning at *L'empio, sleale, indegno* (aaB // ccB). The isometric stanzas, and the rhyme, mean that we are no longer in *versi sciolti*: the poetry dictates a move from recitative to aria. The only slightly odd thing about it is that each stanza does not close with a *verso tronco*, which creates problems for Handel in setting the text when it comes to the final cadences, where the unaccented final *-a* of *mia* and *sia* falls on musically accented downbeats.

Such two-stanza aria texts are typical for Baroque *opera seria*, and they are set in the form of the *da capo* aria: a musical section A for the first stanza of the text, a musical section B for the second stanza, and then a reprise of section A (and therefore the first stanza) indicated by the instruction *da capo* (from the beginning) at the end of the B section (sometimes the instruction is *dal segno*, i.e., from a sign marked after the beginning of the A section, usually so as to remove the instrumental introduction on the reprise). The reprise of the A section is musically the same as that section's first appearance, from beginning to end (unless abbreviated by starting *dal segno*), and it is hardly ever written out again in the score. However, the convention was that the singer would improvise embellishments the second time round, potentially changing its content and dramatic meaning quite significantly.

These embellishments on the reprise of the A section offer at least a partial solution to the obvious problem of the *da capo* format. For the poet, the difficulty is that a two-stanza text is set to a three-part form (ABA) that ends with the first stanza, not the second. Therefore, the first stanza must be a self-contained textual unit, and while the second stanza can continue, or contrast with, its sentiments, it cannot in itself function as a grand rhetorical conclusion given that there must be a return to the first. If the sentiment of the second stanza in some sense contrasts with that of the first, the literal return to the first must somehow be rendered plausible—if it is not just accepted as a fact of operatic life—by way of intensification or of some manner of ironic subversion: hence the potential of added musical embellishment to generate a different reading. However, the problem is not so great in Tolomeo's "L'empio, sleale, indegno": in the first stanza he rages against Cesare's apparent wickedness, and for the second, his thoughts shift (cued by a typical *Ma*—"But") to the Roman's death. The first stanza can be repeated in the same way as before (Cesare is still wicked so far as Tolomeo is concerned), it can be more vindictive (Tolomeo's rage turns into vengeful triumph after imagining Cesare's death), or it can be more scornful or dismissive (it does not really matter how wicked Cesare is once he dies). There are, of course, other possibilities as well.

In musical terms, the A section will be in one key, and the B section in a related one: "L'empio, sleale, indegno" is in E flat major, with the second section in its relative minor, C minor. The A section will be tonally closed (beginning and ending in the same key), whereas the B section can be tonally open (in "L'empio, sleale, indegno" it ends in G minor, the dominant of C minor) given that it is followed by the reprise of the A section. The A section is normally longer than the B section, and the instruments also usually participate more actively within it. It also tends to be more formally articulated, typically by way of three instrumental ritornellos (R^1, R^2, R^3) that partition two vocal episodes (S^1, S^2), each of which states the first stanza of the text. R^1 and R^3 will usually be in the tonic key, and R^2 will usually begin in a different key (in a major-key aria, in the dominant); R^1 and R^3 will also tend to be longer. Therefore, one musical function of S^1 is to modulate from the tonic (the key of R^1) to the key of R^2, whereas S^2 modulates from the key of R^2 back to the tonic (for R^3). The ritornellos establish keys, while the solo sections move between them; this determines the kinds of melodic patterns they adopt, with strong triadic material common in ritornellos and scalewise sequences in the solo sections. These sequences also allow the voice to show off its abilities across a varied range, while their musical modulations from one key to another allow for some kind of dynamic representation of nuanced emotional states.

In the case of "L'empio, sleale, indegno," then, the A section breaks down as follows:

R^1 instrumental ritornello; E flat major (mm. 1–12)

S^1 voice (the instruments continue in an accompanying role)—*L'empio, sleale, indegno, l'empio, sleale, indegno, vorria rapirmi il regno, e disturbar, e disturbar così, e disturbar così la pace mia*; E flat major modulates to B flat major (mm. 12–32)

R^2 instrumental ritornello; B flat major returning to E flat major (mm. 32–35)

S^2 voice (instruments continue)—*L'empio, sleale, indegno vorria rapirmi il regno, e disturbar così la pace mia. L'empio, sleale, l'empio, sleale, indegno vorria rapirmi il regno, e disturbar così la pace mia*; E flat major moving to F minor, A flat major, and back to E flat major (mm. 36–61)

R^3 instrumental ritornello; E flat major (mm. 61–68 = mm. 1–2, 5–7, and a three-measure cadence)

The voice sings for forty-six measures out of sixty-eight (it is silent in mm. 1–9, 15, 33–35, and 62–68). The subsequent B section has twenty-three measures (just over a third of the A section), with two statements of the second stanza (plus an internal repetition). Here the voice sings continuously and therefore needs the break provided by the nine measures of instrumental music at the beginning of the A section on the *da capo* reprise.

Given the two statements (at least) of the first stanza of the text in the A section (S^1, S^2), plus additional internal repetitions, that first stanza is delivered at least four times in all taking the *da capo* into account, whereas the second stanza is delivered twice. Handel's treatment of the first stanza on its two statements in the A section bears closer examination, however. In S^1 we have an angry repetition of the first line ("The wicked, disloyal, unworthy one, the wicked, disloyal, unworthy one") before Tolomeo continues his thought ("would wish to seize my kingdom from me") and then breaks down into raging incredulity ("and disturb, and disturb thus, and disturb thus my peace"). The musical modulation to the dominant (for R^2) reflects his instability, but the fact that R^2 returns to the tonic prematurely (meaning that S^2 begins, somewhat unusually, in the tonic) suggests Tolomeo's attempt to regain emotional control (though his music soon modulates again). Now he has a full statement of the stanza in order, but then he returns obsessively to the opening: "The wicked, disloyal, unworthy one would wish to seize my kingdom from me, and disturb thus my peace. The wicked, disloyal, wicked disloyal unworthy one would wish to seize my kingdom from me, and disturb thus [pause for a cadenza] my peace." How those words are delivered depends significantly, of course, on the musical setting; how they are delivered differently, if they are, on the *da capo* reprise is a matter for the performer on the one hand, and the stage director on the other.

One can see why modern productions are somewhat distrustful of *da capo* arias, and therefore of late Baroque opera in general: the text repetitions are inconvenient for those seeking motivations for a character's every word and (musical) gesture, and the orchestral ritornellos pose the question of what to do in terms of stage action other than fill it with superfluous business. The stand-and-deliver approach to performing an aria that no doubt was adopted in the early eighteenth century—with restrained, if still expressive, gesture and only a small amount of movement—does not suit the modern ideal of opera as drama. All this has led to the criticism of *opera seria* as being little more than a concert in costume. But while the *da capo* aria certainly serves its purpose of showing off the voice, it also allows the unfolding of emotional states—and any distinctions within them—in real time: in effect, the character can be shown working not just to activate an emotional reaction but also to respond to it. It takes a good singer to pull it off, but paradoxically, the apparent dramatic stasis of the aria turns into something supremely dynamic in terms of how characters are seen to feel and think. The quicksilver emotional shifts of later opera are presented at a much more leisurely pace here, but perhaps a more effective one, and also, odd though it may seem to say it, in a more realistic way.

The impact of performance also helps explain another paradox, or at least an apparent contradiction. One can read into "L'empio, sleale, indegno" a range of attempts by Handel to characterize Tolomeo at this particular moment in the drama of *Giulio Cesare in Egitto*. Yet he originally composed the aria for Senesino to insert in Act III, scene 8 of the opera *Ottone* in March 1723 (well before Handel began work on *Giulio Cesare* that summer). It was then considered (again for Senesino) for *Flavio* (premiered on 14 May 1723), and its music formed the basis of an aria (with the text "Fato, tiranno e crudo"—inveighing against tyrannous, cruel fate) for the character Ugone in the latter opera's Act II (sung by the tenor Alexander Gordon). Senesino's title roles in *Ottone* and *Flavio* involved him representing, respectively, a Holy Roman Emperor and a king of Lombardy (and Ugone is the king's counselor). Handel may have shown good judgment in seeing how the aria might suit a pagan ruler of Egypt—and a different singer—and he certainly modified the music for its new purpose, shortening both parts. But the aria could work equally well in a number of quite different contexts: the emotions it represents are not specific to a singular character or dramatic situation. It takes the singer—on set, in costume—to put them to particular use.

SOME ALTERNATIVES

These *da capo* arias are almost always followed by the character's exit unless some means can be found to remain onstage (e.g., the character is prevented by another from leaving). Thus a scene-complex (a succession of scenes done on a single set) will gradually bring characters onstage scene by scene—if they are not already present—while those already there diminish in number aria by aria unless they are minor characters who leave on a recitative, as Achilla does in the Tolomeo scene just discussed. Usually, at the end of this process just one character is left onstage with, in effect, a soliloquy. This final aria will mark the end of the scene-complex, which is followed by a set change: so, Tolomeo's "L'empio, sleale, indegno" has the character alone onstage and is the second of two arias in the second scene-complex in Act I.

The librettist must therefore lay out the drama accordingly—with almost every scene building to an exit aria—and must also consider the distribution of arias through the opera in terms both of the appropriate number required for each character (according to that character's status in the cast, and also, of course, the singer's). Act I of *Giulio Cesare in Egitto*, for example, has four scene-complexes—a bank of the Nile (scenes 1–4); Cleopatra's study (5–6); Cesare's headquarters (7–8); and a hall in Tolomeo's palace (9–11)—all arranged to allow convenient set changes. It also contains twelve arias—for Cesare (four, although the first is foreshortened, as we shall see), Cleopatra (three), Sesto (two), and Achilla, Cornelia, and Tolomeo (one each)—plus an *arioso* (Cornelia) and a final duet (Cornelia and Sesto). One might expect Tolomeo to be a larger role—and the fact that he is not creates some dramatic problems in the opera—but that is a question of casting against the *primo uomo* (Cesare) and *prima donna* (Cleopatra). The librettist also needs to distribute these arias in terms of emotional, and therefore musical, variety: it would not do to have two arias with the same affective content (rage, love, pity, etc.) one after the other. None of this is easy to achieve.

The aria texts themselves are often fairly generic. Tolomeo's "L'empio, sleale, indegno" does not name Cesare, and while its content reflects the Egyptian's position at this moment in the drama, we have seen that it could also serve for any would-be ruler threatened by a rival, and there are plenty of them in Baroque *opera seria*. Conversely, one could slot in its place any analogous aria from any other opera by any other composer of the period. The same is true of so-called simile arias, such as where Cesare compares himself to a cautious hunter trying to catch his prey ("Va tacito e nascosto" in Act I, scene 9), or where Cleopatra likens her return to good fortune in Act III, scene 7 to a ship surviving a storm and arriving safely in harbor ("Da tempeste il legno infranto"), although the latter, at least, has distinctly Cleopatra-like music. For that matter, the same aria could serve two quite different characters: later sources for *Giulio Cesare in Egitto* have an aria, "La speranza all'alma mia" ("Hope proclaims and says to my soul that I shall one day be happy"), allocated both to Nerina, Cleopatra's maidservant (replacing Nireno), in a later (1725) version of the opera (in G major), and to Cornelia in 1730 (in F major) to replace Sesto's "Cara speme, questo core" (I.8). Likewise, Cesare's "hunting" aria, "Va tacito e nascosto" was originally composed (as "Va tacito e soletto") for Cleopatra's cousin and confidante, Berenice, in Handel's first version of Act I. Such substitutions doubtless occurred, in particular as the singers most in demand took their favorite party-pieces—fitting their range or particular vocal abilities, or favored by audiences from prior performances—from opera to opera (these are known as "suitcase" arias). This further explains Handel's well-known self-borrowings (there are a number in *Giulio Cesare*), in which he draws on

music written for other occasions. It is unlikely that such an eclectic approach
would have struck contemporary listeners as incongruous or incoherent.

Of course, some of the arias in *Giulio Cesare in Egitto* are more closely
tied to the plot, and therefore their textual and musical design needed some
consideration. Pompey's death leaves behind his widow, Cornelia, and their
son, Sesto. The latter is an impetuous youth whose ardent desire to avenge
his father's death is the subject of his monologue at the end of Act I, scene 4:

	Vani sono i lamenti;	7	Laments are in vain;
	è tempo, o Sesto, ormai	7	it is time, o Sesto, now
	di vendicar il padre;	7	to avenge your father.
	si svegli alla vendetta,	7	Wake up to vengeance,
5	l'anima neghittosa,	7	my indolent spirit,
	che offesa da un tiranno	11	for when offended by a tyrant, it
	invan riposa.		can take no rest.
	Svegliatevi nel core,	7	Awake in my heart,
	furie d'un'alma offesa,	7	furies of an offended soul,
	a far d'un traditor aspra vendetta.	11	to take upon a traitor bitter revenge.
10	L'ombra del genitore	7	The ghost of my father
	accorre a mia difesa,	7	runs to my defense,
	e dice: a te il rigor, figlio, si aspetta.	11	and says: "Harshness, my son, is
			expected of you."

In the aria "Svegliatevi nel core," the first stanza has Sesto girding his
loins: Handel provides an energetic setting in C minor and also omits the
middle ritornello, as if the character cannot wait to take action a minute
longer than necessary. The question, however, is what might best be done for
the second stanza. Continuing in that energetic mode would be one option,
but Handel instead puts on the brakes, providing a 3/8 Largo and adding
flutes to the instrumental mix, the latter usually (for Handel) some sign of
pathos. This allows Sesto a sentimental moment as he imagines the ghost
of his father; it also puts clearer emphasis on the words that Sesto imagines
it speaking. Two-tempo arias are not unusual for Handel, especially when
the text allows for some kind of emotional contrast. Of course, the typical
problems with how to manage the *da capo* reprise remain, and indeed are
perhaps heightened: the reading of the first stanza on the reprise must somehow be different in light of the different emotion presented in the second.

The exit convention is a very powerful one, both in dramatic terms (it would be hard to return to recitative after an aria) and also as a way of managing the applause that will invariably follow the final instrumental ritornello of an aria, or with which the audience will interrupt that ritornello if it is too eager to congratulate the singer. Yet sometimes the beginning of a scene requires something stronger than recitative. In the Bussani-Sartorio *Giulio Cesare in Egitto*, Act I, scene 1 begins (after the overture) with Cesare's entrance, where he speaks to Curio in recitative: *Curio, Cesare venne, e vide, e vinse* (an eleven-syllable line)—"Curio: Cesare came, and saw, and conquered"—identifying the Roman leader by his well-known catchphrase (which, however, Caesar was reported to have uttered on his defeat of Pharnaces II of Pontus in 47 BCE). Haym and Handel, however, seem to have felt the need for a stronger opening, stretching the convention of including a dance movement in an overture by turning it into a triumphal chorus, which the composer scores as a formal minuet with a majestic quartet of French horns (they return in the final scene of Act III):

CHORUS

Viva, viva il nostro Alcide!	8	Live, long live our Alcides,
goda il Nilo in questo dì!	8t	let the Nile celebrate this day!
Ogni spiaggia per lui ride,	8	Every riverbank smiles for him,
ogni affanno già sparì.	8t	all troubles disappear.

GIULIO CESARE

Presti omai l'Egizia terra	8	Let the land of Egypt now yield
le sue palme al vincitor.	8t	its palms to the victor.
Curio, Cesare venne, e vide e vinse;	11	Curio: Caesar came, and saw, and conquered.
già sconfitto Pompeo invan ricorre	11	Already the defeated Pompey in vain seeks help,
per rinforzar de' suoi guerrier lo stuolo	11	to reinforce his troop of soldiers,
d'Egitto al re . . .	. . .	from the Egyptian king . . .

The eight-syllable lines for the chorus are conventional enough, and they continue into the beginning of Cesare's speech, giving him what could be the first (if short) stanza of a two-stanza *da capo* aria ("Presti omai l'Egizia terra"). Handel provides in effect the A section of such an aria, with plenty of florid ornamentation as Cesare flaunts his victory (this was the composer's second attempt at the piece; the first ended up being reworked for Tolomeo's "Belle dee di questo core" in Act II, scene 9). But there is no B section, and therefore no *da capo*—Cesare continues straight into recitative after his foreshortened entrance-aria. Thus he can stay onstage for the rest of scene 1 through scene 2 (with the arrival of Cornelia and Sesto) to scene 3 (Achilla enters, bearing Pompey's head). Only then does Cesare have a full-fledged *da capo* aria ("Empio, dirò tu sei") for his exit.

Such start-of-scene half arias as "Presti omai l'Egizia terra" are very useful for establishing a dramatic position at the beginning of a scene-complex, to mark the change of set (with the instrumental introduction allowing time for it to occur), and to set a different mood. Often referred to as cavatinas (not to be confused with later uses of that term), they also granted singers a near-aria moment without disrupting the balance of arias among differently ranked members of the cast. Cornelia's two cavatinas fulfill all those functions. We have already seen her "Nel tuo seno, amico sasso" at the beginning of Act I, scene 8 as she mourns before Pompey's monument, and she has another cavatina at the head of Act II, scene 3 ("Deh piangete, o mesti lumi"), again the start of a scene-complex. In the latter case, Cornelia then stays onstage through scenes 4–6, when she exits after her aria "Cessa omai di sospirare"; in Act I, scene 8, however, she leaves in silence.

Cesare's recitative following "Presti omai l'Egizia terra" is in the declamatory style (for voice and basso continuo) known as *recitativo semplice* (or *secco*—"dry"—recitative). This is the predominant form of recitative, and for setting *versi sciolti*, within Baroque and Classical opera. For heightened emotional moments, however, another form of recitative is available: *recitativo stromentato* (also termed *recitativo obbligato* or *recitativo accompagnato*; sometimes called "accompanied recitative") uses not only a continuo but also additional upper instrumental parts providing sustained chords or rhythmic punctuations. In Act II, scene 8, Curio interrupts Cesare and Cleopatra to warn him of an impending attempt on his life by Tolomeo's guards; Cesare decides to fight, with an aria, "Al lampo dell'armi," that ends, somewhat unusually with the offstage cries of the assassins (Haym took them from Bussani). Cesare runs off, leaving Cleopatra alone onstage:

Che sento? Oh dio! Morrà Cleopatra ancora.	11	What do I hear? Oh god! Cleopatra will yet die.
Anima vil, che parli mai? Deh taci!	11	Cowardly soul, what do you say? Ah, silence!
Avrò, per vendicarmi	7	I will have, for my revenge
in bellicosa parte,	7	in time of war,
di Bellona in sembianza un cor di Marte.	11	in the guise of Bellona the heart of Mars.

Intanto, o numi, voi che il ciel reggete,	11	Meanwhile, o gods, you who rule the heavens,
difendete il mio bene!	7	defend my beloved!
Ch'egli è del seno mio conforto e speme.	11	For he is the comfort and hope of my breast.

Cleopatra's aria "Se pietà di me non senti" follows, in a wonderfully pathetic F sharp minor.

The *versi sciolti* in this soliloquy cue recitative, but they merit more than just *recitativo semplice*. Cleopatra is at a low point: she questions herself but recovers her courage (she will take the guise of the female god of war and the heart of the male one), she invokes the gods who rule the heavens, and she ends on an altruistic note (she is more concerned for Cesare than for herself), although the aria will put her back at center stage. Handel's choice of a *recitativo stromentato* makes perfect sense. The delivery of the text is slower paced, over an accompaniment that ranges widely in harmonic terms (G minor to C sharp minor) and with strong dissonances. Further, the instrumental gestures seem to represent (to us or to her?) what Cleopatra is feeling at any given moment: after the opening halo of sound, fast repeated notes precede her *Anima vil, che parli mai?* (line 2)—Handel sets it as *vile*—as if they are her "cowardly soul" speaking, to which she responds, while her decision to adopt the heart of Mars (line 5) is marked by an accented cadence before the pace slows again as she switches from the future to the present at *Intanto* (Meanwhile).

The decision to set *versi sciolti* as *recitativo stromentato* is largely the composer's, whether in response not just to the content of the poetry but also to its form (e.g., a greater preponderance of weighty eleven-syllable lines or stronger rhymes). This kind of recitative also seems to isolate the character from the main action. At the beginning of Act III, scene 7, Cleopatra is surrounded by her faithful (but silent) former handmaidens: she thinks that Cesare is dead, and she is set to take her own life. Her *recitativo stromentato* addressing her entourage, "Voi che mie fide ancelle un tempo foste," begins with ten-measure sinfonia marked *Adagio, e piano* (slow, and soft)—it was originally composed as the ritornello to the first version (in F minor) of Cornelia's "Nel tuo seno, amico sasso" (I.8)—that presumably also covers the scene change (from a wood to Cleopatra's apartment). The queen bids a sad farewell to her servants, blames Tolomeo for her misfortune (sustained chords in the instruments), hears the sound of arms in the distance (the instruments play fast fanfares, in effect creating the offstage sounds), and is on the verge of taking her last breath (the instruments gasp with her) before Cesare enters safe and sound (in *recitativo semplice*), saving the day. Cleopatra rejoices with the aria "Da tempeste il legno infranto."

As an important halfway point between "simple" recitative and aria, *recitativi stromentati* also established a set of melodic, harmonic, rhythmic, and textural vocabularies that would be put to good operatic use well into the nineteenth century, not least as *recitativo semplice* disappeared from the reckoning (we shall see the consequences in Verdi's *Rigoletto*). Handel seems to have enjoyed the freer expressive and musical possibilities they offered, even if they could not be allowed to supplant the arias that were the raison d'être of the genre. At the beginning of Act I, scene 7, Cesare muses over the urn containing Pompey's remains ("Alma del gran Pompeo") and on the fragility of human fortune, although he is soon to be distracted from such fine thoughts by the arrival of Cleopatra (disguised as Lidia). The orchestral strings set the scene with a gentle rocking motion but then move to sustained chords, providing a halo of sound around Cesare's soliloquy: this is just about as reflective as opera gets in this period. Handel also emphasizes the gravity of the moment by a quite extraordinary key scheme in terms of its distance from tonal norms, and also its range: he starts and ends in G sharp minor (but the ending is notated in the enharmonic equivalent, A flat minor), passing through E major, E flat minor, C minor, and F minor. The later eighteenth-century music historian Charles Burney thought this the "finest piece of accompanied recitative, without intervening symphonies, with which I am acquainted," calling the modulations "learned, and so uncommon, that there is hardly a chord which the ear expects." For Burney, "it had an effect, when recited on the stage by Senesino, which no recitative, or even air, had before, in this country."

Duets, on the other hand, are relatively rare in *opera seria*: there are only two in *Giulio Cesare in Egitto*: one for Cornelia and Sesto at the end of Act I, and the other for Cleopatra and Cesare before the final chorus in Act III. The Baroque style (unlike, we shall see, the Classical one) does not easily allow the presentation of contrasting emotions in very close succession, so duets only work if their characters are in exact, or at least close, agreement and therefore can sing more or less the same words and music. In the Act I duet, Haym varies the words slightly for Cornelia and Sesto: she begins *Son nata a lagrimar* ("I am born to weep"), whereas he

(*LEFT*) EBERHARD WÄCHTER AND IRMGARD SEEFRIED AS CESARE AND CLEOPATRA (VIENNA STAATSOPER, 1959) AND (*RIGHT*) NATALIE DESSAY AND LAWRENCE ZAZZO (PARIS OPÉRA, 2011)

Production styles for Baroque opera have transformed significantly over the last fifty years, alongside changes in performance practices to include countertenors (Zazzo) rather than baritones (Wächter).
Vienna, 1959: AKG-IMAGES/Imagno/Barbara Pflaum; Paris, 2011: AKG-IMAGES/Marion Kalter.

has *Son nato a sospirar* ("I am born to sigh"), but they continue with the same text. Handel has somewhat more of a problem with giving them the same music because Cornelia is an alto and Sesto a soprano, so their voice ranges differ by about a third: Cornelia begins in E minor, then Sesto takes her music into G major (three steps higher). But they are still able to sing in parallel thirds, signifying their common response to the dismal events in the opera thus far.

"FLY, MY HEART, TO THE SWEET ENCHANTMENT"

Despite the prevalence, and acceptance, of "singing," rather than just musically "speaking," in Baroque *opera seria*—and while there was no longer much limitation on who might sing—the genre still occasionally betrays a degree of nervousness about the consequences. Moments of "real" music—that is, performed as music, to be heard as such by the characters—are relatively rare in *opera seria*, but that makes them all the more striking. *Giulio Cesare in Egitto* has a perfect example.

At the beginning of Act II, Cleopatra has decided to stage a pageant as a way of charming her way into Cesare's heart. She will do so in the guise of Lidia playing the part of Virtue sitting on Parnassus and surrounded by the nine Muses. The latter are represented by an onstage orchestra consisting of nine (it seems) instruments: oboe, two violins, viola, harp, viola da gamba, theorbo, bassoon(s), and cello(s). Her servant Nireno is in on the game, and in scene 2 he draws Cesare to the appropriate spot:

NIRENO

| Da Cleopatra apprenda | 7 | From Cleopatra, let he |
| chi è seguace d'amor l'astuzie e frodi. | 11 | who is a follower of love learn its wiles and deceits. |

CESARE (*entra*)   (*enters*)

| Dov'è, Niren, dov'è l'anima mia? | 11 | Where, Nireno, where is my beloved? |

NIRENO

In questo loco in breve	7	In this place soon
5 verrà Lidia, signor.	→	will come Lidia, sire.
(*Qui s'ode vaga sinfonia di vari strumenti.*)		(*Here is heard a delightful sinfonia of various instruments.*)

CESARE

| Taci! | → | Silence! |

NIRENO

| Che fia? | 11 | What is it? |

CESARE

| Cieli, e qual delle sfere | 7 | Heavens! and what harmonious sound |
| scende armonico suon, che mi rapisce? | 11 | descends from the spheres to enrapture me? |

NIRENO

| Avrà di selce il cor chi non languisce. | 11 | He who is not moved will have a heart of stone. |
| (*S'ode nuovamente una sinfonia; s'apre il Parnasso, e vedesi in trono la Virtù, assistita dalle nove Muse.*) | | (*A sinfonia is heard again; Parnassus opens, and Virtue is seen on her throne, surrounded by the nine Muses.*) |

CESARE

| Giulio, che miri? e quando | 7 | Giulio, what do you see? And when |

10	con abisso di luce	7	with such great light
	scesero i numi in terra?	7	did the gods descend thus to earth?

CLEOPATRA (*nelle vesti di Virtù*)   (*dressed as Virtue*)

	V'adoro pupille,	6	I adore you, eyes,
	saette d'amore,	6	arrows of love,
	le vostre faville	6	your sparks
15	son grate nel sen.	6t	are welcome in my breast.
	Pietose vi brama	6	Searching for your pity
	il mesto mio core,	6	is my sad heart,
	ch'ogn'ora vi chiama	6	which forever calls you
	l'amato suo ben.	6t	its beloved.

CESARE

20	Non ha in cielo il Tonante	7	The Thunderer [Jove] in heaven
	melodia che pareggi un sì bel canto.	11	does not have a melody to match so beautiful a song.
	Vola, mio cor, al dolce incanto! . . .	→	Fly, my heart, to the sweet enchantment! . . .

(*Mentre Cesare corre a Cleopatra, si chiude il Parnasso e torna la scena come prima.*)   (*While Cesare runs to Cleopatra, Parnassus closes, and the scene returns as before.*)

	E come?	11	But what?
	Ah, che del mio gioir invido è il Nume!	11	Ah, the goddess is jealous of my joy!

This scene-within-a-scene plays quite knowingly with various operatic conventions. It also invokes the long-standing Neoplatonic debate in terms of what might best inspire "true" love: sight or sound (we have already seen the Accademia degli Incogniti elaborate upon it in Venice during Monteverdi's time there). Handel's first "delightful sinfonia"—a stately triple-time sarabande (nine measures) in F major—is presumably heard without being seen: Cesare is aware of the sound—and his exchange with Nireno (*Taci! Che fia?*) is sung over it—but he does not know its source, comparing it (in a brief recitative: *Cieli . . .*) to some celestial harmony of the spheres. The second sinfonia, a longer version of the sarabande (seventeen measures), allows for the revealing of Parnassus, and thence Cleopatra/Lidia as Virtue with the Muses. Cesare moves from hearing to seeing (*Giulio, che miri?*—Giulio, what do you see?—he asks). Cleopatra then begins her "song," "V'adoro pupille," to the same sarabande and accompanied largely by the onstage band. This is cast as a *da capo* aria, albeit without strong ritornellos. The key (F major) is not one of Cleopatra's typical extremes in the opera (A major or E major; see below); but then, she is not Cleopatra at this particular moment.

The B section (for the second stanza of the text) is in the relative minor key (D minor) as one would expect, although it cadences in A minor. This could move easily enough back to the *da capo*, but Handel has other ideas. First we need to consider the first three of Cesare's lines in the libretto following Cleopatra/Lidia's aria as he enjoys the ravishing vision but then sees it disappear:

Non ha in cielo il Tonante	7	The Thunderer [Jove] in heaven
melodia che pareggi un sì bel canto.	11	does not have a melody to match so beautiful a song.
Vola, mio cor, al dolce incanto! . . . E come?	11	Fly, my heart, to the sweet enchantment! . . . But what?

At some point, the internal rhyme *canto–incanto* prompted a change to line 3 (adding an additional *vola*) to produce a full-fledged rhyming couplet that, in turn, left the final *E come?* hanging as an irregular line:

Non ha in cielo il Tonante	7	The Thunderer [Jove] in heaven
melodia che pareggi un sì bel canto.	11	does not have a melody to match so beautiful a song.
Vola, *vola*, mio cor, al dolce incanto! . . .	11	Fly, *fly*, my heart, to the sweet enchantment! . . .
E come?	?	But what?

This is not so unusual, and the added *vola* may have been Handel's for rhetorical reasons rather than metrical ones. Less common, however, is what happened at some other point (whether before or after is unclear), when Handel decided to take Cesare's two lines about the melody unmatched in heaven (*Non ha in cielo . . . un sì bel canto*) and to insert them between the B section of Cleopatra's "V'adoro pupille" and the *da capo* reprise of its A section. There are four measures of *recitativo semplice* in D minor, closing off the tonal space of the B section as Cesare makes his rapturous claim. He then hears that song again, as, of course, do we.

When operatic characters speak to themselves, as do Nireno and Cesare in this scene, they also speak to the audience. Such asides therefore serve several purposes beyond allowing the expression of some reaction or comment: they also draw the audience into the action, in effect bringing us onto the stage. For Nireno, Cleopatra/Lidia's little scene allows the followers of love to discover its "wiles and deceits": watch, listen, and learn, he tells us. But there is more. Of course, we are witness to Cleopatra/Lidia/Virtue's performance as much as is Cesare, and we are meant to be seduced by it just as he is. The first Cleopatra, Francesca Cuzzoni, must have thoroughly enjoyed the moment, and also the empowerment that it represented. But so, too, did Handel, whose strategy is transparent enough. Interposing Cesare's two lines between the B section and the *da capo* reprise allows the return of the A section to emphasize still more the qualities of "so beautiful a song." But it is not just Cesare who makes the comparison with heavenly music; rather, Handel does so as well.

Opera usually seeks to maintain the affectation that it is some form of drama—indeed, to do so is essential to the genre—and we willingly indulge it. It also inhabits a world imagined as verisimilar, however inverisimilar it might be to us. However, sometimes all pretenses are dropped, and the genre exposes a rather knowing self-awareness—or self-reflexivity, if you prefer. In the performance-within-a-performance in Act II, scene 3 of *Giulio Cesare in Egitto*, both Cesare and Handel wink at the audience, saying that they, and we, know it is all a game. It is none the worse for that.

TAMING CLEOPATRA

Like the protagonist of Monteverdi's *L'incoronazione di Poppea*, Cleopatra would seem to be one of those "dangerous" women that have populated the operatic stage almost from the beginnings of the genre's history. A queen of Egypt is even more exotic than an empress of ancient Rome and can plausibly be expected use all her sexual and musical wiles to wheedle her way into a Western ruler's heart. However, when Cleopatra sings not in disguise (as Lidia) but as an "Eastern" queen, her music needs to be distinguished as such. It is probably no coincidence that Handel writes her arias often in exotic sharp keys (A major, E major), especially when she is singing to another character. This takes her to the edge, and beyond, of typical tuning and temperament systems of the period, thereby making Cleopatra's music sound especially strange. And although Handel's arias in general for the singer Francesca Cuzzoni (the first Cleopatra) tended to range quite widely in terms of key, *Giulio Cesare in Egitto* has the highest number of sharp-key arias for her in a single opera. The composer must have seen the advantage to be gained by limiting such remote tonal regions to Cleopatra, even if it took time to do so. For example, the first version of what became Cornelia's "Priva son d'ogni conforto" was originally written in E major (not its final

D major), and that of her duet with Sesto, "Son nata a lagrimar," in F sharp minor (not E minor): here the keys seem chosen for extreme affective reasons (as they are, too, for Cleopatra), but Handel seems in the end to have found them inappropriate for a Roman widow (or, perhaps, for the singer who took the role). Likewise, the idea of moving Cleopatra into exotic tonal areas came slowly: the first version of her aria "Non disperar chi sa" (I.5) was in D major, and her next aria (I.7), "Tutto può donna vezzosa," in A major, was originally intended for the queen's confidante, Berenice, for which role it was written in G major.[2] "Tutto può donna vezzosa" certainly seems more appropriate for a confidante (urging her mistress to action): giving it to Cleopatra makes her seem too proud, on the one hand, and too scheming, on the other.

This reflects a problem with Cleopatra as a whole in the opera. It would be easy just to dismiss her as a sexual predator—ever ready to turn her feminine charms to devious ends—but that would weaken the outcome of the plot: we may in the end not have much sympathy for Nerone's dalliances with Poppea, but Cesare should be made of sterner stuff. Therefore *Giulio Cesare in Egitto* tends to walk a thin line between representing Cleopatra as an alluring, and therefore dangerous, vamp, and showing her as a dignified queen fighting for what should be hers by right of age, though not of gender (the "real" Cleopatra's brother, Ptolemy XIII, was eight years younger than her). She is no Poppea, nor was she in historical terms, for we also know that in the end she died well: suicide by asp is a more noble outcome than being kicked to death. Even just within Handel's opera, the character is nowhere near as evil as her brother, Tolomeo, who behaves according to the Eastern stereotype in wholly reprehensible ways by decapitating Pompey (after his death) and by seeking to usurp his sister's rule over the Nile. Of course, none of this could happen in modern (1724) England, which had more or less renounced the chopping off of noble heads, and had also recently had a sister (Queen Anne) follow her brother-in-law to the throne. Given that King George I and his son, Prince George (later George II), and younger daughter, Princess Sophia Dorothea, attended the premiere of *Giulio Cesare in Egitto*, one would also expect certain proprieties to be observed. There are plenty of political allegories in the opera relevant to England in the mid-1720s if one wishes to look for them. But the Egyptian queen cannot be made to appear all bad.

2. But Handel kept Cleopatra's "Tu la mia stella sei" (I.8), in a more "normal" B flat major (she is left alone on the stage); it derives from an aria written for Berenice in F major, which in turn drew on at least three earlier pieces by Handel.

Her fortunes are closely linked to Cesare's and move inversely to Tolomeo's. Thus, when Cleopatra's naval forces are routed by Tolomeo's (at the beginning of Act III) and Cesare appears lost in the fray, she is at her lowest point, appearing in scene 3 in chains with guards at her side. At this point, Bussani and Sartorio had represented her as feisty (as they do throughout their opera): she warns Tolomeo that fortune and fate will give her the means for revenge, given that they are fickle mistresses turning tables on a whim. But a London audience in 1724 would expect something more submissive, and this is the classic place for a lament. Haym and Handel duly oblige, although they made two other attempts before coming up with one of Cleopatra's greatest arias:

	E pur così in un giorno	7	And so in a single day
	perdo fasti e grandezze? Ahi fato rio!	11	have I lost honors and greatness? Ah harsh fate!
	Cesare, il mio bel nume, è forse estinto;	11	Caesar, my beloved, perhaps is dead;
	Cornelia e Sesto inermi son, né sanno	11	Cornelia and Sesto are helpless, and do not know
5	darmi soccorso. Oh dio!	7	how to help me. Oh god!
	Non resta alcuna speme al viver mio.	11	There remains no hope for me to live.
	Piangerò la sorte mia,	8	I will lament my fate,
	sì crudele e tanto ria,	8	so cruel and so harsh,
	finché vita in petto avrò.	8t	for as long as I have life in my breast.
10	Ma poi morta d'ogn'intorno	8	But when dead, all around
	il tiranno e notte e giorno	8	and night and day will I the tyrant [Tolomeo]
	fatta spettro agiterò.	8t	haunt as a ghost.

A brief *recitativo semplice* sets the scene: Cleopatra has already had a *recitativo stromentato* toward the end of Act II (before the aria "Se pietà de me non senti"), and she will soon have another (in Act III, scene 7, when she bids farewell to her maidservants as she prepares for death, interrupted by Cesare's return). In part, it seems, the recitative in scene 3 is underplayed so as not to slow the pace of the act (there is plenty more to come), although the cadences in the still more exotic keys of C sharp minor and G sharp minor take us so deep into unfamiliar tonal realms that Cleopatra's typical E major of her aria seems almost normal. Handel also sneaks the aria in by avoiding an opening ritornello (as he does also in Cornelia's lament over the dead Pompey in Act I). It appears almost as an extension to the recitative (although the tempo slows to *Largo*), with minimal instrumental accompaniment and, at the beginning, a restricted vocal range that only gradually takes lyric flight. Having a flute (*flauto traverso*) double the first violins is a marker of pathos (Handel also uses it for Cornelia in Act I). One might also see some semiotic significance in the descending bass line at the beginning, moving steadily downward by step from tonic to dominant, with one pitch per measure. We have already encountered this pattern (a descending tetrachord) in *L'incoronazione di Poppea*, both in the minor key (where it seemed at times to signify lament) and in the major (in the final love-duet between Nerone and Poppea, among other examples). Which, if any, of its potential meanings might apply to "Piangerò la sorte mia" is open to debate, but Handel certainly makes a point of its presence: in the first part of the aria the bass line descends seven times from E(–B), and once from C♯(–G♯), occupying some three-fifths of the A section.

This A section is not constructed over a ground bass, strictly speaking, but with those obsessive descending tetrachords, it comes close. The text of the second stanza, however, demands some kind of change. Having decided to spend the rest of the time available to her in lamentation, Cleopatra then resolves on what to do after her death: to haunt her tyrannical brother without end. The shift to the relative minor key (C sharp minor) is conventional enough, but Handel also changes meter (from 3/8 to C) and tempo (to *Allegro*), and the furious sixteenth notes in the strings (including a cello part separate from the bass line) and in the voice fly around like demented spirits as Cleopatra imagines what her ghost will do to Tolomeo. Hell hath no fury like a woman scorned.

This of course raises once more the typical problem of the formulaic *da capo*. Cleopatra now has to rein in her feverish imaginings and reprise her lament. There are several ways to play this on the stage if the simple stand-and-deliver approach probably adopted in Handel's time is thought unsatisfactory for modern audiences. For example, in the A section the first time round Cleopatra can in some way challenge her (supernumerary) guards—adding strength to her dignity—and on the reprise fall into greater, more internalized despair. Or she can do the reverse: Cleopatra's initial despair can gain new strength from the B section and therefore, on the reprise, become a cue for positive action rather than being just a negative response: lament may be all that is left to her, but she will do it bravely and well. Following the aria, she must exit, but how she does so—head held high or dragged by her guards—will depend on the performance interpretation given to the aria. The choice between these two readings, or for any other, will also have a significant impact on the kinds of embellishment the singer decides to add on the *da capo* reprise.

In terms of the lament convention, however, this reprise acts as the typical moment of womanly recantation: we saw it already in the case of Ottavia in *L'incoronazione di Poppea*, albeit in a very different musical context. Haym no longer needs to articulate the shift by way of words: the trope is strong enough that it can be conveyed just in a musical return. Cleopatra's fortunes may be about to change again: Cesare has, of course, survived, and he will win the day. He will also win Cleopatra once and for all, but only now that she has learnt to behave in the manner of a proper Western woman.

CESARE RETURNS

There is a problem with the staging here. According to Handel's autograph score, the set at the beginning of Act III is a wood outside the city of Alexandria; according to the libretto (following Bussani and Sartorio), it is "the port of Alexandria," although we shall see that the full harbor view was probably reserved for the final scene of the opera. Either way, Cleopatra is outdoors for "Piangerò la sorte mia" prior to her exit at the end of scene 3. Because of a major cut to the Bussani libretto—including two scenes for Tolomeo, Cornelia, and Nireno between Cleopatra's exit and Cesare's appearance—Haym and Handel's next scene (scene 4) stays in the wood, but with what seems to be a different view on one side, of the port of Alexandria where Achilla lies mortally wounded—even though he was alive enough in Act III, scene 1 to sing an aria. The complete change of personnel on a single set (if modified in some way) is unusual: Cesare enters (presumably after Cleopatra is well out of sight) and in some confusion wanders around the battlefield, which is strewn with corpses (though he does not notice them at first); Achilla must strike his pose (it is not clear how); and Sesto and Nireno must later appear so as to encounter Achilla (but not yet Cesare). We also need to shift from the E major of "Piangerò la sorte mia" to less exotic, more stable tonal realms. Handel deals with the shift in mood and pace, and also the difficult staging, by providing a gentle sinfonia in F major marked *Andante, e piano*, with twenty-two 3/8 measures, which is unusually long. The instruments continue into a *recitativo stromentato* as Cesare reports how he almost drowned but rescued himself from the waves, notes that fate has been on his side but fears that he is left alone, asks the breezes for pity, wonders where Cleopatra might be, and only then sees the dead soldiers lying around him:

Italian	Syllables	English
Dall'ondoso periglio	7	From the perilous depths
salvo mi porta al lido	7	safe has brought me to shore
il mio propizio fato.	7	my propitious destiny.
Qui la celeste Parca	7	Here heavenly Fate
5　non tronca ancor lo stame alla mia vita.	11	does not yet cut the thread of my life.
Ma dove andrò? E chi mi porge aita?	11	But where shall I go? And who helps me?
Ove son le mie schiere?	7	Where are my troops?
Ove son le legioni,	7	Where are the legions
che a tante mie vittorie il varco apriro?	11	who opened the way to so many of my victories?
10　Solo in quest'erme arene	7	Alone on these desert sands
al monarca del mondo errar conviene?	11	will the emperor of the world be left to roam?
Aure, deh per pietà	7t	Breezes, ah for pity
spirate al petto mio,	7	breathe on my breast
per dar conforto, oh dio,	→	to give comfort, oh god,
15　al mio dolor.	11t	to my grief.
Dite, dov'è, che fa	7t	Tell me, where is, what does
l'idolo del mio sen,	7t	the idol of my breast,
l'amato e dolce ben	→	the beloved, sweet darling
di questo cor.	11t	of this heart.
20　Ma d'ogni intorno i' veggio	7	But all around I see
sparse d'arme e d'estinti	7	bestrewn with arms and corpses
l'infortunate arene:	7	these dismal sands:
segno d'infausto annunzio al fin sarà.	11t	this must be a sign of ill-omened portent.

This is an addition to the Bussani libretto (which has only a version of line 1, then going in a different direction as Cesare addresses the dying Achilla), and the text is not as straightforward as it might seem. On the face of it, we have a recitative in *versi sciolti*, with rhyming couplets to mark the rhetorical pauses, and a reasonably standard two-stanza aria (*pace* the predominant *versi tronchi*). Then there are four concluding lines in what would seem to be verse for recitative, were it not for the final eleven-syllable *verso tronco*. Those last lines are somewhat odd: after his aria Cesare should leave the stage, yet here he needs to remain for the next scene. A cavatina might have done the trick (we saw it in Act I, scene 1), but Cesare has not been onstage for six scenes—since Act II, scene 8—and he sings less in Act II as a whole than does Cleopatra, with two arias versus her three. It is time to give the character, and the singer, some space.

Again, Handel has the aria sneak in. There is no clear cadence at the end of the *recitativo stromentato*, which instead leads straight into the unaccompanied exclamation, *Aure* (Breezes). The instruments then start to play what seems to be a reprise of the sinfonia beginning the scene, but it turns out to be a foreshortened opening ritornello for the aria (so, in the same 3/8 and F major). The A section of the aria (*Aure, deh per pietà*) is not strongly articulated in tonal terms, for although the first statement of the first stanza gets to the dominant—C major—via its minor, there is no clear middle ritornello in the new key. The B section (*Dite, dov'è, che fa*) is in the customary relative minor key (D minor)—and continues the mood of the first stanza—but then instead of an immediate *da capo*, it moves into another *recitativo stromentato* for the four lines beginning at *Ma d'ogni intorno i' veggio* (But all around I see . . .). Only then do we have the reprise of the A section (starting at m. 3).

The *recitativo stromentato* separating the B section from the reprise works in a similar way to the one we saw in Act II, scene 2, as Cesare commented on the beauty of Cleopatra/Lidia's Parnassian pageant prior to the return of the first stanza of her "V'adoro pupille." In that case the decision to manipulate the convention may have been Handel's. Here, however, it seems to have been Haym's (whether or not in consultation with the composer): the final eleven-syllable *verso tronco* (*segno d'infausto annunzio al fin sarà*) only makes sense by virtue of a planned return to a rhyming *verso tronco* (*Aure, deh per pietà*).

The effect is one of there being some kind of aria—but a loosely articulated one—in the overall context of *recitativo stromentato*. This grants Cesare a moment of pathos (which he does not have at this point in the Bussani-Sartorio opera) but allows him to remain onstage, watching as Sesto and Nireno arrive, and then to take from Sesto the seal (given to him by Achilla) that will allow access to soldiers to defeat Tolomeo. Only after all that action does Cesare have a fully formed *da capo* aria prior to his conventional exit ("Qual torrente, che cade dal monte," in impetuous ten-syllable lines). However, Haym's strategy also serves to justify the *da capo* in "Aure, deh per pietà." This is a typical invocation aria (to the breezes), marked by Cesare's peremptory vocative (*Aure*), before the aria proper starts. The first time around, Cesare wallows in his personal grief—or self-pity—at seemingly being left all alone in the world. His thoughts then turn outward, first to Cleopatra in the B section, and then, of course, to the dead bodies around him, at which point the grief requiring pity becomes all the greater and, in the end, humane. It will be tricky to make the difference in performance, although a good stage director could help. But for a character who has spent much of the opera praising his own military prowess or swooning over an Egyptian beauty, it is about time that he, too, found his nobler side through altruism. Cleopatra may need taming, but Cesare needs to grow.

ALL'S WELL . . .

The Bussani-Sartorio *Giulio Cesare in Egitto* ends at Act III, scene 17, just after Tolomeo has been dragged off in chains. Cleopatra and Cesare declare their love for each other; she grants freedom to Cornelia and Sesto; Cornelia agrees to marry Curio; Cesare once more extols Cleopatra's beauty (comparing her to Ariadne crowned in heaven); and the new queen of Egypt swears fealty to Rome and sings of her joy on the one hand, and her beauty on the other. This was not quite going to work in London. First Sesto needs to proclaim his revenge: he has just killed Tolomeo, which Haym explained in the preface to the first edition of the libretto as a necessary fiction ("it was thought necessary in the present drama to make Sestus the instrument of Ptolomey's death in revenge for his father's murder, varying from history only in circumstances of action"). Cornelia must remain a noble widow (so Cesare simply praises Curio's valor); then Cesare, Cornelia, and Sesto must finally be reconciled. As for Cesare and Cleopatra, although he can hand her the symbols of Tolomeo's reign and she can declare herself loyal to Rome, the queen cannot appear too proud. This revised scene is prepared by a regal opening sinfonia, with the return of the four horns not heard since the opening of the opera (they may represent the trumpets and drums cued in the stage direction): that sinfonia must have been intended in part to allow the audience to wonder at the full stage set (the port of Alexandria). And instead of Cleopatra's vainglorious aria, we have a predictable love-duet:

CLEOPATRA			
Caro!			Dear one!
	Più amabile beltà	7t	No more lovable beauty
	mai non si troverà	→	will ever be found
	del tuo bel volto.	11	than your fair face.
5	In me non splenderà	7t	In me will never shine forth

	né amor, né fedeltà	→	either love or loyalty
	da te disciolto.	11	if parted from you.

CESARE

	Bella!		Fair one!

	Più amabile beltà	7t	No more lovable beauty
10	mai non si troverà	→	will ever be found
	del tuo bel volto.	11	than your fair face.

	In te non splenderà	7t	In you will never shine forth
	né amor, né fedeltà	→	either love or loyalty
	da me disciolto.	11	if parted from me.

The text is not Haym's best, and it is also ungrammatical (Cleopatra's *disciolto* should be *disciolta*). Both characters have more or less the same text—as is required by the single affect of the music—save Cesare's switching of pronouns (Cleopatra's *me* becomes *te* as Cesare rather imperiously turns her sentiment into an instruction). But the words serve their generic purpose: the union of two lovers. We do not know who decided to add those nonmetrical vocatives at the beginning (Cleopatra's *Caro!* and Cesare's *Bella!*): there is nothing similar in the cantata movement which provided Handel with the opening of this duet (the aria "Quando ritornerò" from *Stelle, perfide stelle*, HWV168). But it likely was Handel himself, who certainly draws them out in his new setting.

All is prepared for the conventional conclusion. Cesare proclaims that peace will reign in Egypt and that Rome's fame will spread far and wide. The "chorus"—made up of the rest of the characters on the stage (and the singer who played Tolomeo in the wings)—celebrates the return of joy and pleasure in a dignified bourrée (usually performed too fast) in *da capo* form, the B section of which gives Cesare and Cleopatra a final moment to declare their happiness. One should not read anything into the B section's shift from G major to G minor (often considered a "sad" or tragic key in a later period, if not entirely correctly): grief is gone, replaced by love, constancy, and fidelity. The bourrée was French dance, but the political overtones of the final chorus are clear, and were made still more apparent in a performance of *Giulio Cesare in Egitto* in Hamburg on 9 June 1727 in honor of King George I's birthday. This had an additional prologue and epilogue (text by Thomas Lediard and music by Georg Philipp Telemann) entitled *The Joy and Happiness of the British Nation*.

Writing in the 1780s, the music historian Charles Burney said that Cesare's "Dall'ondoso periglio"—where the emperor is just saved from a watery death but still uncertain of his future—enabled Senesino to gain "so much reputation as an actor, as well as singer." The scene is often considered one of the finest musical moments in *Giulio Cesare in Egitto*, no doubt for two separate but related reasons: that convention seems to give way to a stronger sense of drama, and that the music appears to take over from the words. By Burney's time, however, opera had changed quite radically. On 1 March 1787, the English composer Samuel Arnold produced in London a supposed revival of *Giulio Cesare in Egitto* that was, in fact, a pasticcio drawing on music from a range of Handel operas: he was honest enough to admit that because the original offered "a great number of incongruities, both in the language and in the conduct, several material alterations have been thought absolutely necessary, to give the piece a dramatic consistency, and to suit it to the refinement of a modern audience." What suited the "refinement" of any audience in 1724 was hardly likely to have the same appeal in the last quarter of the eighteenth century. *Opera seria* was now reformed, and in some quarters, at least, *opera buffa* was starting to rule the roost, with far-reaching consequences.

FURTHER READING

The rather complex history of Handel's *Giulio Cesare in Egitto* is outlined in Winton Dean and John Merrill Knapp, *Handel's Operas, 1724–1726* (Oxford: Clarendon Press, 1987), 483–526 (plus the list of borrowings in the opera in ibid., Appendix D). See also Craig Monson, "*Giulio Cesare in Egitto*: From Sartorio (1677) to Handel (1724)," *Music and Letters* 66 (1985): 313–43; and the discussion of Handel's opera in Thomas Forrest Kelly, *First Nights at the Opera* (New Haven, CT: Yale University Press, 2004), 3–61. Antonio Sartorio's *Giulio Cesare in Egitto* (libretto by Giacomo Francesco Bussani) is edited by Craig Monson in the series Collegium Musicum Yale University 2, no. 12 (Madison, WI: A-R Editions, 1991); it is also discussed in Tim Carter, "Mask and Illusion: Italian Opera after 1637," in *The Cambridge History of Seventeenth-Century Music*, edited by Tim Carter and John Butt (Cambridge: Cambridge University Press, 2005), 241–82, at 259–70. C. Steven LaRue, *Handel and His Singers: The Creation of the Royal Academy Operas, 1720–1728* (Oxford: Clarendon Press, 1995), discusses the original performers. For the extent of the broader repertoire, see Claudio Sartori, *I libretti italiani a stampa dalle origini al 1800: catalogo analitico con 16 indici*, 7 vols. (Cuneo: Bertola and Locatelli, 1990–94). Peter Sellars's staging of *Giulio Cesare in Egitto* (first aired at the PepsiCo SummerFare at the State University of New York at Purchase in 1987) in an unspecified Middle Eastern country, with Cesare as the U.S. president and Tolomeo a tinpot dictator, has been a source of boundless controversy; it is available on DVD.

CHAPTER 4

Lorenzo da Ponte and Wolfgang Amadeus Mozart, *Le nozze di Figaro* (Vienna, 1786)

WOLFGANG AMADEUS MOZART
(SILVERPOINT DRAWING BY DORA
STOCK; APRIL 1789)

Stock's portrait was done when Mozart, on his way to Berlin, passed through Dresden, where he visited her home and, by report, kept everyone away from dinner while he improvised at the piano. This was a few months before Le nozze di Figaro *was revived in Vienna.*

AKG-IMAGES/Imagno/k. A.

Count Almaviva: Stefano Mandini (baritone)
Countess Almaviva [Rosina]: Luisa Laschi-Mombelli (soprano)
Susanna, maid to the Countess, engaged to Figaro: Anna (Nancy) Storace (soprano)
Figaro, valet to the Count: Francesco Benucci (bass)
Cherubino, page to the Count: Dorothea Bussani-Sardi (mezzo-soprano)

Marcellina, housekeeper to Bartolo: Maria Mandini (soprano)
Bartolo, a doctor from Seville: Francesco Bussani (bass)
Don Basilio, a music master: Michael Kelly (tenor)
Don Curzio, a magistrate: Michael Kelly (tenor)
Barbarina, daughter of Antonio; Anna Gottlieb (soprano)
Antonio, a gardener and uncle of Susanna: Francesco Bussani (bass)
Villagers, peasants, servants.

SETTING: The castle of Aguafrescas, near Seville, (roughly) the present day.

SOURCE: Pierre Augustin Caron de Beaumarchais (1732–1799), *La Folle Journée, ou Le Mariage de Figaro* (1781; first performed 1784).

FIRST PERFORMED: Vienna, Burgtheater, 1 May 1786 (postponed from 28 April). The opera had nine performances from then to 18 December. It was done in Prague in December (or perhaps from late November) 1786 and January 1787 (Mozart conducted it on 22 January). It was revived in Vienna on 29 August 1789, with twenty-eight or so performances up to early 1791; here Mozart replaced Susanna's two arias with new ones for the singer now taking the role, Adriana Ferrarese del Bene (who would be Fiordiligi in *Così fan tutte*), and he rewrote some of the music for Countess Almaviva (now Catarina Cavalieri, Konstanze in Mozart's *Die Entführung aus dem Serail* of 1782) and the Count (a higher baritone, though the singer is not known).

ACT I. (*An unfurnished room, with a chair in the center.*) (No. 1, *Duettino*, "Cinque . . . dieci . . . venti . . . trenta . . .") Figaro measures the space for a bed, while Susanna urges him to compliment her bridal bonnet. Figaro likes the room, but Susanna is more cautious when she hears it is to be theirs, and although Figaro feels that the room is convenient for them to serve the Count and Countess (no. 2, *Duettino*, "Se a caso madama"), Susanna points out that it is also very handy for the Count to get up to no good. She tells him that the Count is tired of his wife and wants to bed Susanna according to the *droit du seigneur*, even though it has been officially abolished in his lands: the music teacher Basilio is acting as go-between. Left alone, Figaro now realizes what the Count means by proposing to take him to London with Susanna as a "private attaché." (No. 3, Cavatina, "Se vuol ballare") He vows to make the

Count dance to his tune, and leaves in a rage. Bartolo enters with his old housekeeper, Marcellina, and they discuss her claim on Figaro by virtue of a signed contract to repay money she has lent him by a set date (today) or to take her hand in marriage. Bartolo in turn is happy at the chance to punish the man who helped the Count steal his ward, Rosina, and (no. 4, Aria, "La vendetta, oh la vendetta!") he rejoices that vengeance is at hand. Marcellina, talking to herself, complains about her rival, Susanna, who enters and overhears her diatribe: (no. 5, *Duettino*, "Via resti servita") they trade insults as Marcellina takes her leave. The young page Cherubino rushes in to tell Susanna a sorry tale: yesterday the Count caught him with Barbarina and has dismissed him from service—he must leave unless the Countess can intercede, and he will never see Susanna again. Susanna knows that he is really sighing for her mistress, and Cherubino admits it, snatching from Susanna one of the Countess's ribbons and giving her, in return, a "canzonetta" that she can sing to all the women in the palace, for (no. 6, Aria, "Non so più cosa son, cosa faccio") he is overwhelmed by strange feelings of love. He makes to leave but sees the Count coming and hides behind the chair. The Count presses his suit with Susanna but is interrupted by the arrival of Basilio; he hides behind the chair as Cherubino slips in front and Susanna covers him with a dress. Basilio asks Susanna if she has seen the Count, and also about Cherubino, who clearly, as everyone says, is in love with the Countess. The Count emerges in a rage and (no. 7, *Terzetto*, "Cosa sento! Tosto andate") threatens to have Cherubino chased from the castle; Basilio apologizes for his intrusion; Susanna faints, but recovers when they lead her to the chair; the Count explains how he caught Cherubino hiding under a table in Barbarina's room, and as he acts out the discovery by lifting the dress from the chair, he finds the page yet again—Susanna exclaims that things could not be worse while Basilio is quite happy at the visible proof that "all women are like that" (*Così fan tutte le belle*). Cherubino, although discovered, has a weapon up his sleeve given that he has just heard the Count propositioning Susanna, at which point the Count appoints him an officer in his regiment in Seville. (No. 8, *Coro*, "Giovani liete") Figaro leads in a chorus singing in praise of the Count in an attempt to get his wedding underway, but the Count prevaricates, hoping to find Marcellina.

Figaro hears from Susanna the details of Cherubino's new military appointment, and after he tells the page to see him before he leaves, he extols the virtues of army life (no. 9, Aria, "Non più andrai, farfallone amoroso").

ACT II. (*A magnificent room with an alcove, the entrance door on the right, a closet on the left, a door at the rear which leads to the maids' rooms, and a window at the side.*) (No. 10, Cavatina, "Porgi, amor, qualche ristoro") The Countess seeks comfort from grief: let her husband return to her or may she die. Susanna enters and the Countess asks her to finish her story: that the Count is proposing to pay for the maid's sexual favors. Figaro enters singing, recapitulates matters, and explains that they are natural enough and can easily be resolved: he has arranged for Basilio to receive an anonymous letter arranging an assignation with the Countess. This will confound the Count and make him easier to manipulate. Figaro also proposes telling the Count to await Susanna in the garden this evening, although Cherubino, dressed as a woman, should go in her place. The Countess and Susanna agree that it is not a bad plan, and Figaro exits to fetch Cherubino, singing once again that he will make the Count dance to his tune. The Countess wonders why Cherubino did not come to her to ask her to intercede over his initial expulsion from the castle; she asks about the canzonetta, which Susanna suggests they make him sing. Cherubino enters, and despite his nervousness, takes up the tune to the accompaniment of Susanna's guitar (no. 11, *Canzone*, "Voi che sapete"). They decide to find women's clothes for the page; Susanna locks the main door to the room lest they be discovered; and the Countess sees the commission appointing Cherubino an officer, which she notices lacks an official seal. (No. 12, Aria, "Venite . . . inginocchiatevi") Susanna dresses Cherubino, even though he cannot keep his eyes off the Countess. The two women admire their handiwork, then the Countess notices that Cherubino has a ribbon tied around his arm (the one he snatched from Susanna in Act I) which he has used as bandage to cover a scratch because of the reputed powers of a ribbon that has touched the hair or skin of a . . . "stranger," the Countess interjects. She sends Susanna off to find another one.

Cherubino bursts into tears, the Countess wipes his eyes, and he moves to kiss her just as there is a knock at the door. It is the Count, and the Countess and Cherubino fly into a panic: he hides in the closet, and she locks the door and removes the key, then unlocks the door to her own room and lets the Count in. He is surprised that the Countess's own door was locked, but she says that she was trying on a dress and that Susanna has just gone to her room. The Count is wary at seeing her so flustered; he shows her the anonymous letter he has received; and then a noise is heard from the closet, which the Countess says must be Susanna. The Count now is even more suspicious given that Susanna is supposed to be elsewhere. The Countess tries to pass it off as her mistake, while Susanna enters from the rear and hides. (No. 13, *Terzetto*, "Susanna, or via sortite!") The Count orders Susanna to come out of the closet, and the Countess says that she cannot because she is trying on a dress, while Susanna comments on the scene; he then asks just to hear her voice, but the Countess forbids it, standing on her dignity; and both husband and wife warn each other of the danger of scandal. Given the Countess's refusal to open the door, the Count decides to call his servants to break it down, but she says that this would be an unwarranted attack on her honor. He agrees and decides to fetch tools himself, taking the Countess with him and making sure all the entries to the room are secure. (No. 14, *Duettino*, "Aprite, presto, aprite!") Susanna leaves her hiding place and tells Cherubino to come out of the closet; they realize that he has no escape save to jump out the window, which he does, running off safe and sound. She then goes into the closet herself. The Count and Countess return, and he notes that all is as he left it. The Countess, distraught, admits that Cherubino is in the closet, and the Count is furious, thinking that this confirms the content of the anonymous letter. (No. 15, Finale, "Esci, ormai, garzon malnato!") He orders Cherubino to come out; the Countess begs her husband's indulgence given that the page is only half dressed; and the Count orders her away from his sight. But when he opens the closet door, he is shocked to see Susanna, as is the Countess. He goes inside to check that there is no one else there, while Susanna explains to her mistress how Cherubino escaped; the Count emerges confused and asks his wife for forgiveness, although the women chide that he does not deserve it. He declares his love for the Countess and appeals to her former self as Rosina, although she rejects the name. The Count asks about her prior confusion, but she says that it was just a joke; as for the anonymous letter, she and Susanna claim that it was written by Figaro to be delivered by Basilio. The Count threatens to punish his servant and the music master, but the Countess and Susanna remind him that he who wants forgiveness must first forgive others, and the Count agrees: all seems to end in harmony. Figaro enters announcing that the musicians await outside to celebrate the wedding, and the Count once more prevaricates, asking him about the anonymous letter. Figaro pretends to know nothing of it, despite Susanna's and the Countess's promptings (for they have already revealed its source). The Count accuses Figaro of lying, and the Countess and Susanna want to bring the theatricals to an end, which, Figaro suggests, they should do in typical stage fashion, with a wedding. All three plead with the Count, while he hopes that Marcellina will soon arrive. Instead, Antonio the gardener suddenly enters, bearing a broken flowerpot with carnations in it: he has seen anything and everything thrown out of the castle windows, but only now a man. The Count's suspicions are aroused once more, and Susanna and the Countess tell Figaro that it was Cherubino, although he had already seen him. After trying to defuse the situation by claiming that Antonio is drunk, Figaro admits that he himself was the one who jumped, although Antonio thinks it was someone smaller, perhaps Cherubino. Figaro says that one crouches when jumping, and that anyway, Cherubino has gone off to Seville on horseback: this leaves Antonio confused, because no horse jumped out of the window. Figaro explains to the Count that he had been waiting in Susanna's room, had been frightened by the Count and Countess's argument—also bearing in mind the anonymous letter—and so he jumped, twisting his ankle in the process. Antonio then produces a document that he had found left by the jumper in the garden; the Count grabs it, dismisses Antonio, and subjects Figaro to an inquisition. Aided by Susanna and the Countess, Figaro works out that the document is the page's commission, which lacked the proper seal. The Count is beaten on all sides, but rescued by the sudden appearance of Bartolo, Basilio, and Marcellina, who appeal to him for judgment on what to do with the lawsuit, which he says must proceed in due order. They rejoice while the Countess, Figaro, and Susanna are left in confusion.

ACT III. (*A rich hall, with two thrones, prepared for the wedding ceremony.*) The Count reflects on recent events: he is perplexed but cannot quite bring himself to distrust the Countess, who surely respects his honor—though what price honor now? As he continues musing—he has sent Basilio to Seville to check on Cherubino—the Countess urges Susanna on. The maidservant catches the Count's attention by asking for a flask of smelling salts and (no. 16, *Duetto*, "Crudel! perché finora") leads him to believe that she will meet him in the garden that evening. The Count is delighted but then overhears Susanna telling Figaro that his case is won: he realizes that he has fallen into a trap and (no. 17, *Recitativo ed Aria*, "Hai già vinto la causa! Cosa sento!"–"Vedrò, mentre io sospiro") rages against the idea that he might be bested by his servant. Don Curzio, the judge, enters with Bartolo, Figaro, and Marcellina to announce that the court has decided in her favor: Figaro must pay his debt or marry her. The Count thinks the verdict just, but Figaro says that he cannot fulfill its terms without the consent of his lost parents, given that he was kidnapped as a child. He points to a birthmark on his right arm, and Marcellina realizes that she is his mother, and Bartolo his father. (No. 18, *Sestetto*, "Riconosci in questo amplesso") The family is happily reunited, while the Count and Don Curzio look on in dismay; Susanna enters with money to pay Figaro's debt but sees him embracing Marcellina and assumes the worst until everything is explained to her. As the Count and Don Curzio leave in a huff, the newly reconciled family, with Susanna now a part of it, express their happiness at the turn of the events. Barbarina leads Cherubino to her house so as to dress him in female garb for a celebration being prepared for the Countess. Meanwhile (no. 19, *Recitativo ed Aria*, "E Susanna non vien! Son ansiosa"–"Dove sono i bei momenti"), the Countess anxiously awaits Susanna for news of recent events, and worries about the plan for them to swap roles in the garden so as to catch out the Count; it is a bad state of affairs when she has to seek the help of her maidservant, and she longs for former happier times, but perhaps her constancy in love will prompt her husband to reform. Antonio tells the Count that Cherubino is still in the castle and is being dressed as a woman. The Countess hears from Susanna how the Count received her proposition to meet in the garden, and (no. 20, *Duettino*, "Che soave zeffiretto") she dictates a letter that will confirm the arrangement. The letter will be sealed by a pin which the Count can return as a sign of his agreement. (No. 21, *Coro*, "Ricevete, o padroncina") A group of peasant girls enters to present flowers to the Countess. She is captivated by one of them, whom the Count and Antonio quickly unmask as Cherubino. The Count threatens the page one more time, but Barbarina exerts her own pressure to have him promise her Cherubino as her husband. Figaro enters, once again trying to get the wedding underway, and when confronted with the sight of Cherubino, he tries to bluff his way out of the now evident lies he told earlier: if he jumped out the window, then Cherubino could just have easily done so as well. (No. 22, Finale, "Ecco la marcia . . . andiamo") A march heard in the distance provides a distraction, and the Countess leads her husband to honor a double wedding: for Figaro and Susanna, and Bartolo and Marcellina. Two peasant girls and then the chorus sing in praise of the Count's renunciation of the *droit du seigneur*, and the company starts to dance a fandango. Susanna passes her letter to the Count, and Figaro sees him reading it and pricking his finger on the pin. The Count announces that the weddings will be celebrated this evening with a banquet and dancing, and the girls and the chorus repeat their song of praise.

ACT IV. (*A dense garden with two accessible pavilions, one on the right and the other on the left. Night.*) (No. 23, Cavatina, "L'ho perduta, me meschina") Barbarina has lost the pin that the Count gave her to return to Susanna. Figaro enters with Marcellina and asks the young girl what is wrong: as Barbarina explains, Figaro realizes that the letter he saw the Count reading was from Susanna. He "finds" the pin and drags the whole story out of Barbarina, who leaves to find Susanna and then Cherubino. Figaro is devastated and heads off to take his revenge on behalf of all husbands. Marcellina, however, trusts Susanna more and decides to warn her, given that women must unite against ungrateful men: (no. 24, Aria, "Il capro e la capretta") animals of either sex coexist peaceably—it is only women who are abused by their male counterparts. Barbarina enters carrying fruit and cakes, which she is to deliver to the pavilion on the left; she is glad to have Cherubino even if it cost her a kiss from the Count. But hearing people approach forces her to take refuge. Figaro is joined by Bartolo and Basilio, whom he has summoned to witness his exposure of Susanna. He leaves to make the necessary preparations, and Basilio presents to Bartolo his basic philosophy of life: that one should never play games with noblemen, and anyway (no. 25, Aria, "In quegli anni in cui val poco") he has always found it better to be phlegmatic and to cover himself with an ass's skin (i.e., play the fool). (No. 26, *Recitativo ed Aria*, "Tutto è disposto: l'ora"–"Aprite un po' quegli occhi") Figaro announces that everything is ready; he inveighs against Susanna, and then warns all men to beware of women. The Countess and Susanna enter dressed in each other's clothes, accompanied by Marcellina, who reveals that Figaro is eavesdropping and then goes into the (left) pavilion, where Barbarina is hiding. The Countess withdraws, and Susanna decides to make Figaro pay for his distrust. (No. 27, *Recitativo ed Aria*, "Giunse alfin il momento"–"Deh vieni, non tardar, o gioia bella") The moment has come for her to delight in being in the arms of her beloved: let joy delay no more, for the time and the place are right. Figaro hears (but cannot see) her, and he is shocked. Cherubino enters in search of Barbarina, but he sees the Countess (whom he takes to be Susanna). (No. 28, Finale, "Pian, pianin le andrò più presso") He starts making amorous advances that she tries to resist, fearful that the Count might approach, as he does, with Figaro and Susanna each watching from a distance. The Count chases Cherubino away; makes his own advances to "Susanna," giving her a ring; and tries to lead her into a pavilion. Figaro passes by noisily; the Countess hides in the pavilion on the right, while the Count heads off. Figaro laments that he is about to become Vulcan to Venus's new lover, Mars. Susanna enters, and Figaro, taking her to be the Countess, tells her that she is about to see the Count and Susanna in action. But he quickly recognizes her voice and decides to turn the tables, throwing himself at her feet in pretend adoration. Susanna thinks that he is wooing the real Countess and starts to beat him, but they make peace. The Count returns in search of "Susanna," who Susanna reveals to Figaro is the Countess, and they decide to act out a seduction scene. The Count, thinking that he has finally caught his wife in the act, calls for all to assemble, then pulls out from the pavilion on the left Cherubino, Barbarina, Marcellina, and Susanna (as the Countess). All ask forgiveness, but the Count denies it until the real Countess appears from the right pavilion, to everyone's surprise. The Count must now beg her forgiveness, which she grants. All decide that only love can turn this day of torments, caprices, and madness into happiness and joy: they decide to leave to the sound of a march to start the wedding celebrations.

WOLFGANG AMADEUS MOZART (1756–1791) wrote his first dramatic work, *Apollo et Hyacinthus* (1767), at the age of eleven, and his last, *Die Zauberflöte* (1791), when he was thirty-five. His twenty or so operas (depending on what one includes within that term) ranged from *opere serie* and *buffe* in Italian to *Singspiele* in German, the latter mixing music with spoken dialogue (instead of recitative). The lack of French operas is typical for an operatic world that, outside of France, remained strongly Italian. Mozart's *opere serie* reveal the influence of various reform movements within the genre in the third quarter of the eighteenth century: *Idomeneo* (Munich 1781) is usually regarded as the best example—for all the tussles over it that the composer had with his librettist, Giovanni Battista Varesco—and it is often counted as the first of Mozart's "mature" works for the stage. His comic *opere buffe*, however, took advantage of the popularity of a relatively new genre often considered—if not quite correctly—to be more in keeping with Enlightenment sensibilities.

Chief among the reformers was Christoph Willibald von Gluck (1714–1787). Although he was brought up in German-speaking Bohemia, he studied in Italy and wrote Italian operas that premiered in London, Dresden, Copenhagen, Prague, and Vienna before he moved to Paris in 1773 and turned to the French *tragédie lyrique* and related genres. Those Italian operas were largely *opere serie*, though Gluck gradually tried to purge the genre of its abuses, which for him included vain singers, illogical *da capo* arias, and other dramatic absurdities: his *Alceste* (1767) is generally regarded as a prime example of his "reform" operas. Their influence spread both to France and in the German-speaking lands: in 1781 Gluck revised his French *Iphigénie en Tauride* (Paris, 1779) for the Burgtheater in Vienna as the "tragisches Singspiel" *Iphigenie auf Tauris*. But Italian *opera buffa* was soon to take over the stage in Vienna, as it did elsewhere in Europe.

That production of *Iphigenie auf Tauris* fit a pattern, however. For a while the Habsburg Emperor Joseph II briefly flirted with German theater and opera, in part for political reasons: he dissolved the Italian opera company in Vienna in 1776 and turned the Burgtheater into a "National Theatre" devoted to spoken plays in German and, starting in 1778, *Singspiele*. This is one reason Mozart was tempted to move there from his native Salzburg in 1781: much to the dismay of his father, Leopold, he engineered his own dismissal from his position among the court musicians of Prince-Archbishop Colloredo of Salzburg in the hope of gaining fame and fortune in one of the leading cultural capitals of Europe. It also explains why his first opera for Vienna was indeed a *Singspiel*, *Die Entführung aus dem Serail* (*The Abduction from the Seraglio*), premiered on 16 July 1782.

But emperors have a tendency to change their minds, and Mozart had no choice but to acknowledge the fact in a letter to his father of 7 May 1783 as he struggled to adapt to new circumstances:

> Well, the Italian *opera buffa* has started again here and is very popular. The *buffo* is particularly good—his name is Benucci. I have looked through at least a hundred libretti and more, but I have scarcely found a single one with which I am satisfied; that is to say, so many alterations would have to be made here and there, that even if a poet would undertake to make them, it would be easier for him to write a completely new text—which indeed it is always best to do. Our poet here is now a certain Abbate da Ponte. He has an enormous amount to do in revising pieces for the theatre and he has to write *per obbligo* an entirely new libretto for Salieri, which will take him two months. He has promised after that to write a new libretto for me. But who knows whether he will be able to keep his word—or will want to? For, as you are aware, these Italian gentlemen are very civil to your face. Enough, we know them! If he is in league with Salieri, I shall never get anything out of him. But indeed I should dearly love to show what I can do in an Italian opera! So I have been thinking that unless Varesco is still very much annoyed with us about the Munich opera [*Idomeneo*], he might write me a new libretto for seven characters. Basta! You will know best if this can be arranged. In the meantime he could jot down a few ideas, and when I come to Salzburg we could then work them out together. The most

LE NOZZE
DI FIGARO,
O SIA
LA FOLLE GIORNATA.
COMEDIA per MUSICA
TRATTA DAL FRANCESE
IN QUATTRO ATTI.

DA RAPPRESENTARSI
Nei Teatri di Praga
l'Anno 1786.

Preso Giuseppe Emanuele Diesbach.

Title page of the libretto of *Le nozze di Figaro* printed for the Prague production (1786)

From the first operas on, librettos were printed in cheap editions for the audience to follow (theaters remained lit throughout the performance) and to keep. Often they do not reflect last-minute changes in rehearsal.
AKG-IMAGES.

essential thing is that on the whole the story should be really *comic*; and, if possible, he ought to introduce *two equally good female parts*, one of these to be *seria*, the other *mezzo carattere*, but both parts equal *in importance and excellence*. The third female *character*, however, may be entirely buffa, and so may all the male ones, if necessary. If you think that something can be got out of Varesco, please discuss it with him soon.

Mozart's anxieties are clear: he needed to secure a commission for a new Italian opera but needed something special to beat the competition. He was also uncertain of whether he would gain the support of the newly appointed poet at the court theater, Lorenzo da Ponte (1749–1838), not just because he was busy writing new librettos and revising old ones for performances at the Burgtheater, but also given that Mozart feared he was in cahoots with Antonio Salieri, the musical director of, and chief composer for, the Italian opera in Vienna. However, da Ponte did write three complete librettos for Mozart, beginning with *Le nozze di Figaro*, an adaptation of a highly controversial French play, *La Folle Journée, ou Le Mariage de Figaro*, by Pierre Augustin Caron de Beaumarchais (1732–1799). *Figaro* was followed by *Don Giovanni* (Prague, 1787), and *Così fan tutte* (Vienna, 1790), although for the latter, it seems that Salieri was originally to be its composer. All three operas are set in some version of Spain (*Così* in Naples, which was under Spanish rule), presumably because it was European enough to present realistic characters but also sufficiently exotic to allow their somewhat licentious behavior.

LORENZO DA PONTE (ENGRAVING
BY MICHELE PEKENINO,
AFTER NATHANIEL ROGERS; C1820)

Da Ponte wrote some twenty-eight opera librettos and adapted many more. He left Vienna in 1791 (following the death of Emperor Joseph II in 1790) and moved first to London and then, fleeing bankruptcy, to the United States. He was the first professor of Italian literature at Columbia College.
AKG-IMAGES.

As for Mozart's ideas for a new libretto in 1783—with three female characters and four male ones—they have often been read as somehow prophetic: for example, the Mozart-da Ponte operas each have two "equally good female parts," one *seria* (Countess Almaviva, Donna Anna, Fiordiligi) and one *mezzo carattere* (Susanna, Donna Elvira, Dorabella), plus a third who is *buffa* (Marcellina, Zerlina, Despina)—though we can argue over Susanna's position in this taxonomy. These character types reflect the influence on Italian *opera buffa* of the prominent playwright and librettist Carlo Goldoni (1707–1793). He had established the *dramma giocoso* (one of his preferred terms) as something comic rather than tragic and in a "modern" setting, but with characters across the social range and with farce tempered by a strong element of sentimentality on the one hand, and a "moral" message on the other. However, and logically enough, Mozart's shopping list, as it were, also reflects the constitution of the new opera company at the Burgtheater and the expectations that audiences had of it: Mozart had to write for specific singers and inevitably wanted to play to their strengths, while Viennese *opere buffe* in the 1780s rang the changes on a set of very specific dramatic and musical conventions.

In the end, *Le nozze di Figaro* needed nine singers plus a chorus and dancers: Basilio/Don Curzio and Bartolo/Antonio were doubled roles, which is why Antonio has to make a seemingly premature exit in the Act II finale before Bartolo appears (although the libretto turns that exit into a comic moment), and why all four characters could not appear at the end of the Act IV finale, *pace* any stage direction to the contrary (and Mozart provides music only for Basilio and Antonio). To judge by his letter of 7 May 1783, Mozart was already impressed by the comic bass singer Francesco Benucci, who would create the role of Figaro and then that of Guglielmo in *Così fan tutte* (and who was Leporello in the revised *Don Giovanni* staged in Vienna in 1788). He seems to have been fond of the English soprano Anna (Nancy) Storace, who was the first Susanna; he later wrote a poignant concert aria for her, "Ch'io mi scordi di te?" (How can I forget you?), for her farewell concert in Vienna in February 1787, with a prominent piano part that Mozart no doubt played alongside the orchestra. He worked again with the other singers in *Figaro*, too: Luisa Laschi-Mombelli (Countess Almaviva) was Zerlina in the Vienna *Don Giovanni*; Dorothea Bussani (Cherubino; a trouser role) was Despina in *Così fan tutte*; and her husband, Francesco (Bartolo, Antonio), was the Vienna Commendatore and Masetto, and Don Alfonso in *Così*. Husband-wife pairings were not unusual in the theatrical world—Stefano Mandini (Count Almaviva) was also married to Maria (Marcellina)—as a way of allowing women to perform onstage after marriage. But perhaps the most revealing example of Mozart's collaboration with singers is Anna Gottlieb, who was just two days past her twelfth birthday when she played Barbarina. Five years later, at the age of seventeen, she was Pamina in *Die Zauberflöte*. Although Barbarina has only a cameo role in *Figaro*, it is worth comparing her cavatina "L'ho perduta, me meschina" (at the beginning of Act IV) with Mozart's music for Pamina (for example, her "Ach, ich fühl's, es ist verschwunden")—there are striking musical similarities, in part because they are for the same (if developing) voice, but also, it seems, because Mozart made an in-joke of the connection.

The fact that the same performer could play Countess Almaviva in *Figaro* and Zerlina in *Don Giovanni* reveals that singers were not strongly typecast in this period. It is true, however, that Luisa Laschi-Mombelli may have had problems as the Countess: in the Act II trio ("Susanna, or via sortite!"), Mozart originally made her sing above Susanna but then had to switch their musical lines, meaning that Susanna ended up with the scale going to up to top G first time round, and an even higher top C the second, despite the fact that she is meant to be hiding in the wings and so should not draw attention to herself (some modern productions revert to the original). This was a last-minute fix. But when *Figaro* was revived at the Burgtheater in 1789, the presence of singers new to their roles forced more significant adjustments (which was by no means unusual). In addition to revising the endings of the Count's "Vedrò, mentre io sospiro" and the Countess's "Dove sono i bei momenti," Mozart wrote two arias for the new Susanna—Adriana Ferrarese del Bene—replacing "Venite . . . inginocchiatevi" in Act II with "Un moto di gioia," and "Deh vieni, non tardar, o gioia bella" in Act IV with "Al desio di chi t'adora." Del Bene tended to play on her virtuosity, as we see also in Mozart's next operatic role for her, Fiordiligi in *Così fan tutte*. As a result, "Al desio" is an elaborate two-tempo *rondò* that significantly changes Susanna's character (even though she is pretending to be the Countess at this point). This also means that one can feasibly choose to perform either the 1786 *Figaro* or the 1789 one, with interesting consequences in terms of preferring Mozart's "first" or "last" thoughts, although the 1786 version is the one most commonly done.

Figaro is very much an ensemble opera, but each of its original singers needed at least one aria. Alas, Marcellina's "Il capro e la capretta" and Basilio's "In quegli anni in cui val poco," both in Act IV, tend to be cut nowadays because they are considered redundant, and the opera already runs long. This leaves two holes in the middle of that act (they are very noticeable), and at least in the case of "Il capro e la capretta," it means that we lose the clearest statement of one important message of the opera: how women deserve better than being oppressed by men. But other arias were clearly intended to make an effect, and the Irish tenor Michael Kelly (the first Basilio and Don Curzio) left a vivid account of one of them:

> I remember at the first rehearsal of the full band, Mozart was on the stage with his crimson pelisse and gold-laced cocked hat, giving the time of the music to the orchestra. Figaro's song, "Non più andrai, farfallone amoroso," Benucci gave, with the greatest animation, and power of voice.
>
> I was standing close to Mozart, who, *sotto voce*, was repeating, "Bravo! Bravo! Benucci"; and when Benucci came to the fine passage, "Cherubino, alla vittoria, alla gloria militar," which he gave out with Stentorian lungs, the effect was electricity itself, for the whole of the performers on the stage, and those in the orchestra, as if actuated by one feeling of delight, vociferated "Bravo! Bravo! Maestro. Viva, viva, grande Mozart." Those in the orchestra I thought would never have ceased applauding, by beating the bows of their violins against the music desks. The little man acknowledged, by repeated obeisances, his thanks for the distinguished marks of enthusiastic applause bestowed upon him.

Figaro fared well in Prague later in 1786—so Mozart reported with excitement in his letters—where its success led to the commission of *Don Giovanni*. It also quite quickly became part of the repertory in European opera houses, if less so in Italy, where Mozart was often regarded as too complex and "instrumental" a composer to be able to write good (i.e., singable) operas. In France, the opera was often done for a while as an *opéra comique*, replacing the recitative with Beaumarchais's original spoken dialogue; in London in 1819, Henry Rowley Bishop produced at Covent Garden an English version (competing with the Italian one at the Theatre Royal, Haymarket) with spoken dialogue that also reworked the plot, dropped many of the larger ensembles, revised the surviving music, and included new arias. Nevertheless, the standard (1786) version of *Figaro* was well established by the early nineteenth century—though *Don Giovanni* had more performances—and it attained classic status. Even nowadays, however, opera houses tend to accept some cuts that may have been sanctioned early on but make scant musical sense (e.g., within Susanna and Cherubino's "Aprite, presto, aprite!"), and as noted above, we are shortchanged by the common omission of Marcellina's and Bartolo's Act IV arias. But *Figaro* is probably the best loved of Mozart's operas, and with good cause.

"These Italian gentlemen are very civil to your face"

It was not clear at the outset, however, that *Figaro* was ever going to gain such approval. The chief opera composers in Vienna were all Italian—whether Salieri or the imperial Hofkapellmeister, Giuseppe Bonno—or had been taught there (the Spanish Vicente Martín y Soler). Mozart's father knew the game and sought to give his son the next best thing to an Italian training by taking him on three extended trips to Italy in 1769–71 (Mozart was thirteen when he started out), later in 1771, and in 1772–73, each time ensuring that he was commissioned to write an *opera seria* or some other theatrical piece. Once the Italian opera was reestablished in Vienna, however, Mozart knew that while leaving Salzburg might have seemed a good decision at the time, it was about to turn against him.

He made two false starts on an *opera buffa* for Vienna: *L'oca del Cairo* (to a libretto by Varesco, who did indeed respond positively to the composer's request in his letter of 7 May 1783), and then *Lo sposo deluso* (perhaps by Lorenzo da Ponte)—there is not enough of them to perform in full, although they are interesting for Mozart's exploration of ensemble writing, and also for how he was trying to design roles for Benucci and Storace. Meanwhile he honed his theatrical skills by writing substitute arias and ensembles for insertion into operas at the Burgtheater. But the delays in receiving an ever elusive commission weighed heavily on him, forcing Mozart to earn money largely by teaching and by subscription concerts (including performing his own piano concertos). He also made the mistake of allowing himself to be pitted against Salieri on 7 February 1786 in what was set up as a competition between German opera (Mozart's *Der Schauspieldirektor*) and Italian (Salieri's satirical *Prima la musica e poi le parole*): the vote went to Salieri. In the case of *Le nozze di Figaro*, then, Mozart needed to work hard to make an impression.

One move he made was canny enough: one of the more popular *opere buffe* on the boards was Giovanni Paisiello's *Il barbiere di Siviglia* (St. Petersburg, 1782), staged frequently in Vienna beginning in 1783 with a number of singers who would be in *Figaro*. *Il barbiere* was based on Pierre Augustin Caron de Beaumarchais's play *Le Barbier de Séville, ou La Précaution inutile* (1775)—also the source for Rossini's more famous setting (1816)—which concerns Comte Almaviva's attempts to elope with Rosine under the eyes of her guardian, Dr. Bartholo, and with the aid of the barber, Figaro. Beaumarchais wrote a sequel, *La Folle Journée, ou Le Mariage de Figaro*, by 1781, although it was first performed at the Comédie Française only in April 1784: here the Comte and Comtesse have been married for some three years, and Figaro and Suzanne are employed as their servants. Mozart was clearly hoping to ride on the coattails of Paisiello's success, while also having individual singers repeat their former roles: Stefano Mandini was a Count Almaviva in Paisiello's opera, and Luisa Laschi-Mombelli sometimes played Rosina, as did Nancy Storace (although Francesco Benucci was Dr. Bartolo, and Francesco Bussani, Figaro). But his choice of setting *Le Mariage de Figaro*—and da Ponte claimed that it was the composer's—was not unproblematic. The play was condemned across Europe for lèse-majesté—Napoleon later called it "the revolution in action"—and performances of it had been banned in Vienna in February 1785.

The idea of a count's being given his comeuppance by a servant may have suited one tenor of the times—and Mozart almost certainly felt some sympathy with the idea given his own tribulations in Salzburg—but it may not have been the wisest of subjects. Da Ponte tells in his memoirs of how he needed to persuade the court authorities, up to the emperor himself, that the play had been toned down in its musical adaptation, and, for that matter, that what could not be said could still be sung (presumably because the words would be less clear). Certainly the librettist played up the comic aspects of the text, also cutting down the more overt of Figaro's diatribes against the false privileges of the nobility (whether Mozart reinserted them by way of the music is a matter for debate). However, the "political" content of the work under the guise of an Italian comic opera does not seem to have caused problems at the time: one of the later Prague performances (on 14 October 1787) was in honor of Archduke Franz (later Emperor Franz II) and his sister, Archduchess Maria Theresia. Indeed, if, as has been suggested, *Figaro* was originally intended as an opera for Carnival, its topsy-turvy satire would have been even less offensive.

Da Ponte's memoirs further report—whether accurately or not is unclear—how those opposed to Mozart in Vienna (or more partisan in favor of the Italians) tried to sabotage the opera not just by complaining about its subject but also by taking issue with the fact that it contained a ballet (in the Act III finale), even though the emperor had prohibited such dancing in operas because it caused them to be overlong. By this account, Mozart ensured that in a rehearsal attended by the emperor, the music would stop at the beginning of the ballet, leaving the action mute for no apparent reason, with the result that the music was quickly restored by imperial fiat. It is unclear whether the story is true, but what lies behind it squares with the reports of Mozart's father to the composer's sister about a number of cabals mounted against him in Vienna.

The initial reception of *Le nozze di Figaro* may not have been quite as enthusiastic as Michael Kelly would have us believe. The Viennese opera fan Count Carl Zinzendorf was "bored" by the opera on its opening night, though he may have been distracted by the company in his box (Louise von Diede, Baroness Fürnstein), and repeated hearings made him more favorable to the work. The fact that Emperor Joseph II was moved to ban encores of ensemble numbers in the Burgtheater on 9 May 1786 (*Figaro* was performed on 1, 3, and 8 May) suggests that the opera was making an impact. A later article in the *Wiener Realzeitung* (11 July 1786) noted that the opera had faced some opposition, that "the first performance was none of the best, owing to the difficulty of the composition," and that the public was uncertain about its quality; but that "now, after several performances, one would be subscribing either to the *cabal* or to *tastelessness* if one were to maintain that Herr *Mozart's* music is anything but a masterpiece of art."

TRANSLATING BEAUMARCHAIS

Leopold Mozart wrote to his daughter on 11 November 1785 that at last he had heard from his son, who was hard at work on his adaptation of Beaumarchais:

> I know the piece; it is a very tiresome play and the translation from the French will certainly have to be altered very freely, if it is to be effective as an opera. God grant that the text may be success. I have no doubt about the music. But there will be a lot of running about and discussions before he gets the libretto so adjusted as to suit his purposes exactly. And no doubt according to his charming habit he has kept on postponing matters and has let the time slip by.

Turning a spoken play into a libretto was a common enough strategy in this period. Especially for *opera buffa*, it had the advantage of providing a strong dramatic framework and also a basis for the situational and verbal commentary, and even slapstick, that lay at the heart of the genre. And despite Leopold Mozart's dire predictions, da Ponte and Mozart had a good model from which to work.

Da Ponte clearly knew French, and he followed Beaumarchais's prose word for word where it suited him. However, *Le Mariage de Figaro* was already a long play, and given that it always takes more time to sing something than to say it, da Ponte needed to cut things down. He explains the matter in the preface to his libretto, where he also seeks to preempt criticisms of the play itself:

> The duration prescribed as being usual for dramatic performances, a certain number of characters generally introduced into the same, and some other prudent considerations and exigencies imposed by morality, place, and spectators, were the reasons why I did not make a translation of this excellent comedy, but, rather, an adaptation or, let us say, an extract.
>
> To this end, I was obliged to reduce the sixteen characters of which it consists to eleven, two of which may be performed by a single person [*recte* four by two], and to omit, apart from an entire act, many a very charming scene and a number of good jests and sallies with which it is strewn, in place of which I had to substitute canzonettas, arias, choruses, and other forms and words susceptible to music, things that can be supplied only by verse, but never by prose. In spite, however, of every effort, and of all the diligence and care taken by the composer and by myself to be brief,

the opera will not be one of the shortest to have appeared on our stage, for which we hope sufficient excuse will be found in the variety of the threads from which the action of this play is woven, the vastness and grandeur of the same, the multiplicity of the musical numbers that had to be made in order not to leave the actors too long unemployed, to diminish the vexation and monotony of long recitatives, and to express with varied colors the various emotions that occur, but above all in our desire to offer, as it were, a new kind of spectacle to a public of so refined a taste and such just understanding.

This rhetoric may help explain why da Ponte called his libretto a *commedia in musica* rather than an *opera buffa* (as Mozart styled the work), if the different label means anything at all. But he did not have much trouble reducing Beaumarchais's five acts to four, even if three or even two would have been normal for an *opera buffa*. Removing the more seditious episodes helped, and da Ponte probably assumed that the play and its predecessor, *Le Barbier de Séville*, were sufficiently well-known to allow some abbreviation of the plot and of the motivations of its characters: thus, *Le Barbier* explains why Bartolo so desires revenge against Figaro (because the latter helped Almaviva lure away his ward). One of the "prudent considerations and exigencies" to which da Ponte refers was presumably the toning down of the Countess's burgeoning relationship with Cherubino—in the third of Beaumarchais's Figaro plays, *L'Autre Tartuffe, ou La Mère coupable* (1792) she has a child by him—although modern productions often tend to play it up again. But the biggest problem in the adaptation is the removal of the trial scene where Marcellina's lawsuit against Figaro is heard, with the verdict reached in her favor. Beaumarchais used this scene (his Act III, scene 15) to project a satire of corrupt judiciary—which may be one reason da Ponte cut it, although it is hard enough to imagine setting a trial to music (*pace* Gilbert and Sullivan), with long recitatives for the plaintiff, defendant, and judge and no place for a musical number. However, he created problems given that there now seems to be scant time for the trial to take place between the Count's rage aria, "Vedrò, mentre io sospiro," and the entrance of the characters announcing the verdict, soon to be voided by the discovery that Marcellina and Bartolo are Figaro's long-lost parents. There is also an additional issue of when and where Susanna gets the money to pay Figaro's debt (she has it when she enters during the Act III "recognition" sextet).

All this has led some to argue for reorganizing Act III, moving the Countess's soliloquy ("E Susanna non vien! Son ansiosa" leading to "Dove sono i bei momenti") from scene 8 to between scenes 4 and 5, so that it separates the Count's aria and the sextet and in effect covers the time of the trial offstage. This has the further advantage of keeping "Dove sono" apart from the Letter Duet, "Che soave zeffiretto," for the Countess and Susanna (in scene 10): having the two so close together makes life very hard for the singer. But there is no real historical or other justification for the shift, and it cannot operate with the double-casting used in 1786 (Bartolo and Antonio would appear almost in successive scenes). As for the "missing" trial itself, Gustav Mahler, who often conducted *Le nozze di Figaro* at the Vienna Staatsoper, had a different solution: he composed a new scene (1906) in a fairly credible Mozart pastiche.

In turning spoken French into sung Italian, da Ponte had to simplify things. He also, of course, needed to locate the arias and ensembles expected in an *opera buffa*. Beaumarchais included various musical episodes in the play: a conventional *vaudeville* at the end (the characters have a final chorus); a fandango, a duet, and other music for the would-be nuptials in the middle of Act IV (the Act III finale in the opera); and in Act II, Chérubin's sentimental ballad sung to the Comtesse, with Suzanne accompanying him on the guitar ("Mon coursier hors d'haleine," sung to the tune of "Marlbroug s'en-va-t'en guerre," i.e., "For he's a jolly good fellow"), which da Ponte replaced with "Voi che sapete." Elsewhere, however, da Ponte needed to find some cue within Beaumarchais's dialogue for where a musical number might occur, either by temporarily freezing the action or somehow enabling it to continue in more developed musical terms rather than in recitative.

Act III, scene 2 provides a straightforward example. The act begins with the Count alone onstage, musing on the events thus far. Then Susanna enters to collect smelling salts for her mistress, although it is just a pretext to arrange the assignation in the garden that will soon prove to be the Count's downfall. Da Ponte cuts down Beaumarchais's Act III, scene 9 (he removes the passages in italic, below) and also finds a place for the duet "Crudel! perché finora" (within the bracket):

SUZANNE: My Lord—*Oh, beg pardon!*
COMTE (*ironically*): What is it, *young lady?*
SUZANNE: You are angry!
COMTE: You were wanting something, *apparently.*
SUZANNE (*shyly*): The Mistress has the vapors. I was coming to ask
    you to lend us your smelling salts. I'll return them immediately.

COMTE (*handing her the vial*): Keep them for yourself. *No doubt you'll soon find them useful.*

SUZANNE: Do you imagine that women of my class have the vapors? *It's a genteel malady. They only catch it in drawing rooms.*

COMTE: A loving bride, and she's losing her young man . . .

SUZANNE: But by paying Marceline with the dowry that you promised . . .

COMTE: I promised?

SUZANNE (*lowering her gaze*): My Lord, I thought I heard so.

COMTE: Ay!—if only you would hear me . . .

SUZANNE (*eyes on the ground*): Is it not my duty to listen to Your Lordship?

COMTE: Then why, *child*, didn't you say so before?

SUZANNE: Is it ever too late for the truth?

COMTE: Will you be in the garden this evening?

SUZANNE: Don't I walk there every evening?

COMTE: Why were you so obstinate this morning?

SUZANNE: *This morning*—with the page behind the chair?

COMTE: *She's quite right. I had forgotten. But why this persistent refusal* when Bazile, on my behalf . . .

SUZANNE: What need of a Bazile?

COMTE: She's right *again. But there's a certain Figaro to whom I fear you may have told things!*

SUZANNE: *Why, of course! I tell him everything—except what he ought not to know.*

COMTE: *Charming!* And you promise me? If you go back on your word, *let us be clear,* my dear: *no rendezvous no dowry—no dowry no marriage.*

SUZANNE (*curtseying*): *But no marriage also means no "Droit de Seigneur,"* My Lord!

COMTE: *Where does she pick it all up? Upon my word I shall dote on her!* But your Mistress is waiting for the vial . . .

SUZANNE (*laughing and handing it back*): I had to have some excuse to talk to you . . .

COMTE (*trying to kiss her*): Delicious creature!

SUZANNE (*evading him*): Someone is coming.

COMTE (*aside*): She's mine. (*Goes off.*)

SUZANNE: *I must go and tell Her Ladyship.*

The passages cut by da Ponte are redundant (save that they pace the dialogue), off the point, or too nuanced for easy comprehension. Moving from recitative to the duet at "Then why . . . didn't you say so before?" also makes sense. Here the Comte changes tack as Suzanne indicates her willingness to "listen": he asks her a leading question, to which she cunningly responds by way of another question. He then asks a still more leading question ("Will you be in the garden this evening?"), which Suzanne again answers with a question. These two question pairs are nicely balanced; the Comte's next question, however, is more prosaic and refers to the past rather than the future, so less needs to be made of it.

The dialogue in this scene is mostly translated into *versi sciolti* (for recitative). But da Ponte then turns each of those two question pairs into a four-line stanza and invents a third four-line stanza (not taken from Beaumarchais) where the Count and Susanna express their reactions to the situation in asides (two lines each). He also finds a stronger opening for the duet by way of a typical vocative: *Crudel! perché finora* (*Cruel one*, why). However, da Ponte knows the musical rules: the paired-question format would be awkward for music by requiring one open-ended phrase after another, disallowing strong cadences. So he turns Susanna's questions-as-answers into statements that are made even stronger by contrasting her *versi tronchi* with the Count's wheedling *versi piani*. The technique is clear in the second stanza:

CONTE		
Dunque in giardin verrai?	7	Then you will come to the garden?
SUSANNA		
Se piace a voi, verrò.	7t	If it pleases you, I will come.
CONTE		
E non mi mancherai?	7	And you will not fail me?
SUSANNA		
No, non vi mancherò.	7t	No, I will not fail you.

This makes Susanna appear more brazen, although Mozart finds a glorious, and wonderfully comic, way to temper the effect. He composes a kind of seduction duet in the typical key of A major (albeit starting in A minor), the same key used for almost all such duets in his Italian operas (and often in those of other composers): Don Giovanni and Zerlina's "Là ci darem la mano" (in *Don Giovanni*) and Ferrando and Fiordiligi's "Fra gli amplessi in pochi istanti" (in *Così fan tutte*) are obvious examples. To reduce the danger of Susanna's appearing too forward, however, Mozart repeats that second stanza (after a statement of the third) and extends it by having the Count repeat his questions in shorter form, while Susanna gives *sì* (yes) and *no* responses (added to the libretto, for they do not fit the poetic meter), first in the correct order and then wrongly. This makes her initially appear unsettled (a nice touch) but then manipulative, which is how Beaumarchais represented her all along, if by way of a different rhetoric.

Sometimes, however, da Ponte can take one of Beaumarchais's speeches and turn it almost directly into an aria text. In Act I, scene 7 of the play, Chérubin is in the throes of strange feelings that he cannot quite understand:

> I no longer know what I am. But for some time I have felt an agitation in my breast. My heart quivers at the very sight of a woman. The words "love" and "pleasure" make it throb and confuse it. In fact, the need to say to someone "I love you" has become so pressing for me that I say it to myself as I run through the park, to your mistress, to you, to the trees, to the clouds, to the breeze which carries them off with my fleeting words.

This works well enough as the basis for a typical "I"-song (one of the standard justifications for an operatic aria), although da Ponte needed to refocus the ending to provide for a more effective climax:

	Non so più cosa son, cosa faccio,	10	I no longer know what I am, what I do;
	or di fuoco, ora sono di ghiaccio,	10	now I burn, now I freeze.
	ogni donna cangiar di colore,	10	Every woman makes me blush,
	ogni donna mi fa palpitar.	10t	every woman makes me tremble.
5	Solo ai nomi d'amor di diletto,	10	At the mere words "love" and "delight"
	mi si turba, mi s'altera il petto,	10	my breast heaves and pounds,
	e a parlare mi sforza d'amore	10	and there forces me to speak of love
	un desio ch'io non posso spiegar.	10t	a desire which I cannot explain.
	Parlo d'amor vegliando,	7	I speak of love when I am awake,
10	parlo d'amor sognando,	7	I speak of love when I am asleep,
	all'acque, all'ombre, ai monti,	7	to the streams, to the shade, to the mountains,

	ai fiori, all'erbe, ai fonti,	7	to the flowers, to the grass, to the fountains,
	all'eco, all'aria, ai venti,	7	to the echo, to the air, to the breezes
	che il suon de' vani accenti	7	which bear away the sound of my
15	portano via con se . . .	7t	fleeting words . . .
	E se non ho chi m'oda,	7	And if I have no one to hear me,
	parlo d'amor con me.	7t	I speak of love to myself.

Two stanzas of ten-syllable lines each with the same *verso tronco* rhyme at the end ("palpi*tar*," "spie*gar*") are followed by a middle section in seven-syllable ones, then a two-line *envoi*; the middle section and *envoi* both end with a *verso tronco* rhyme. Those ten-syllable lines have a clear influence on Mozart's gushing melody (which, indeed, is inconceivable without them). But the poetic form of the aria also has other rhetorical and musical consequences that need exploring in some detail.

ARIA FORMS

This kind of extended poetic structure is quite striking compared with the typical two-stanza forms of earlier *opera seria* that we saw in Handel's *Giulio Cesare in Egitto*. However, it is not untypical for *opera buffa*, where librettists (from Carlo Goldoni on) started to loosen the formalities, created patter-style lyrics, and also generated a rhetorical progression from the beginning of a text to its end, something not possible within a *da capo* aria text destined to finish with the first stanza rather than the second.

A few of the arias in *Le nozze di Figaro* retain more conventional stanzaic structures. The Countess's "cavatina" at the beginning of Act II, "Porgi, amor, qualche ristoro," marks her late entrance into the action (Beaumarchais has her appear earlier). It sets but a single stanza of text and thus serves a similar purpose to Giulio Cesare's entrance in Act I, scene 1 of *Giulio Cesare in Egitto*, allowing the Countess to remain onstage. There is a quite long orchestral introduction, presumably to allow for the change of set from Act I; the music is also strongly and no doubt deliberately reminiscent of a cavatina for Rosina in Paisiello's *Il barbiere di Siviglia* ("Giusto ciel, che conoscete," in Act I, scene 18). Barbarina's cavatina at the beginning of Act IV, "L'ho perduta, me meschina" (one stanza), also has an introduction for similar reasons, although the smaller scale of her piece is probably because the singer who took the role (Anna Gottlieb) was so young.[1]

The other, by now standard, form was the *rondò* (not to be confused with the instrumental rondo), which usually has a text in three stanzas, the first two of which are intended to be set in a slower tempo, and the third, in a faster one. By the 1780s this had become a typical operatic showpiece, usually for the *prima donna*: the Countess's "Dove sono i bei momenti" in Act III, scene 8 is a good example. The slight oddity of giving a *rondò* to Marcellina ("Il capro e la capretta" in IV.4), presumably to emphasize one of the messages of the opera, makes one regret still more the fact that that it is often cut. Mozart and da Ponte also originally intended a *rondò* for Susanna in Act IV, scene 10 ("Non tardar, amato bene"): Mozart sketched the music for the first two stanzas but not the faster concluding section for the third. This may have been intended to give Nancy Storace a chance to shine following Luisa Laschi-Mombelli's aria in Act III, or perhaps it was because Susanna is indeed pretending to be the Countess at this point and therefore should adopt her musical manners. "Non tardar amato bene" was dropped, of course, in favor of "Deh vieni, non tardar, o gioia bella," which is the polar opposite of a virtuosic piece, even if the autograph score has a cadenza at the end that is almost never performed nowadays. But when it came to revising *Le nozze di Figaro* in 1789, Mozart replaced it with, precisely, a *rondò* ("Al desio di chi t'adora") for the new singer—and unquestionably a *prima donna*—Adriana Ferrarese del Bene.

The three-stanza *rondò* certainly allowed for a vocally climactic conclusion that might also be put to dramatic purpose, as with the Countess's decision, in the third stanza of "Dove sono i bei momenti," to stay constant in her love for her husband in the hope that it might change his ungrateful heart (*Ah se almen la mia costanza*). The bigger question, however, was what to do in the slower opening section in terms of text repetition so as to allow for a balanced musical form. In the case of the Countess's *rondò* (and in the initial sketch for Susanna's), Mozart brings back the first stanza after the second (in Marcellina's, the stanzas run 1–2–1–2). In effect, "Dove sono" becomes a *da capo* aria (stanzas 1–2–1) with a faster coda (stanza 3). Stanza 1 is presented in the tonic, and stanza 2 prompts a move to a new key, the dominant, followed by a return to the tonic for the reprise of stanza 1. Thus,

---

1. The third use of the term "cavatina" in *Le nozze di Figaro*, for Figaro's "Se vuol ballare" (I.2), is less usual, given that the piece is an exit aria.

in its simpler forms (there are more complex ones), the slower section of the *rondò* tends to be tonally closed, which has an impact on the musical and rhetorical shift to the faster conclusion.

The same concerns—where to modulate and what, if anything, to repeat—underpin all the arias. Cherubino's *canzone* "Voi che sapete" is a "real" song (literally performed onstage, and heard as such by all the characters), and da Ponte follows Beaumarchais by providing a straight-forward strophic text (seven four-line stanzas in five-syllable lines). Mozart could have composed music just for one stanza and repeated it for all the rest, but instead he opts for a through-composed setting, even if the stanzaic structure of the poetry remains clearly articulated in the music. Stanza 2 marks the shift to the dominant, while stanzas 3–7 move quite widely before being stabilized by a reprise of stanza 1 (back in the tonic). We do not know whether this return was da Ponte's idea or Mozart's, but either way, the young page is clearly more sophisticated than his demeanor might suggest.

However, it is Cherubino's "Non so più cosa son, cosa faccio" that provides the more common model for the arias in *Figaro*. As we have seen, it begins with two four-line stanzas, in ten-syllable lines, then a middle section (seven lines) in seven-syllable ones, and a two-line *envoi*. Mozart does what might now be expected: stanza 2 initiates the move to the dominant, and stanza 1 is then repeated prior to the middle sec-tion. As for the *envoi*, it has some similarities with the musical setting of the opening in a somewhat stretched out form, providing additional clo-sure. A similar approach appears in Figaro's "Se vuol ballare," which has three stanzas (five-syllable lines) prior to the faster middle section where Figaro creates a list of how he will make his attack (*L'arte schermendo, / l'arte adoprando*), leading to a typical (for da Ponte) sequence of a *verso sdrucciolo* and a *verso tronco* as he vows to turn all the Count's machi-nations on their head (*Tutte le macchine / rovescierò*). Here, however, the first stanza is repeated not in the middle but the end: Figaro will make the Count dance to his tune, and the return to the courtly minuet (prior to a fast instrumental coda) enhances the threat while also suggesting his reining in his anger so as to take more effective control of the action to come.

In the aria that immediately follows—Bartolo's "La vendetta, oh la ven-detta!"—on the other hand, there is no text repetition for the sake of a broader musical structure, which turns the aria into mere bluster. Rather, the musical return of the opening material is instead worked into the *envoi* as

Bartolo proclaims that all Seville knows him, and that the scoundrel Figaro will be defeated (*Tutta Siviglia / conosce Bartolo / il birbo Figaro / vinto sarà*).[2] This requires music designed for one line length (eight-syllable lines) being reworked for another (five-syllable ones), though that is an easier task than we will find, below, in the case of the Act III sextet. In the Count's equivalent rage aria in Act III, scene 4, on the other hand, Mozart runs through stanzas 1–2 twice, then the middle section and the *envoi* twice, with the repetitions turning rage into obsession.

The Count's "Vedrò, mentre io sospiro" (III.4) is preceded by a *recitativo stromentato*, enhancing still further the seriousness of the situation; the Countess also has one prior to "Dove sono i bei momenti." More unusual, perhaps, are the two such recitatives in Act IV for Figaro (scene 8, before "Aprite un po' quegli occhi") and Susanna (scene 9, before "Deh vieni, non tardar, o gioia bella"). One would not normally expect servants to enjoy such elevated musical language. But it also reveals one of the problems of the original casting of *Le nozze di Figaro*. Francesco Benucci (Figaro) and Nancy Storace (Susanna) were clearly the stars of the production, yet their characters in the opera are lower in social status than the Count and the Countess, who should, in principle, be given the most "serious" music—unless Mozart is trying to convey some broader political message by suggesting otherwise.

A DUET, A TRIO, AND A SEXTET

In fact, *Le nozze di Figaro* is fairly democratic in so far as the allocation of arias is concerned, with three for Figaro; two each for Cherubino (he lost a third at a late stage),[3] the Countess, and Susanna; and one each for Barbarina, Bartolo, Basilio, the Count, and Marcellina. This accounts for half of the opera's twenty-eight numbers (separated by recitative): the other half is made up of six duets, two trios, one sextet, two choruses, and three finales. Susanna's first aria, "Venite . . . inginocchiatevi" (no. 12), comes quite late and is, in effect, a silent duet with Cherubino rather than any grand personal statement. But she has already established herself as perhaps the most significant character in the

2. Mozart's score has *vostro sarà*, i.e., Figaro will be "yours" (Marcellina's) and not "defeated," which raises an interesting question about whether (and when) Marcellina, who is present onstage, is paying attention to the aria.
3. The libretto printed in 1786 has an aria for Cherubino at the end of Act III, scene 7 (6 in that libretto): in "Se così brami" (for which no music survives) the first four-line stanza is addressed to Barbarina (who was present in the scene), while the second is an aside as the page expresses his hope of seeing the Countess again.

opera by her sheer presence—she has the most time onstage—and also by her participation in the ensembles that are often regarded as the glory of *Le nozze di Figaro*. The opera begins with two numbers for Susanna and her fiancé, each labeled *duettino*: such diminutive labels, which appear often in the opera, indicate not only scale but also an intention to keep the action moving. These numbers reveal how the stanzaic and other structures developed for arias could be adapted for two or more characters singing together onstage.

Thus, in their first duet, a minor conflict is set up between Susanna and Figaro, the outcome of which clearly establishes that she has the upper hand in their relationship:

Figaro (*misurando la camera*)		(*measuring the room*)
Cinque . . .dieci . . . venti . . . trenta . . .	8	Five . . . ten . . . twenty . . . thirty . . .
trentasei . . . quarantatre . . .	8t	thirty-six . . . forty-three . . .
Susanna (*fra sé, guardandosi nello specchio davanti al quale sta provandosi un cappellino ornato di fiori*)		(*to herself, looking at herself in a mirror before which she stands, trying on a little hat decorated with flowers*)
Ora sì ch'io son contenta,	8	Now, yes, I am content,
sembra fatta in ver per me.	8t	it seems just made for me.
(*A Figaro, seguitando a guardarsi*)		(*To Figaro, still looking at herself*)
Guarda un po' mio caro Figaro,	8s	Look, my dear Figaro,
guarda adesso il mio cappello.	8	look here at my hat.
Figaro		
Sì, mio core, or è più bello;	8	Yes, my love, now it's prettier;
sembra fatto inver per te.	8t	it seems to be made just for you.
Figaro, Susanna		
Ah il mattino alle nozze vicino	10	Ah, on this the morning of our wedding
quanto è dolce al mio (tuo) tenero sposo	10	how delightful to my (your) husband
questo bel cappellino vezzoso	10	is this lovely little hat
che Susanna ella stessa si fe'.	10	which Susanna made for herself.

A large amount of information is presented in a very efficient way, not least that Figaro and Susanna are to be married today, and that it is morning—which matters given that the opera is impeccably Aristotelian in adhering to the unity of time (the action of each successive act takes place from morning to evening during a single day). The duet begins with the characters speaking to themselves (two lines each, each pair closed by a *verso tronco*), then Susanna has two lines to call Figaro's attention to herself (with a nice *verso sdruc-ciolo* to make the point), and Figaro responds: these two pairs of lines form a single four-line stanza ending in a *verso tronco*. Then they have another four-line stanza in which each says almost exactly the same thing, stating their response to the situation. Mozart adds spice to the mix by extending the tussle between Figaro's stolid measuring and Susanna's pleas for atten-tion and taking it to the dominant—in which key Figaro sings Susanna's melody (*Sì, mio core, or è più bello*)—prior to the return to the tonic for the final four lines of the text. Now the music brings that melody back in the home key: Figaro's plodding measuring has been forgotten. The composer's only problem is that da Ponte has moved from eight- to ten-syllable lines, suggesting that he may have envisaged some kind of musical shift (e.g., to a faster tempo) for the closing section. However, Mozart sticks with his orig-inal material—keeping the setting more unified—given that the melody he wrote for Susanna's eight-syllable lines (which on the whole has two notes for every syllable) can quite easily be adjusted rhythmically to fit:

| O- | ra | sì | __ | ch'io | __ | Son | ___ | con- | ___ | ten- | ta |
| Al | mat- | tin' | __ | al- | le | noz- | ___ | ze | vi- | ci- | no |

This duet presents the typical pattern of (statement + statement + . . .)–action–reaction, where the number of initial statements depends on the num-ber of characters in the ensemble. The unanimity of the reaction will depend on the accord reached by the characters, but it usually comes down to two individuals (or groups) either sharing a common idea or contradicting each other, that is, being in harmony or at odds. The sequence can also be repeated, so that an ensemble can include two or more statement–action–reaction chains. This is the case of the Act II trio (no. 13). The Countess and Susanna have been dressing Cherubino as a maid, Susanna has left to get a ribbon and a dress, the Count knocks on the door, and Cherubino hides in a closet. The Count enters, sees his wife flustered, and hears a noise from the closet, which the Countess says has been caused by Susanna, who is in there. The Count, suspicious, orders her to come out, and the Countess has to block the move. Meanwhile, Susanna enters from another room, unseen by either character:

CONTE

| Susanna, or via sortite! | 7 | Susanna, come out now! |
| Sortite, così vò. | 7t | Come out, I order it. |

CONTESSA (*al Conte, affannata*) — (*to the Count, agitated*)

| Fermatevi . . . sentite . . . | 7 | Stop . . . listen . . . |
| sortire ella non può. | 7t | she cannot come out. |

SUSANNA

| 5 (Cos'è cotesta lite? | 7 | (What is this argument? |
| Il paggio, dove andò?) | 7t | Where did the page go?) |

CONTE

| E chi vietarlo or osa? | 7 | And who dares to forbid it? |

CONTESSA

Lo vieta l'onestà.	7t	Honesty forbids it.
Un abito da sposa	7	A bridal outfit
10 provando ella si sta.	7t	is she trying on.

CONTE

| (Chiarissima è la cosa: | 7 | (The affair is clear: |
| l'amante qui sarà.) | 7t | a lover is in there.) |

CONTESSA

| (Brutissima è la cosa: | 7 | (The affair is ugly: |
| chi sa cosa sarà?) | 7t | who knows what will happen?) |

SUSANNA

| 15 (Capisco qualche cosa, | 7 | (Now I understand things, |
| veggiamo come va.) | 7t | let us see what happens.) |

CONTE

| Dunque parlate almeno, | 7 | Well, at least speak, |
| Susanna, se quì siete . . . | 7 | Susanna, if you are there . . . |

CONTESSA

Nemen, nemen, nemmeno,	7	Not at all, not at all, not at all,
(*verso la porta*)		(*toward the door*)
20 io v'ordino, tacete.	7	I order you: be silent.

SUSANNA (*nascondendosi entro l'alcova*) — (*hiding herself within the alcove*)

(Oh cielo! un precipizio,	7	(O heavens! a crisis,
un scandalo, un disordine	7s	a scandal, an upset
qui certo nascerà.)	7t	will certainly happen here.)

CONTE, CONTESSA

	Consorte mia (mio), giudizio!	7	My wife (husband), be careful!
25	Un scandalo, un disordine	7s	a scandal, an upset
	schiviam, per carità.	7t	let us avoid, for pity's sake.

The text proceeds in *versi piani–versi tronchi* pairs save for the final three-line groupings, and the *versi tronchi* are rhymed, first with -*ò* endings and then (after the first set of statements, or, in this case, two instructions and a statement) -*à* ones. For those final reactions, the Count and Countess are paired—even though they are on opposite sides, they urge caution on each other—while Susanna remains apart (just as she is on the stage). But those two sets of reactions match up in terms of lines and rhymes and even share some common words (*un scandalo, un disordine*), which means that the characters can sing them together.

In these ensembles, text repetition on any larger structural scale (as in the stanza 1–2–1–3 arias) is usually inappropriate given the dramatic situation and its progression. Mozart therefore must decide whether he still needs musical repetition, reworking music setting one part of the text so as to fit another. In the case of the Act II trio, Mozart divides the text into two unequal halves, each beginning with the Count's imperative: first, that Susanna should come out (*Susanna, or via sortite!*—the vocative kickstarts the trio), and then, that she should speak (*Dunque parlate almeno*; line 17). The prior move to the dominant occurs at what in effect is the beginning of the second stanza (after the first three pairs of lines), heightening the aggressiveness of the Count's question as to who or what prevents Susanna from appearing (line 7: *E chi vietarlo or osa?*) and establishing a tension between the tonic and dominant keys. The music returns firmly to the tonic, with the opening musical material, for the second half of the setting (the Count's second imperative at line 17), then veers away into darker tonal areas (at the Count's warning to his wife, *Consorte mio, giudizio!*), then returns to the tonic with the music first heard in the dominant transposed into the home key: so, the Countess's rising scale (which Mozart later gave to Susanna) is heard in two different keys, in the dominant and, transposed (up!), in the tonic.

For Susanna to sing that rising scale, therefore putting her at the top of the texture, would seem to create a dramatic problem: she is in hiding, so might better also stay hidden within the musical texture. But the solution adopted in some productions—to restore Mozart's first idea—is no less problematic: the first time round, at least, the Countess is also singing an aside that is not meant to be heard by her husband. Indeed, for a good part of this trio (eleven lines out of twenty-six), the characters are singing (or if you prefer, speaking) just to themselves rather than to each other. But it is not a distinction that can be made easily in musical terms; rather, it is up to the stage director to sort things out.

Thus the trio does not so much stage the action as create a space within which the action might be staged. But that space is clearly articulated by way of some kind of dramatic or emotional arc extending beyond the dark tonal shift as the Count warns his wife to be careful (*Consorte mia, giudizio!*). Three separate processes come into play here, one after the other: first, a strongly articulated move to the dominant; second, a clear tonal return (to the tonic), and also a thematic one (the initial material), two-thirds of the way through the piece; and third, material presented in a foreign key (the dominant) being repeated in the tonic. The scheme is also characteristic of sonata form (also called the sonata principle, or sonata style), usually found in the first movements (and some others) of instrumental pieces written during the Classical and Romantic periods, either in a three-part version (exposition, development, and recapitulation) or in an "abridged" one (in which the development section is replaced by a shorter preparation for the recapitulation), as here in the Act II trio. While identifying this trio as being in sonata form would not have been contentious a few decades ago, it has become so now, in part because it seems a misapplication of the term (which does not quite fit anyway) but more because critics have come to resent the assumption that opera draws its inspiration, and its models, from instrumental music—or, to put it another way, that instrumental music (for which read Beethoven) is the paragon against which opera must be measured. Mozart of course would not have known the term "sonata form" in any context, whether vocal or instrumental—it was formulated by theorists only later—although he certainly understood the musical grammars on the one hand, and rhetorics on the other, that underpin it: this was one of the principal ways in which any composer in the latter part of the eighteenth century constructed a musical argument. The more specific problem, however, is the assumption that the tonal and thematic elements of a recapitulation somehow present and enable closure, meaning that large-scale dissonances have been resolved, and instabilities rendered stable. This clearly does not work in dramatic terms in the case of the Act II trio, where things are even more up in the air at the end than they were at the beginning. It is a simple fact of musical life, however—at least in the eighteenth century—that pieces must end in the key in which they began. The apparent contradiction between open-ended dramatic situations and closed musical forms is one that animates the history of opera in various ways.

Many of these issues come to a head in perhaps the greatest ensemble in *Le nozze di Figaro*: the Act III sextet (no. 18). Despite Figaro's defeat in the lawsuit pursued by Marcellina, all is suddenly resolved by the discovery that she is his long-lost mother, and Bartolo his father. The Count, supported by Don Curzio, laments the wrecking of his plan to get Figaro out of the way (by marrying Marcellina) so that he could have free rein with Susanna. Susanna herself enters midway through the action, having found (from where is not at all clear) a thousand doubloons to pay Figaro's debt. She sees him embracing Marcellina and Bartolo and assumes the worst—that she has been pushed aside—until Marcellina explains the newly discovered family circumstances. Susanna is at first skeptical, then persuaded, then overjoyed. The Count and Don Curzio are left in confusion that all their plans have come to naught.

The plot device—a sudden recognition that turns the tables—is so conventional that one has a clear sense of da Ponte, and still more Mozart, poking fun at the device itself. As occurs in a number of moments in *Le nozze di Figaro*, the sextet becomes almost metatheatrical: theater plays with itself as theater rather than as some representation of particular dramatic situations. The text follows what will by now be a fairly familiar pattern, with opening statements by each of five characters (Susanna has yet to appear) in couplets linked by the *verso tronco* rhyme, *-ir*:

MARCELLINA		
Riconosci in questo amplesso	8	See in this embrace
una madre, amato figlio.	8	your mother, beloved son.
FIGARO (*a Bartolo*)		(*to Bartolo*)
Padre mio, fate lo stesso,	8	Father, do the same,
non mi fate più arrossir.	8t	let me blush with shame no longer.
BARTOLO (*abbracciando Figaro*)		(*embracing Figaro*)
5 Resistenza la coscienza	8	My conscience will not let me
far non lascia al tuo desir.	8t	resist your desire.
DON CURZIO		
(Ei suo padre, ella sua madre,	8	(He his father, she his mother,

l'imeneo non può seguir.)	8t	then the wedding cannot take place.)

CONTE

(Son smarrito, son stordito,	8	(I am shocked, I am astounded,
10 meglio è assai di qua partir.)	8t	it is better to leave here.)

MARCELLINA

Figlio amato!	?→	Beloved son!

FIGARO

Parenti amati!	?	Beloved parents!

That *Figlio amato!/Parenti amati* exchange is odd given that it does not fit the prevailing poetic meter: one suspects that Mozart has added the words on his own to suit his dramatic or musical purposes.

The Count makes to leave, but Susanna enters suddenly and stops him (the music shifts to the dominant) because she now has money to pay off Figaro's debt. The text remains in eight-syllable lines, though the *verso tronco* rhyme changes to -à. Da Ponte also gives Susanna a delicious *verso sdrucciolo–verso tronco* pair that is beautifully matched in the music.

SUSANNA

Alto, alto, signor Conte,	8	Stop, stop, my lord Count,
mille doppie son quì pronte,	8	I have a thousand doubloons here,
a pagar vengo per Figaro	8s	I come to pay for Figaro
15 ed a porlo in libertà.	8t	and to free him.

CONTE, DON CURZIO

Non sappiam com'è la cosa,	8	We do not understand what is going on,
osservate un poco là.	8t	but look over there.

SUSANNA (*si volge e vede Figaro che abbraccia Marcellina. Vuol partire.*)

(*turns and sees Figaro embracing Marcellina. She makes to leave.*)

Già d'accordo con la sposa:	8	Already he has agreed the marriage:
giusti dei, che infedeltà.	8t	ye gods, what faithlessness.

But here the text (and the music) start to reveal one problem for large ensembles: save where characters sing one after the other, such as at the beginning of the sextet, it is almost impossible to keep them distinct. Prior to Susanna's entrance, Mozart establishes one group of three characters (Bartolo, Figaro, Marcellina) and one of two (the Count and Don Curzio), with each group given its own distinct material. Susanna upsets the applecart—the music shifts to the dominant to mark her appearance—and as she gets hold of the wrong end of the stick (on seeing Figaro embracing Marcellina), she joins the Count and Don Curzio as they shake and rage in fury (*Fremio, smanio dal furore*): the characters are now grouped as three plus three. For Susanna, this is an unholy alliance, but it also enables the most striking dramatic (and musical) event in the sextet as Susanna soon moves to the "right" side of the equation.

The poetic meter shifts (though the *-à* rhyme remains) as Marcellina explains matters to her:

26	Lo sdegno calmate,	6	Calm your anger,
	mia cara figliuola,	6	my dear daughter,
	sua madre abbracciate,	6	embrace his mother,
	che or vostra sarà.	6t	who now will be yours too.

Mozart plays up Susanna's realization that Marcellina is indeed Figaro's mother, and Bartolo his father, with a very funny sequence of *Sua madre* and *Suo padre* repetitions across the characters that may again have been the composer's additions to the libretto (once more, the words do not fit the poetic meter). She then joins the family: the three-plus-three grouping shifts to one of four-plus-two in the final two quatrains, as Bartolo, Figaro, Marcellina, and Susanna are united in their "sweet contentment" (*Al dolce contento*)—with Susanna floating ecstatically above the texture—and the Count and Don Curzio remain in "harsh torment" (*Al fiero tormento*).

This shift to six-syllable lines is striking. As in the case of the metrical shift in the first duet in the opera, "Cinque ... dieci ... venti ... trenta ... ," da Ponte may have expected Mozart to begin a new musical section here, and were this an end-of-act finale, the composer would probably have done so, we shall see. Mozart's decision not to change pace must have been deliberate. He treats Marcellina's six-syllable *Lo sdegno calmate* as the point of tonal return (to the tonic) to create a parallelism between this moment in the sextet and the beginning (having revealed herself to Figaro, she now does so to Susanna). This works in a manner similar to the Act II trio (the Count's two imperatives), although the tonal resolution in the sextet better reflects the dramatic situation as Susanna's initial tensions (at her entrance in the dominant) now turn into relief. But while that is a very smart move on

Mozart's part, it creates problems, because (unlike "Cinque ... dieci ... ") the melody designed for Marcellina's eight-syllable lines will not fit the new six-syllable ones—the verbal stresses are in the wrong place. Inevitably, Mozart finds an elegant solution to the problem: that first melody is placed instead in octaves in the orchestral woodwinds (flute, oboe, bassoon).

One can see why the Act III sextet was Mozart's favorite piece in the opera (so Michael Kelly said). But the larger problem is that it brings the action of the opera almost to a halt: the main impediment to Figaro and Susanna's wedding has been removed. Da Ponte has to work quite hard to regain momentum as the tale switches first to the Countess and then to the humiliating of the Count. But perhaps the main story of *Le nozze di Figaro* has been that of the Count and Countess all along.

FINALES

Da Ponte's technique for structuring single-movement ensembles could be extended quite easily for the chain finales that were a feature of later eighteenth-century *opera buffa*. There are two in *Le nozze di Figaro*, one each at the end of Acts II and IV: the Act III finale, with its ballet incorporating dramatic action over a fandango (the one concession in *Figaro* to local Spanish color), is somewhat different. Da Ponte noted in his memoirs the difficulties involved in constructing such extended sequences:

A *finale*, which has to be closely connected with the rest of the opera, is a sort of little comedy in itself and requires a fresh plot and a special interest of its own. This is the great occasion for showing off the genius of the composer, the ability of the singers, and the most effective "situation" of the drama. Recitative is excluded from it; everything is sung, and every style of singing must find a place in it—*adagio, allegro, andante, amabile, armonioso, strepitoso, arcistrepitoso, strepitosissimo*, and with this the said finale generally ends. This in the musicians' slang is called the *chiusa* or *stretta*—I suppose because it gives not one twinge but a hundred to the unhappy brain of the poet who has to write the words. In this finale it is a dogma of theatrical theology that all the singers should appear on the stage, even if there were three hundred of them, by ones, by twos, by threes, by sixes, by tens, by sixties, to sing solos, duets, trios, sextets, sessantets; and if the plot of the play does not allow of it, the poet must find some way of making the plot allow of it, in defiance of his judgment, of his reason, or of all the Aristotles on earth; and if he then finds his play going badly, so much the worse for him!

He might have been speaking directly of the Act II finale (no. 15) in *Le nozze di Figaro*, which follows the pattern very clearly in terms of the incremental increase in the number of characters onstage (even if, we have seen, Antonio has to leave to allow the same singer to return as Bartolo). As for the sequence of "every style of singing," da Ponte enables it by shifts of poetic meter that, by and large, prompt Mozart to move to a new musical section distinguished by tempo, musical meter, or general character, varying the pace and then building it up to the *prestissimo* (da Ponte's *strepitosissimo*) at the end:

(Scene 8) *Allegro* (**C**); E flat major; eight-syllable lines. Count, Countess
(Scene 9a) *Molto andante* (3/8); B flat major; six-syllable lines. Plus Susanna
(Scene 9b) *Allegro* (**C**); B flat major; six-syllable lines (the Count briefly leaves, then returns)
(Scene 10a) *Allegro* (3/8); G major; six-syllable lines. Plus Figaro
(Scene 10b) *Andante* (2/4); C major; eight-syllable lines
(Scene 11a) *Allegro molto* (**C**); F major; ten-syllable lines. Plus Antonio
(Scene 11b) *Andante* (6/8); B flat major; ten-syllable lines (Antonio soon leaves)
(Scene 12) *Allegro assai* (**C**)–*Più allegro* (**C**)–*Prestissimo* (**C**); E flat major; eight-syllable lines. Plus Bartolo, Basilio, Marcellina

Mozart's decision to split scene 10 into two sections reflects the change of poetic meter (from six- to eight-syllable lines). On the other hand, his splitting of scenes 9 and 11, even though the poetic meter remains the same in each, responds to the dramatic situation: in scene 9 the Count goes into the closet, leaving the Countess in agitation (so, *Allegro*) until Susanna explains matters to her; and in scene 11, the *Andante* is needed to draw out Figaro's triumph over the Count in finding a reason for him to carry Cherubino's commission (given that it lacked an official seal). It would also seem from the poetic design that da Ponte intended some continuity from the end of scene 9 through the beginning of scene 10 (despite Figaro's entrance), since the six-syllable lines continue until the Count slows matters down by interrogating Figaro over whether he recognizes the anonymous letter he has received raising suspicions about the Countess (*Conoscete, signor Figaro*). But Mozart marks Figaro's appearance with a new section, which makes sense given that it is an interruption. It is also a break in tonal terms: the finale starts in the tonic and moves to the dominant (E flat major to B flat major), and then there is a very abrupt tonal shift from B flat major to G major, whence the finale moves in a carefully constructed sequence (down the circle of fifths) to get back to the original tonic.

The Act IV finale (no. 28) is more diffuse, which is not to say that it is worse: indeed, such looser structures become the norm in the next two Mozart-da Ponte operas, such that the Act II finale, for all the praise lavished on it in the scholarly literature, seems to be the exception, perhaps because it was Mozart's first large-scale attempt at the genre. Now the drama is more complex: in addition to the Count's humiliation, Cherubino must put in a final appearance, and a tiff between Figaro and Susanna—based on his having misread her previous actions—needs to be resolved. Furthermore, the staging is less straightforward (characters move on and off in the nighttime confusion), and even the tonal scheme wanders, for all that scholars have often tried to find connections with keys used earlier in the opera:

> (Scene 11a) *Andante* (**C**); D major; eight-syllable lines. Cherubino, Countess (as Susanna); then the Count, Figaro, and Susanna each observe from a distance
>
> (Scene 11b) *Con un poco più di moto* (**C**); G major; seven-syllable lines. Count, Countess (as Susanna); Figaro and Susanna observe; then Figaro enters noisily, and the Count and Countess retreat
>
> (Scene 11c) *Larghetto* (3/4); E flat major; seven-syllable *versi sdruccioli*. Figaro (alone)
>
> (Scene 11d) *Allegro di molto* (3/4); E flat major; seven-syllable lines. Plus Susanna (as the Countess)
>
> (Scene 11e) *Andante* (6/8); B flat major; ten-syllable lines. Figaro, Susanna (recognized as herself); then the Count observes from a distance (as Susanna reverts to playing the Countess)
>
> (Scene 12a) *Allegro assai* (**C**); G major; eight-syllable lines. Count, Figaro, Antonio, (Bartolo), Basilio, (Don Curzio), servants; then (emerging from one of the side pavilions) Cherubino, Barbarina, Marcellina, and Susanna; then (from the other pavilion) the Countess
>
> (Scene 12b) *Andante* (**C**); G major; six-syllable lines. Count, Countess, all
>
> (Scene 12c) *Allegro assai* (**C**); D major; eight-syllable lines. All

It would seem that here Mozart took a greater number of structural decisions on his own, perhaps because the action is less orderly, but also, it seems, because he sees a different outcome to the events of this "mad day."

READINGS AND MESSAGES

The most striking disagreement—if disagreement it is—between da Ponte and Mozart in the Act IV finale seems to be the handling of the ending. The Count pulls one character after another out of the pavilion but finally thinks that he has caught the "Countess" (i.e., Susanna) in the act. All ask for forgiveness (*Perdono!*), but the Count refuses it. Then the real Countess emerges, casting everyone not in the know into total confusion:

Oh cielo! che veggio!	6	Oh heavens! what do I see!
deliro! vaneggio!	6	a delusion! a vision!
che creder non so.	6t	that I cannot believe.
CONTE (*in tono supplichevole*)		(*in a tone of supplication*)
Contessa, perdono.	6	Countess, forgive me.
CONTESSA		
Più docile io sono	6	I am meek
e dico di sì.	6t	and say yes.
TUTTI		
Ah! tutti contenti	6	Ah! all happy
saremo così.	6t	shall we be thus.

This rather perfunctory resolution, and the brief stanza that follows, come straight from Beaumarchais, who does not seem to have attached great weight to the outcome of what he had set in train. Mozart, however, presses hard on the musical brakes (creating problems for conductors in the process), turning the Countess's act of forgiveness—or clemency—into a transcendent moment of reconciliation. It is an extraordinarily powerful gesture that almost, but not quite, hides the awkward questions that follow.

In Enlightenment terms, clemency was a desirable virtue usually attached to male rulers and generally associated with wisdom: the Count, however, is neither clement nor wise, which is in part the point of Beaumarchais's satire. It has often been tempting to treat the Countess as his better half—displaying the qualities so notably lacking in her husband—although her final concession, at least as da Ponte (following Beaumarchais) presents it, seems more dictated by convention: his Italian makes her *docile*, meaning meek, malleable, and obedient in the manner expected of eighteenth-century women. Nor is she terribly wise, at least in some of her earlier actions in the play. Much depends on how one plays the role. She is meant to be young rather than matronly—the action takes place just a few years after that of *Le Barbier de Séville*—which might grant her a certain leeway in her japes, and also greater familiarity with her maidservant than one would expect in a typical noble household of the time: in the case of the Letter Duet in Act III, "Che soave zeffiretto" (no. 20), they present themselves almost as equals, which is in part Mozart's point.

Susanna, too, steps beyond the typical role of the wisecracking, manipulative female servant—Despina in *Così fan tutte* is the obvious example. This surely has something to do with Nancy Storace, a *prima donna* not in a *prima donna* role; but Mozart's music for Susanna also moves beyond the type. While one can imagine a Despina singing "Venite . . . inginocchiatevi," the same hardly applies to "Deh vieni, non tardar, o gioia bella," an aria that is as unusual in its text (ten eleven-syllable lines in rhyming couplets, with nary a *verso tronco* in sight) as in its handling of its 6/8 rhythms in ways so different from the more rustic 6/8 of the peasant choruses in the opera. The impulse is in part pastoral—the action in the final act moves from repressive indoor settings to the freer space of a garden at night—which is also reflected in Marcellina's Act IV aria, "Il capro e la capretta." But Susanna is also painted as being smarter than any Despina: she saves the day toward the end of Act II, and her gloriously pointed minuet in that act's finale as she emerges from the closet instead of the expected Cherubino, is a noble dance that—as many have noted—turns the tables on the Count in ways far beyond Susanna's social station.

Figaro has already used the same device in Act I, with "Se vuol ballare," where he vows to teach the *Contino* (an offensive diminutive) to dance. But compared with Susanna's minuet, this is a more clodhopping example in terms both of the poetry (prosaic five-syllable lines as distinct from Susanna's more elegant six-syllable ones) and of the music (phrases tend to start on the downbeat rather than Susanna's upbeats). Figaro's rhetoric also exceeds the bounds of the style—Mozart adds a *sì* to the libretto, which is then repeated—and descends into verbal and musical bluster. Although, by comic convention, he should be the chief engineer of the action, as in *Le Barbier de Séville*, his story ends too soon, with the Act III sextet. By that time, anyway, he has already started to lose the plot—despite his impressive saves in the Act II finale—and he is too quick to distrust Susanna toward the end of the opera. Shorn by da Ponte of his political diatribes, it becomes hard for him to keep the upper hand. Benucci may have been good at delivering arias across the footlights and inveighing against women's inconstancy, as in his Act IV aria "Aprite un po' quegli occhi": Mozart and da Ponte gave him one in similar vein in *Così fan tutte* with Guglielmo's "Donne mie, le fate a tanti." But Figaro's invective starts to sound empty-headed.

Of course, it may be unreasonable to expect anything more. We have already seen how the Act III sextet seems to revel in its absurdity, and there are several moments in *Le nozze di Figaro* when the audience is reminded that all we are seeing is only an opera. For example, in the Act II finale the Countess and Susanna declare their wish to bring the comedy to a close (*la burletta ha da finir*), and Figaro asks that it be done in the traditional theatrical fashion (*Per finirla lietamente / e all'usanza teatrale*): with a wedding. This is a typical operatic ploy that in turn reflects the genre's nervousness about itself. It also discourages any attempt to delve into the characters' subconscious thoughts, to attribute to them intentions that they cannot possibly have, to grant them agency to act in any way other than how they are represented by their creators, or to imagine any future they might have outside the opera. Yet it says something for Mozart's music that we are constantly inclined to do all four. For those who might want to find a message in *Le nozze di Figaro*, however, the most obvious is Marcellina's proto-feminist observation, if one chooses to read it that way, that while billy goats and nanny goats, rams and ewes, and even both sexes of the most ferocious animals seem to get along amicably enough, only in the case of humankind do men treat their women badly: it is better, she suggests, that we should all somehow find a way to get along. But that is not a bad lesson to take away from a particularly "mad" day in Spain.

FURTHER READING

The quotations here from the letters between Mozart and his father are taken (with minor adjustments) from Emily Anderson, ed., *The Letters of Mozart and His Family*, 3rd ed. (London: Macmillan, 1985); Lorenzo da Ponte's memoirs have been translated by Elisabeth Abbott (1929; New York: Da Capo Press, 1988); for Michael Kelly, see his *Reminiscences*, edited by Roger Fiske (London and New York: Oxford University Press, 1975). Other relevant documents quoted here are in Otto Erich Deutsch, *Mozart: A Documentary Biography*, translated by Eric Blom, Peter Branscombe, and Jeremy Noble (London: Simon and Schuster, 1990). Useful introductions to the opera are provided by Tim Carter, *W. A. Mozart: "Le nozze di Figaro"*, Cambridge Opera Handbooks (Cambridge: Cambridge University Press, 1987), and Andrew Steptoe, *The Mozart-da Ponte Operas: The Cultural and Musical Background to "Le nozze di Figaro," "Don Giovanni," and "Così fan tutte"* (Oxford: Oxford University Press, 1988), although they are now a little dated. John Rice, *Mozart on the Stage* (Cambridge: Cambridge University Press, 2009) also covers important ground (and it situates *Figaro* as an opera potentially for Carnival).

For the opera's use of specific musical tropes (in particular, dance patterns) to dramatic effect, see Wye J. Allanbrook, *Rhythmic Gesture in Mozart: "Le nozze di Figaro" and "Don Giovanni"* (Chicago: University of Chicago Press, 1983). For opera in Vienna in the 1780s, see Dorothea Link, *The National Court Theatre in Mozart's Vienna: Sources and Documents, 1783–1792* (Oxford: Clarendon Press, 1998), and Mary Hunter, *The Culture of Opera Buffa in Mozart's Vienna: A Poetics of Entertainment* (Princeton, NJ: Princeton University Press, 1999). Mozart's creation of *Le nozze di Figaro* as reflected in the musical and other sources is covered in the relevant essays in Daniel Heartz, *Mozart's Operas*, edited by Thomas Bauman (Berkeley and Los Angeles: University of California Press, 1990), and in Alan Tyson, *Mozart: Studies of the Autograph Scores* (Cambridge, MA: Harvard University Press, 1987); the latter also discusses variants introduced early in the performance history of the work, some of which are in Alan Tyson, ed., *W. A. Mozart, "Le nozze di Figaro": Eight Variant Versions* (Oxford and New York: Oxford University Press, 1989). Dorothea Link, "The Fandango Scene in Mozart's *Le nozze di Figaro*," *Journal of the Royal Musical Association* 133 (2008): 69–92, also offers an account of the Act III finale that somewhat contradicts da Ponte's.

CHAPTER 5

Francesco Maria Piave and Giuseppe Verdi, *Rigoletto* (Venice, 1851)

GIUSEPPE VERDI (CI853)

Verdi was the most successful composer of Italian operas in the mid-nineteenth century; he also became a major cultural and political icon during the Risorgimento.
AKG-IMAGES.

Duke of Mantua: Raffaele Mirate (tenor)[1]
Rigoletto, court jester: Felice Varesi (baritone)
Gilda, daughter of Rigoletto: Teresina Brambilla (soprano)

1. This list of singers follows the posters made by the Teatro La Fenice for the opening run of *Rigoletto*. Some later sources give Paolo Damini as the first Sparafucile, with Feliciano Pons taking the role of Monterone. The singer playing the latter role is not named in the posters but Damini is given in the first edition of the libretto (from which the variant spellings of names in

Sparafucile, a hired assassin: Feliciano Pons (Ponz; bass)
Maddalena, sister of Sparafucile: Annetta Casaloni (contralto)
Giovanna, duenna to Gilda: Laura Saini (mezzosoprano)
Count of Monterone: [Paolo Damini?] (baritone)
Marullo, a knight: Francesco De Kunert (Francesco Kunerth; baritone)
Matteo Borsa, a courtier: Angelo Zuliani (tenor)
Count of Ceprano: Andrea Bellini (bass)
Countess of Ceprano, wife of the Count of Ceprano: Luigia Morselli (mezzo-soprano)
Usher of the court: Antonio Rizzi (bass)
Page of the duchess: Annetta Modest Lovati (Modes Lovati; mezzo-soprano)
Knights, ladies, pages, halbadiers

SETTING: The city of Mantua and its surroundings, the sixteenth century.
SOURCE: Victor Hugo (1802–1885), *Le Roi s'amuse* (1832).

FIRST PERFORMED: Venice, Teatro La Fenice, 11 March 1851, with another thirteen performances that same month (to the end of the season). The sets were done by Giuseppe Bertoja (under the supervision of the chief scene designer for La Fenice, Francesco Bagnara); Gaetano Mares conducted. By the end of 1852 the opera had been staged widely across Italy under various different titles (for reasons of censorship); by 1854 it had reached Alexandria and Istanbul and, by 1855, Latin and South America. It was first done at the Theatre Royal, Covent Garden, in London on 14 May 1853, and in New York (at the Academy of Music) on 19 February 1855.

ACT I. (Scenes 1–6: *A magnificent hall in the ducal palace, with doors in the rear that lead to other rooms, all brightly lit.*) (Nos. 1–2: *Preludio ed Introduzione*) The ominous mood of the orchestral prelude is broken by the lively sound of an onstage band supplying the music for a court ball, with a crowd of lords

---

this list, as given in parentheses, are also taken). The brief role of the page (mezzo-soprano) is now sometimes taken by a tenor.

and ladies, pages coming and going, and bursts of laughter heard from time to time. The Duke of Mantua discusses with Matteo Borsa his amorous intentions toward a commoner he has seen every Sunday in church; he has discovered her address but does not know who the man is who enters there every night. The Duke is then distracted by the sight of all the beautiful women at the ball, even if he is most enamored of the wife of the Count of Ceprano. Borsa warns him to be discrete, but the Duke cares not one jot; he is happy to seduce whoever might pass by, for all women are the same to him (*Ballata*: "Questa o quella per me pari sono"). As the dancing continues (a minuet in a stately 3/4), the Duke presses his suit with the Countess, and they leave together. Rigoletto mocks Ceprano, who is in quick pursuit; the jester comments that the Duke is up to his usual festive tricks. The dancing shifts to a *perigordino* (in a faster 6/8). Marullo enters, eager to tell the courtiers of his discovery that Rigoletto seems to have a lover. The Duke returns, followed by Rigoletto: his plans for the Countess have been foiled by the Count, but they discuss tactics in terms of how to move forward, overheard by Ceprano. Rigoletto advises putting the Count in prison, banishing him, or chopping off his head; the Count is furious, and even the Duke warns Rigoletto against going too far, but the jester pays no heed. Ceprano sets in train with his fellow courtiers a plot to take revenge on Rigoletto; they will meet at Ceprano's house tomorrow night. Meanwhile, the court continues the festivities ("Tutto è gioia, tutto è festa"). But the Count of Monterone enters to cast a pall on the proceedings: he wishes to pursue his claim against the Duke for having dishonored his daughter. Rigoletto responds mockingly ("Voi congiuraste contro noi, signore"), which increases Monterone's anger still more; the Duke, tired of the intrusion, orders Monterone arrested; and Monterone utters a curse on both him and the jester. Rigoletto is particularly horrified, but the court is happy to leave Monterone to his fate ("O tu che la festa audace hai turbato").

(Scenes 7–15: *The deserted end of a cul-de-sac; on the left a modest house with a small courtyard surrounded by a wall. In the courtyard, a large, tall tree and a marble bench; in the wall, a door leading to the street; above the wall, an accessible terrace supported by arches; the door of the second floor opens onto the terrace, which is reached by a flight of stairs in front. On the right of the street is the very high wall around the garden and one side of the Count of Ceprano's palace. It is night.*) (No. 3: *Duetto*) Rigoletto is returning home. His musing on the curse ("Quel vecchio maledivami!") is interrupted by Sparafucile, an assassin-for-hire who offers his services: he has been watching Rigoletto's house and has seen someone else doing the same, presumably a rival for the hand of the woman living inside. Rigoletto asks about payment (half in advance, half after the deed is done) and his method of killing: Sparafucile either attacks his target in the city after dark or uses his sister to lure the victim to his home. Rigoletto dismisses him but asks where they might meet should the need arise: "Here, every evening," Sparafucile replies.

(No. 4: *Scena e Duetto*) Rigoletto muses on the encounter and realizes that he and Sparafucile are of a type: one does violence with a dagger and the other with his tongue ("Pari siamo! . . . io la lingua, egli ha il pugnale"). Monterone's curse still haunts him, but he is also outraged by his position at court: deformed and constantly abused by the courtiers, but forced to play the fool to keep the Duke amused. As he opens the door to his house, Gilda runs into his arms, and they greet each other as father and daughter ("Figlia! . . . Mio padre!"). Gilda knows almost nothing about him or her mother and asks to hear more; Rigoletto is more anxious over whether Gilda ever leaves the house; only to go to church, she says. However, he does reveal something about Gilda's deceased mother ("Deh, non parlare al misero"): Gilda is all that is left to him. She is left with mixed feelings of compassion and curiosity. Rigoletto returns to the question of whether Gilda ever leaves the house—he is terrified that she might become a victim of some dishonor—and he summons her duenna, Giovanna, to interrogate her further, and then to urge her to keep careful watch over his daughter ("Veglia, o donna, questo fiore"); Gilda, on the other hand, thinks that her mother in heaven will protect them. The Duke, disguised as a commoner, enters the street; Rigoletto hears a noise and goes out to investigate; and the Duke slips inside the courtyard, hiding behind the tree and throwing a purse to Giovanna to ensure her silence. Rigoletto returns and asks Giovanna whether she and Gilda are ever followed to church; no, she says. He orders her never to open the door to anyone (not even the Duke?—she asks, to which Rigoletto answers a firm "no"). The Duke realizes that he is pursuing his jester's daughter. Rigoletto leaves, repeating his injunction to Giovanna.

(No. 5: *Scena e Duetto*) Gilda tells Giovanna that she feels guilty because she has not told her father about the young man she has seen in church ("Giovanna, ho dei rimorsi"). Giovanna thinks him a great gentleman, but Gilda does not care whether he is a lord or prince, and indeed would love him more if he were poor; she also admits to fantasizing about revealing her feelings to him, which prompts the Duke to burst out of hiding to declare his own love for her, also waving Giovanna away. Gilda is shocked, but as the Duke insists on his love for her ("È il sol dell'anima, la vita è amore"), she is unable to resist his charms. Ceprano and Borsa appear in the street, ready to put their plan into action. Gilda asks to know her lover's name (the Duke makes up "Gualtier Maldè" on the spot and says that he is a poor student); Giovanna returns because she has heard sounds in the street; and the two lovers bid a fond farewell ("Addio! speranza ed anima").

(No. 6: *Scena ed Aria*). Gilda is head over heels in love, and the name Gualtier Maldè is engraved on her heart ("Caro nome che il mio cor"); she goes into the house, then appears on the terrace to try to catch a glimpse of her beloved as he leaves. Ceprano and the courtiers appear, wearing masks and carrying arms, and when they see Gilda from the street, they comment on her beauty. Rigoletto returns—though he does not know why—and recalls the curse once more. He encounters the courtiers, who decide to trick him: they say they have come to kidnap the Countess of Ceprano, and Rigoletto willingly joins in the game; they blindfold him and have him hold a ladder against the wall. (No. 7: *Coro*) The courtiers plot to kidnap Rigoletto's "lover" ("Zitti, zitti moviamo a vendetta"); they enter his house, seize Gilda, and drag her off; she loses a shoe in the process. Her cries for help are heard in the distance. Rigoletto, still holding the ladder, suddenly realizes that he is wearing a blindfold; he tears it off, sees the shoe lying in the street, and also the open door to his house. He tears his hair, cries out against the curse, and collapses.

ACT II. (*A room in the ducal palace. There are two doors on each side, and a larger one in the rear which closes, flanked by full-length*

portraits of the Duke and his consort. There is a high-backed chair
next to a velvet-covered table.) (No. 8: *Scena ed Aria*) The Duke
enters in some agitation; he had returned to Rigoletto's house only
to find Gilda kidnapped ("Ella mi fu rapita!"), and he imagines
her tears ("Parmi veder le lagrime"). The courtiers enter to tell the
story of how they have taken Rigoletto's "lover" ("Scorrendo uniti
remota via"); the Duke, realizing that it is Gilda and that she is now
in the palace, runs off to be with her, summoned, he says, by love
("Possente amor mi chiama"). The courtiers are confused by the
Duke's change of mood, but they turn their attention to Rigoletto
(no. 9: *Scena ed Aria*), who arrives feigning nonchalance while
desperately seeking evidence of his daughter ("La-rà, la-rà"). A page
enters saying that the Duke's wife (the duchess of Mantua) wishes
to speak with him; the courtiers respond that he is unavailable, and
Rigoletto realizes that he is with Gilda. He admits to the courtiers
that she is his daughter and alternates between lambasting their
corrupt life ("Cortigiani, vil razza dannata") and begging for
their mercy.

(No. 10: *Scena e Duetto*) Gilda rushes in and throws herself
into her father's arms. Rigoletto briefly thinks that all is well—it
was only a joke—but Gilda's tears reveal something more, and she
asks to speak with him alone. Rigoletto dismisses the courtiers,
saying that not even the Duke should be allowed into the room.
Gilda tells the whole story, starting from how she met the handsome young man at church ("Tutte le feste al tempio"). Rigoletto
cuts her off, blames himself, and seeks to console his daughter
("Piangi, fanciulla, e scorrere") before deciding what to do. The
Count of Monterone is led through the room on the way to
prison: he stops before the portrait of the Duke and complains
that his curse was in vain, but Rigoletto says that the old man
will have an avenger after all ("Si vendetta, tremenda vendetta").
Gilda, however, would rather have her father forgive the Duke,
whom she still loves.

ACT III. (*A deserted bank of the River Mincio. On the left is a*
two-story house, half fallen into ruin, the front of which—facing
the audience—allows one to see, through a large arcade, the inte-
rior of a rustic hostelry on the ground floor and a rough-hewn

staircase that leads up to the granary, where through a balcony without shutters can be seen a bed. On the facade that faces the street is a door that opens inward; the wall is so full of holes that from outside one can easily see whatever happens within. The rest of the scene reveals the deserted area along the Mincio, which runs in the rear behind a half-ruined parapet; beyond the river lies Mantua. It is night.) (No. 11: *Scena e Canzone*) Rigoletto and Gilda appear before Sparafucile's house. She admits to her father that she still loves the Duke even though Rigoletto has given her time to forget him; he tells her to watch through the hole in the wall to see what happens. The Duke enters the tavern in the uniform of a cavalry officer, demanding a room and some wine. As Sparafucile goes off to get a bottle, the Duke sings of the fickleness of women ("La donna è mobile"). The assassin returns with wine and two glasses, and knocks on the ceiling to summon a young woman dressed as a gypsy (his sister, Maddalena), who flirts with the Duke while Sparafucile steps into the street to speak with Rigoletto, asking whether the man is to live or die. Rigoletto says that he will come back later to conclude their business. (No. 12: *Quartetto*) The focus now splits between the Duke and Maddalena inside the tavern, and Gilda and Rigoletto watching from outside. The Duke continues to flirt with Maddalena ("Un dì, se ben rammentomi"); Gilda is shocked, and still more so when he declares his love ("Bella figlia dell'amore"); Maddalena complains that these protestations are all just a game; Rigoletto tells his daughter that it serves no purpose to weep and that he will avenge her. (No. 13, *Scena, Terzetto, e Tempesta*) He then orders her to return home, dress herself in male garb, and go to Verona, where he will meet her the next day. He goes behind the house and returns with Sparafucile, counting out money (ten *scudi*) into his hands as half payment for the assassination; he will return at midnight to collect the body. Sparafucile asks for the victim's name: Rigoletto says that it is "Crime," while his own is "Punishment" ("Egli è *Delitto, Punizion* son io"). A storm brews, and the Duke decides to stay the night; Sparafucile leads him upstairs to the granary even though Maddalena urges him to leave. The Duke takes off his hat and sword and stretches out on the bed, singing a strain of his ditty on the fickleness of women

("La donna è mobile"). Downstairs, Maddalena admits that she is attracted to the man; Sparafucile tells her to go up and remove his sword; Gilda returns along the street, dressed in male attire, complete with boots and spurs. The storm gets stronger. Maddalena pleads for the young man's life—he is as handsome as a god and she loves him ("Somiglia a un Apollo quel giovine . . . io l'amo")—but Sparafucile will not cheat his client, nor will he lose his money. She first suggests that he should kill Rigoletto, but the assassin has his standards. He suggests instead that if anyone else should arrive before midnight, that person will die in the man's place ("Se pria ch'abbia il mezzo la notte toccato"). They think that the storm is such that no one is likely to appear. The clock chimes the half hour (11:30 p.m.). Gilda, who has overheard all this, decides to sacrifice herself to save the Duke: she knocks on the door of the tavern; Maddalena urges Sparafucile on ("Su, spicciati, presto, fa l'opra compita") and opens the door, then runs to close off the archway that allowed a view of the interior of the inn; the storm rages, then dies down, and the scene remains in silence and darkness.

(No. 14: *Scena e Duetto finale*) As the storm recedes, Rigoletto enters, delighted that this is the hour of vengeance for which he has been waiting thirty days, weeping tears of blood the while ("Della vendetta alfin giunge l'istante!"): this is indeed his moment of greatness. The clock strikes midnight: Sparafucile comes out of the house and hands over a sack containing a body. Rigoletto pays him the second half of the money, refusing his offer of help in disposing of the corpse. He wants to gloat over it but decides not to undo the sack; he can feel the spurs through the fabric. He then starts to drag the sack to the river. But just as he glories in his revenge, he hears the voice of the Duke in the distance ("La donna è mobile"). In shock, Rigoletto cuts open the sack; a flash of lightning reveals his daughter. He is horrified and bangs on the door of the tavern for help, but no one answers. Gilda revives briefly and admits that she deceived her father ("V'ho ingannato . . . colpevole fui . . . "), but she will pray for him alongside her mother in heaven ("Lassù . . . in cielo! . . . vicina alla madre . . . "). She dies, and Rigoletto falls on her body, crying out against the curse.

POSTER FOR THE PRODUCTION OF "RIGOLETTO," MODENA, TEATRO
COMUNALE, 7 MAY 1853

Rigoletto *faced problems from the censors from its inception, and during its
fast spread across Italy it was often staged under a different title and with
cuts, as advertised here (ending the opera with the Act III quartet), even after
a new libretto was printed. "Viscardello" is Rigoletto, his employer is the
Duke of Nottingham, and the opera is set in Boston.*
AKG-IMAGES/De Agostini Picture Library/G. Cigolini.

RIGOLETTO is often counted as the first of the three great "middle period"
works by Giuseppe Verdi (1813–1901), followed by *Il trovatore* (Rome, 19
January 1853) and *La traviata* (Venice, 6 March 1853). He had already written sixteen operas, starting with *Oberto* (Milan, 1839), at a rate—averaging
one every nine months—that was not so unusual for major opera composers
of the seventeenth, eighteenth, and early nineteenth centuries but that seems
quite remarkable nowadays. Several of these operas had been done in collaboration with the resident poet and stage manager at the Teatro La Fenice
in Venice, Francesco Maria Piave (1810–1876)—including *Ernani* and *I due
Foscari* (both 1844), *Attila* (1846), *Macbeth* (1847), *Il corsaro* (1848), and
Stiffelio (1850)—with whom Verdi had developed an amicable professional
relationship. No less remarkable, it seems, is the fact that the music for
Rigoletto was reportedly "composed"—in the sense of drafted almost from
beginning to end—in some forty days and while Verdi was coping with difficult personal circumstances, breaking off relationships with his parents

because of his illicit liaison with the singer Giuseppina Strepponi. But he finished his work on the opera only on 5 February 1851, barely more than a month before the premiere, which allowed for just some three weeks of rehearsal (and the singers did not have the music earlier). The path to the first performance of *Rigoletto*, at La Fenice on 11 March, was not entirely straightforward.

Verdi had had some notable successes with earlier works, including *Nabucco* (Milan, 1842) and *Macbeth* (Florence, 1847), and he was now in a position to make demands both of his librettists and of the theater managers with whom he (or his publisher, Giovanni Ricordi) negotiated: he drove a hard bargain with La Fenice and had no qualms in forcing Piave to make revision after revision of his text in terms of plot treatment, the distribution of numbers (albeit within generic and other constraints), and poetic meters and rhymes. But he also operated within the now very well-oiled Italian opera industry: operatic subjects were chosen not just for their dramatic interest, but also to suit the place of first performance (including the size of the theater) and the singers available, whether contracted to a given opera house or freelancing on the open market. Verdi had his favorites, including the baritone Felice Varesi (1813–1889), the first Rigoletto. Varesi had created the role of Macbeth in Florence in 1847 and would also be the first Giorgio Germont in *La traviata*. Raffaele Mirate (1815–1895; Duke of Mantua) was currently the *primo tenore assoluto* at La Fenice. The first Gilda, Teres(in)a Brambilla (1813–1895), had already sung various Verdi roles (including Abigaille in *Nabucco* in Paris in 1846), although the composer was not enthusiastic about her when the casting for *Rigoletto* was underway.

The nature of the industry tended to encourage what one might call consistent product lines. For example, the distribution of roles in *Rigoletto* and *La traviata* (both written for La Fenice) can easily be mapped one onto the other, despite the quite different subject matters (and save that there is no contralto role in *La traviata* to match Maddalena in *Rigoletto*, though the decision to have Maddalena a contralto was a late one anyway, it seems). Likewise, the emphasis given to these roles worked according to a hierarchy now embedded within fairly precise terminologies: the *primi* singers (the *prima donna*, *primo tenore*, *primo baritono* for Gilda, the Duke, and Rigoletto), the *comprimari* (Maddalena as the *contralto comprimario*, Sparafucile the *basso comprimario*), and the *secondi* (*seconda donna soprano*, *seconda donna mezzo-soprano*, *secondo baritono*, etc.). Singers also became increasingly specialized in terms of voice-types (coloratura soprano, lyric soprano, *tenore spinto*, etc.)—defined by range, flexibility, and character—with performers tending not to cross over between different types of roles, as they might have done in the eighteenth century. This therefore required a certain conformity in operatic plots. One problem with *Rigoletto*, however, is that while the two lovers (Gilda and the Duke) are conventionally the *prima donna* and *primo tenore*, in fact they sing together only once: Gilda's duets are predominantly with her father, the *primo baritono*, which creates difficulties in terms of what their respective ranges let them sing together. Another problem is that the *primo tenore* is cast in a massively unsympathetic role.

The Italian opera industry also depended on facilitating consistent productions within a widespread system. The Ricordi publishing house in effect produced and controlled all the textual and musical materials for staging its operas; the set descriptions and stage directions within these materials became more and more comprehensive (also leading, later, to even more comprehensive production books—*disposizioni sceniche*); and costume illustrations were prepared and distributed. Rather in the manner of modern Broadway or West End musicals, a *Rigoletto* seen in Venice, Rome, or Naples (or Paris, London, or New York) could be very similar in its look, and even in its sound depending on the quality of the singers and the orchestra.

The 1850–51 Carnival season at La Fenice (with performances from 26 December to 30 March) began with Verdi's *Luisa Miller* (its Venetian premiere) and continued with Giovanni Pacini's *Allan Cameron* and Gaetano Donizetti's *Lucia di Lammermoor* before presenting two new works, Francesco Malipiero's *Fernando Cortez* and *Rigoletto*. The same singers appeared in all these productions, performing four or five times per week (although performances were canceled or rearranged in late February because Raffaele Mirate was indisposed). Thus on 9 March 1851, two nights before the opening of *Rigoletto*, Mirate and Brambilla took their last turn as the star-crossed lovers Edgardo and Lucia in Donizetti's opera, with Felice Varesi as Lucia's unpleasant and overprotective brother, Enrico Ashton, and with Andrea Bellini, Francesco De Kunert, Luigia Morselli, and Angelo Zuliani in secondary roles. The comparison with *Luisa Miller* (first performed in Naples on 8 December 1849) is also intriguing: it was based on Schiller's play *Kabale und Liebe* (1784), subtitled a "bourgeois tragedy" (*Ein bürgerliches Trauerspiel*), a genre that had gained some favor in the latter part of the eighteenth century and was emerging as an alternative to the more heroic forms of grand opera. *Luisa Miller* also concerns a commoner in love with a mysterious nobleman and a father who fails to protect his

COSTUME DESIGNS FOR *RIGOLETTO* (GILDA, DUKE, RIGOLETTO, ET AL.)

The Ricordi publishing house kept tight control over much Italian opera in the nineteenth century, providing performance materials (librettos, scores, orchestral parts) as well as production notes and standardized designs (the one here originally in color).

AKG-IMAGES/De Agostini Picture Library/G. Dagli Orti.

daughter from dishonor and death, though Rigoletto's complicity in Gilda's fate makes him a more challenging character, as we shall see.

Operas at La Fenice, as in most Italian houses, were followed by ballets. The one paired with *Rigoletto* in its first run was usually *Faust* (premiered at La Scala on 12 February 1848), with music by Giacomo Panizza, Michael Costa, and Niccolò Bajetti. As for *Rigoletto* itself, it took a while to gain critical success—given the initial hurdles over its morality—but it became a financial one much sooner.

LE ROI S'AMUSE

The somewhat awkward configuration of roles in *Rigoletto* was caused by its source, and also by the treatment to which the libretto was subjected by the censors in Venice. Verdi and Piave had already reworked a play by the French playwright Victor Hugo (1802–1885) in the case of *Ernani* (Venice, 1844), and even before receiving the commission for the opera that became *Rigoletto*, Verdi had been attracted by the idea of adapting Hugo's *Le Roi s'amuse*, which he thought was "a fine play with stupendous situations." That idea had arisen in conjunction with the potential commission for an opera for the Teatro S. Carlo in Naples (following the premiere of *Luisa Miller*) to be done around Easter 1850, and therefore in collaboration with the house poet there, Salvadore Cammarano. That plan fell through—Verdi was instead preoccupied with *Stiffelio* for Trieste (premiered on 16 November 1850)—and the project shifted to Venice. Once a contract had been signed with La Fenice, in April 1850, Verdi wrote to Piave on the 28th: "I have in mind a subject that would be one of the greatest creations of the modern theater if the police would only allow it . . . The subject is grand, immense, and there is a character in it who is one of the greatest creations that the theater of all countries and all times can boast."

Verdi's concern over the police was based on the controversy generated by the play, which had been banned from performance the day after its premiere at the Comédie Française in Paris on 22 November 1832. Hugo's account of the amorous antics of François I, king of France from 1515 to 1547, drew on scandalmongering accounts by the likes of Brantôme (Pierre de Bourdeille; *c*1540–1614) that had then entered the hazy realm between historical truth and fiction: certainly Jean de Poitiers, Seigneur de Saint Vallier (the Count of Monterone in the opera), existed and was imprisoned by the king for conspiracy—which would date the action of the play to around 1524—and his daughter, Diane de Poitiers, was a favorite at court.

In the case of the character that became Rigoletto, Hugo gave him the name of a deformed jester at the court of Kings Louis XII and François I, Triboulet (also known as Feurial; 1479–1536); in addition to the historical evidence, he is described in Rabelais's *Le tiers livre des faicts et dicts héroïques du bon Pantagruel* (1546). But the story about Triboulet's daughter, Blanche, appears to have been invented by Hugo.

The play *Le Roi s'amuse* followed quickly on from Hugo's novel about another deformed antihero in Renaissance France, *The Hunchback of Notre-Dame* (1831), but it trod on more dangerous ground in the context of the July Monarchy (1830–48) under King Louis Philippe, and of the anti-monarchist June Rebellion of 1832. The latter would form the climax of Hugo's epic novel *Les Misérables* (1862), which describes events in terms strongly sympathetic to the republican cause. *Le Roi s'amuse* might also be construed as republican in intent, and it was certainly open to charges of lèse-majesté. The immediate cause for the play's being banned, however, was a claim that Triboulet's remark in Act III that the courtiers' mothers had prostituted themselves with the royal servants was a not-so-veiled comment against Louis Philippe's mother.

All of Verdi's operas save *Aida* had librettos based on preexisting works (other librettos, poems, or for the most part, plays), usually of some significant literary status: those prior to *Rigoletto* include *Ernani* (Hugo), *I due Foscari* and *Il corsaro* (Byron), *Giovanna d'Arco*, *I masnadieri*, and *Luisa Miller* (Schiller), and of course *Macbeth*—Verdi also long harbored plans for an opera based on Shakespeare's *King Lear*. Nor was he the first to take a banned play as the subject for an opera. But he and Piave had a harder time persuading the authorities to accept the idea than did Lorenzo da Ponte with Beaumarchais's *La Folle Journée, ou Le Mariage de Figaro*. Venice was under Habsburg rule, and the Austrian authorities kept a tight rein on stage productions: Hugo's play would be as unacceptable to them as it was in France. Although Piave appears to have assured Verdi that approval of the project would be forthcoming, there were already doubts being raised in August 1850, and the formal denial of permission to stage the opera titled (as it then was) *La maledizione* (The Curse) issued in early December sent the composer into a tailspin. Piave very quickly produced a reworking of the libretto, as *Il duca di Vendôme*, keeping the Paris setting but changing the king to a duke (probably Charles de Bourbon), removing the jester's deformity, cutting out the curse (which the censors presumably considered blasphemous), and making other revisions, to all of which Verdi took strenuous objection.

He was not going to lose the jester's hunchback, nor the curse, nor the sack containing Gilda's body. Triboulet (Triboletto, as Verdi styled him) could easily enough be changed to Rigoletto, the name taken from a French vaudeville, *Rigoletti, ou Le Dernier des fous* (Paris, 1835), concerning a duke and his jester (but otherwise not obviously related to Hugo's play). Verdi also felt that Piave's idea of turning the king of France into a lesser member of the French nobility was inappropriate because the character needed to be an absolute ruler for Monterone's curse to make any sense; he also insisted that he be a libertine. Verdi's initial suggestion for a replacement was Pier Luigi Farnese (1503–1547), duke of Parma and Piacenza, who was famously debauched. In the end, however, he and Piave opted for an unnamed duke of Mantua—probably Vincenzo Gonzaga (1562–1612), who certainly had a reputation as a womanizer. As for the notion of needing a "libertine," Verdi clearly had a figure like Don Juan in mind: the opening scenes of *Rigoletto* refer closely to the Act I finale of Mozart's *Don Giovanni*—with action taking place over onstage dance music—and throughout the opera the Duke has numerous textual and musical echoes of the Don. It was a useful comparison: *Don Giovanni* was the most popular of Mozart's operas in the nineteenth century. However, the absence of any punishment—divine or otherwise—for the Duke is just one of many difficulties presented by *Rigoletto* in terms of what, or whom, the story might be about, and to what end.

CANTABILES AND CABALETTAS

Piave appears to have worked from a printed edition of Hugo's play (in French, it would seem), with the result that passages that even Hugo admitted were dropped in the stage version for reasons of decorum remain in the libretto: one example is Saltabidil's (Sparafucile) account of how his sister, Maguelonne (Maddalena), seduces his potential victims—in the spoken version of the play she was just a fortune teller. But in fact, the shift from the king of France to the duke of Mantua seems to have solved all the problems of the play in so far as the censors were concerned, although we shall see that Piave and Verdi still trod carefully at particularly delicate moments, creating problems as a result and not always solving them. They also needed to reduce the play to a more manageable length for operatic purposes—rather as da Ponte did for Beaumarchais—which was achieved largely by cutting down Hugo's long monologues (and therefore the opportunities for arias, but that is a story to come). The play's five acts are compressed to three (I–II, III, IV–V), but in terms of the action and its presentation, the libretto follows the play quite closely. Only two major scenes are removed. The first (the play's Act III, scene 2) is where the King reveals himself to Blanche (after her kidnap) and offers to make her the royal mistress: she flees to the next room, only to have him gleefully follow her: it is his bedchamber. The second (Act V, scene 5) is the final one where Triboulet appeals to passers-by for help with Blanche until a doctor confirms that she is dead. One scene is added: for the Duke at the beginning of the opera's Act II. This was presumably to give the *primo tenore* an aria, although we shall see that it creates complications in terms of how we might read the character.

Hugo's play is in verse, predominantly the standard alexandrines: lines of twelve or thirteen syllables (iambic hexameters) usually divided into two equal parts with a caesura between the sixth and seventh syllable. This may explain why Piave tended to opt for longer lines in his version—ten-syllable ones are particularly prominent—and also newer (in the nineteenth century) verse forms that double up lines with a medial caesura, as with *quinari doppi* (5 + 5) and *senari doppi* (6 + 6): several examples will be seen below. A similar effect is produced by Piave's chains of seven-syllable lines, which are often in some sense paired in a *verso sdrucciolo*-plus-*verso piano* (or *verso tronco*) combination. These are not *settenari doppi* in the strict sense of the term—that is, two seven-syllable lines paired as one with a caesura. (This would turn them into the Italian version of the alexandrine, also known as the *verso martelliano* after the Baroque poet Pier Jacopo Martello; we shall see plenty of examples in the discussion of *La Bohème*.) But they could just as well be. On the other hand, Piave's evident fondness for *versi sdruccioli* (the end accent on the antepenultimate syllable), shared by other early nineteenth-century librettists, may be a result of more direct musical pressures: the *sdrucciolo* line ending allowed one musical subphrase to flow into the next while also discouraging the singer from breaking the line by taking a breath.

While the distinction between *versi sciolti* and more structured verse continued to operate in Italian librettos, the boundaries were gradually breaking down. We have already seen that the two-stanza aria text had started to disappear toward the end of the eighteenth century, alongside the emergence of more flexible, if still structured, poetic models for both arias and ensembles. This combined with newer notions of how drama might best be created in and through music, and with the search for a more fluid operatic language that broke down the increasingly artificial, it seemed, distinction between recitative and aria/ensemble. If ensembles (and finales) could already present some kind of dramatic arc, why not arias? And how could opera take advantage of musical styles that favored developmental change rather than repetitive consistency.

Act III of Mozart's *Le nozze di Figaro* has already provided one early example of this shift, with a *recitativo stromentato* followed by a three-stanza *rondò* (the Countess's "Dove sono i bei momenti"), the first two stanzas set in a slow tempo (in an ABA form) and the third in a faster one. For the singer, the advantage of the *rondò* form is clear; it displays first lyrical, then virtuosic, abilities, and ends in a manner bound to gain applause. The dramatic question, of course, is what prompts the shift from the first to the second part of the *rondò*. Expanding such moments of change, and enacting rather than imagining what brings it about, became one focus of the typical form for arias (and many ensembles) in Italian opera in the first half of the nineteenth century. A slow *tempo cantabile* (we used to call it a cavatina, but in the case of nineteenth-century opera, that term now tends to be reserved for a character's entrance aria) is followed by a middle section (*tempo di mezzo*) in which some action takes place—usually involving other characters—and leads to a quicker *cabaletta*. The *cabaletta* itself will usually start fast and end faster (with a *stretta*, a term also used for the *cabaletta* section of an ensemble finale): the consequent applause makes for an inevitable break in the action. The tendency for audiences to applaud also after the *tempo cantabile* is more insidious (though Verdi usually expected it)—and very tiresome in modern opera houses—given the need to move on to the action in the *tempo di mezzo*. As for the *cabaletta*, it usually makes most sense for its main character(s) to exit on its conclusion. What to do with any characters entering in the *tempo di mezzo* will exercise a librettist's ingenuity: it leads to some oddities in the case of *Rigoletto*.

This three-part form—*tempo cantabile, tempo di mezzo, cabaletta*—extends to four if there is a prior *recitativo stromentato* (in nineteenth-century terms, a *scena*), or even five if between the *scena* and the *tempo cantabile* there is a *tempo d'attacco* (on which more below). It works not just for arias but also for ensembles, in which case it takes on the character of prior chain finales. It can also be foreshortened, as for example by removing the *cabaletta* if there is no easily created dramatic reason for one, in which case the following scene tends to feel like an ongoing *tempo di mezzo*. Given the potential for new characters to enter the stage in the *tempo di mezzo* (and the *tempo d'attacco*), the *scena*-to-*cabaletta* sequence can span several scenes or even a scene-complex (multiple scenes played on a single set), which in the case of *Rigoletto* is how one might read the first scene-complex in Act I (scenes 1–6). In other words, this modular structure permits great flexibility in manipulating generic conventions—and the audience expectations that arise from them—in support of specific dramatic situations. The predictable allows the unpredictable to occur.

As we have seen, eighteenth-century Italian opera separated the musical numbers (arias, ensembles) by recitative, and usually *recitativo semplice* save where greater intensity was needed for dramatic monologues (as *recitativo stromentato*). Now recitative has been folded into the structure (in the *scena* and sometimes the *tempo di mezzo* or even, we shall see, the *cabaletta*), and it is all *stromentato*—thus operas have orchestral accompaniment throughout. The model came from the so-called reform operas of Christoph Willibald von Gluck (1714–1787) and also reflects a degree of French influence, where the boundaries between different musical styles in opera had always been fuzzier. It gives a stronger sense of dramatic flow and even cohesion within and across scenes; it breaks down the distinctions between operatic action and reaction; it embodies a trajectory that also allows for dramatic shifts or even reversals (in the *tempo di mezzo*); and it contains all the songful elements likely to appeal to an operatic audience, whether the slow and lyrical or the fast and virtuosic. In effect, we are moving toward "continuous" opera. In terms of the libretto, however, these various sections will still be distinguished in poetic terms: the *scena* will be in the *versi sciolti* previously associated with recitative, whereas the *tempo cantabile* and *cabaletta* will always be in structured verse—and the *tempo di mezzo* usually so—sometimes marked by changes of meter and sometimes not.

The beginning of Act II (scenes 1–2) of *Rigoletto* is as good an example as any. A brief, agitated orchestral introduction sets the scene (and allows the audience to admire the set) before accented chords mark the entrance of the Duke, who describes how he had returned to Gilda's house only to find her missing. This is the start of the *scena*, in *versi sciolti*:

Ella mi fu rapita!	7	She was stolen from me!
E quando, o ciel . . . ne' brevi istanti, prima	11	And when, o heavens . . . in the brief moments before
che il mio presagio interno	7	my own inner foreboding
sull'orma corsa ancora mi spignesse!	11	forced me again to retrace my steps!

The musical style is one familiar from earlier *recitativo stromentato*, although, as the Duke considers Gilda's uncommon effect on him, he moves into a more lyrical moment (at *colei che poté prima in questo core*). However, the Duke is brought back down to earth as he repeats his opening:

Ella mi fu rapita!	7	She was stolen from me!
E chi l'ardiva? . . . Ma ne avrò vendetta:	11	And who dared to do it? . . . But I shall have revenge:
lo chiede il pianto della mia diletta.	11	the weeping of my beloved demands it.

The rhyming couplet closes the *scena*, but the argument leads in two directions: the notion of revenge (*vendetta*) and some evocation of the weeping (*pianto*) of the Duke's beloved. Given the nature of the form to come, *pianto* must win out for the moment, although *vendetta* might be saved for any *cabaletta*.

The Duke has a brief notated cadenza for the final phrase of the *scena* (at *della mia diletta*), then launches into the *tempo cantabile* (with the tempo marking *Adagio*—very slow) as he imagines Gilda's tears and her crying out for her Gaultier Maldè (which the Duke had told her was his name):

Parmi veder le lagrime	7s	I seem to see the tears
scorrenti da quel ciglio,	7	falling from her brow,
quando fra il duolo e l'ansia	7s	when amid grief and anxiety
del subito periglio,	7	over the sudden danger,
dell'amor nostro memore,	7s	mindful of our love,
il suo Gualtier chiamò.	7t	she called for her Gualtier.

This is pure self-indulgent fantasy on the Duke's part, and one wonders why Piave added it to Hugo's Act III save, precisely, for the need for a *tempo cantabile*: one might suppose that the Duke's concern for Gilda does him some credit, although in the opera (unlike the play)—and rather curiously—they never actually meet again onstage.

The *tempo cantabile* is made up of two stanzas (a second follows the one given above) set straight through (AB, then a repeat of the final two lines), although Verdi keeps the section tonally closed, with a clear final cadence and a notated pause to allow for applause. He then provides four measures of orchestral music at a new tempo (*Allegro vivo*—fast and lively) for the "hurried" entrance of the courtiers (headed by Marullo, Ceprano, and Borsa). This is the *tempo di mezzo*:

TUTTI

| Duca, duca? | → | Duke, Duke? |

DUCA

| Ebben? | → | What? |

TUTTI

L'amante	8	The lover
fu rapita a Rigoletto.	8	of Rigoletto has been kidnapped.

DUCA

Bella! e donde?	→	Nice! And where?

TUTTI

Dal suo tetto.	8	From her house.

DUCA

Ah, ah! dite, come fu?	8t	Ah, ah! tell me, how did it happen?
(*Siede.*)		(*He sits.*)

TUTTI

Scorrendo uniti remota via,	5 + 5	Passing together down a remote street
brev'ora dopo caduto il dì,	5 + 5t	a short time after sunset,
come previsto ben s'era in pria,	5 + 5	as we had indeed foreseen earlier,
rara beltade ci si scoprì.	5 + 5t	a rare beauty revealed herself to us.

At "Scorrendo uniti remota via" the tempo slows (to *Allegro assai moderato*—somewhat moderately fast) for the courtiers' narrative of the kidnapping. This takes up four stanzas of *quinari doppi* (the first is given above), with the Duke's response—when he realizes that the story concerns Gilda—occupying a fifth as he asks them where the poor girl is and hears that she is in the palace.

The Duke, who has been sitting the while, rises up in joy (*alzandosi con gioia*) at the news, cueing the *cabaletta*, which is faster than the *tempo di mezzo* (*Allegro* rather than *Allegro assai moderato*) and then gets faster still (*Più mosso*):

Possente amor mi chiama,	7	Powerful love summons me,
volar io deggio a lei;	7	I must fly to her;
il serto mio darei	7	I would give my diadem
per consolar quel cor.	7t	to console that heart.

Ah! sappia alfin chi l'ama,	7	Ah! may she know who loves her,
conosca alfin chi sono,	7	may she realize at last who I am,
apprenda ch'anco in trono	7	may she learn that even on the throne
ha degli schiavi amor.	7t	love has its slaves.

Again, this is an addition to Hugo by Piave, and it complicates any view of the Duke: he is certainly an eager lover, but can he also be viewed as an honest one? However, these two stanzas of the *cabaletta* (set AB) are followed by a couplet for the courtiers (in the same meter) as they note his change of mood: *Quale pensiero or l'agita, / come cangiò d'umor!* (What thought agitates him?—how he has changed his mood!). Although that couplet marks the end of the scene in the libretto, the convention is that any such intervention will partition what is a conventional repeat of the *cabaletta* (so, AB . . . AB), ending even faster second time round. Verdi follows. The Duke then leaves hurriedly (*esce frettoloso dal mezzo*), presumably to run to Gilda, so there is (or should be) no chance for the tenor to take a bow.

The courtiers' couplet, however, reveals one problem with the design of the scene—and, for that matter, with "continuous" opera. Having brought them in for the *tempo di mezzo*—and given that they need to be onstage for the next scene—it is hard to know what to do with them during the Duke's *cabaletta*. Arias are usually configured as explicit or implicit soliloquies, defined by some kind of dramatic and musical break or set within a frame. If other characters are present, the stage director has to decide what to do with them, but it is not clear whether, or to what, they should pay attention. The Duke's *scena* and *tempo cantabile* are straightforward enough: he is alone onstage. For the *cabaletta* to be plausible, however, the Duke's claim to be summoned by love (*Possente amor mi chiama*) needs to be configured as an aside (it is marked *da sé*), given that the courtiers are not aware of the Duke's feelings for, or even knowledge of, Gilda: they do not hear his words, but note only his agitation and change of mood. However, it is hard to conceive of an aside being delivered by a tenor singing full throttle, as the music requires. The intelligence of any given production can probably be measured by how an issue such as this is handled save in the case of the commonplace solution: to cut the Duke's *cabaletta* altogether, as often occurs.

The other oddity of the scene lies in the *tempo di mezzo*. In an earlier opera, the courtiers' recounting of their kidnapping of Gilda would have taken place in *recitativo semplice*, with one character speaking for the group (or the characters taking turns to tell the tale). However, continuous opera—at least, of the Italian variety—tends not to allow easily for a long group narrative recounting prior actions. Piave and Verdi have it delivered by the courtiers as a male chorus in perfect homophony. This has the advantage of keeping them occupied even if it lacks something in terms of verisimilitude. This pattern of using the courtiers "speaking" in unison as a male chorus—with named roles sometimes emerging from it—is also apparent in

Act I; we shall see that this male chorus has a very different role in Act III. (Despite the call in the cast list for "ladies" of the court [*dame*], they do not sing: all the chorus parts are for tenors and basses.) It becomes a rather curious feature of *Rigoletto* as a whole. One reading is that it serves to accentuate the isolation of the jester—the chorus comprises the *cortigiani, vil razza dannata* (courtiers, vile, damned mob) against whom Rigoletto inveighs in Act II, scene 4. Another is that it was the only way to keep the chorus of La Fenice occupied absent a more conventional epic-heroic plot.

Bringing more action into the *tempo di mezzo*, however, has the distinct advantages of compressing the drama and of rendering it in larger musical units that, furthermore, tend to flow one into another. *Rigoletto* is still a "number" opera, in that it is made up of musical movements, each with a beginning, middle, and (for the most part) some kind of end, and each separated one from the other, if only by a double bar in the score. But there are fewer of them: *Rigoletto* has fourteen separate numbers (thirteen if one combines the Preludio and Introduzione) distributed over three acts, as compared with, say, the twenty-eight (plus the overture) of *Le nozze di Figaro* over four acts, or for that matter, the twenty-five (also over four acts) of Verdi's *Macbeth*, premiered just four years earlier.

Duets

The *tempo cantabile–tempo di mezzo–cabaletta* structure works equally well for duets or larger ensembles, although the introduction of a second character (if not present onstage at the outset) will usually prompt the insertion of a *tempo d'attacco* between the *scena* and the *tempo cantabile*. In Act I, scene 12, Gilda tells Giovanna of her guilty conscience over not having revealed to her father the truth about having met an attractive young man in church (*scena:* "Giovanna, ho dei rimorsi," in *versi sciolti*). Her claim that she does not care whether he is rich or poor (*tempo d'attacco:* "Signor né principe—io lo vorrei," in *quinari doppi*) prompts the Duke to reveal himself (at which point Giovanna leaves). He declares his love (*tempo cantabile:* "È il sol dell'anima—la vita è amore," continuing the *quinari doppi*), entrancing Gilda with his seductive language. As the Duke asks Gilda to say once more that she loves him (*tempo di mezzo:* "Che m'ami, deh ripetimi," in seven-syllable lines), sounds are heard from the street (the courtiers arriving for the kidnap), and Giovanna rushes back in to warn the lovers, who use the *cabaletta* to bid a fond farewell:

Addio . . . speranza ed anima	7s	Farewell . . . my hope and soul
sol tu sarai per me.	7t	will you alone be for me.
Addio . . . vivrà immutabile	7s	Farewell . . . immutable will remain
l'affetto mio per te.	7t	my affection for you.

The purpose of this entire scene is to seal the Duke's seduction of Gilda (this is the only time we see them together in the opera), and he pulls out all the stops in the *tempo cantabile*: she can hardly resist the tender words she has hitherto only imagined in her dreams. It helps that she is a soprano and the Duke a tenor, so they can sing in unison or very close harmony within the same range (albeit an octave apart). They begin singing different words, but their music starts to come together, and as their melodies intertwine, the dissonances rubbing provocatively together, they shift into a kind of wordless ecstasy: the *tempo cantabile* ends with a notated cadenza—mostly on *ah!*—where Gilda even starts to take a rather brazen lead. By the *cabaletta* there is no need to differentiate their text: the same four-line stanza will work for both of them.

Matters are not quite so straightforward in Gilda's duets with her father. Rigoletto's baritone is the typical paternal voice, but it means that there remains a vocal distance between him and his daughter that also prevents them from singing the same melody in the same key: Verdi has to make some swift modulations, often up a fourth, when he wants Gilda to repeat a musical idea first presented by Rigoletto. In dramatic terms, too, their relationship is somewhat fractured: Gilda knows nothing of her mother, nor even her father's real name, and in both cases Rigoletto is reluctant to give any more information than we in the audience need as minimal background. She does not understand why she has been enclosed in his house for the past three months; nor are we told how or why she was brought there, and from where (according to the play, Blanche has been brought up in the French provinces—Chinon—by neighbors who thought her an orphan). Add to that Gilda's evident deception of Rigoletto, at least until her confession at the end of Act II, and it is clear that their duets will work somewhat differently from the norm.

Their Act I duet (covering scenes 8–11) takes the form of a dialogue much of which, again, would have been carried out in recitative in an earlier opera. The dialogue-duet works well enough when the characters can sing one after the other, with different melodic material according to the content of their texts, but it creates some problems when they have to sing together. Rigoletto starts with a soliloquy as he compares himself with Sparafucile: this is a *scena*, in *versi sciolti* ("Pari siamo! . . . io la lingua, egli ha il pugnale"). Gilda's entrance at scene 9 is the *tempo d'at-tacco* (Rigoletto's "Figlia" and Gilda's "Mio padre!"; in *quinari doppi*) prior to the *tempo cantabile* (Rigoletto's "Deh non parlare al misero"; in seven-syllable lines). Here Rigoletto tells briefly of Gilda's mother's life and death before concluding:

Sola or tu resti al misero . . .	7s	Only you remain for this wretch . . .
O dio, sii ringraziato! . . .	7	May the Lord be thanked! . . .

leaving Gilda to complete the stanza:

Quanto dolor! . . . che spremere	7s	What grief! . . . What can have caused
sì amaro pianto può?	7t	such bitter tears?

Gilda then switches tack at the start of a new stanza:

Padre, non più, calmatevi . . .	7s	Father, no more, calm yourself . . .
Mi lacera tal vista.	7	This sight torments me.
Il nome vostro ditemi,	7s	Tell me your name,
il duol che sì v'attrista.	7	and the grief which so saddens you.

Verdi, however, elides the two stanzas, seemingly to give Gilda more to sing within the *cantabile* (so the *tempo di mezzo* begins at Gilda's *Il nome vostro ditemi*); furthermore, needing to find verbal fodder for Rigoletto, the composer ends up repeating (and superimposing) words to the point of unintelligibility. The poetry disappears, as indeed does the idea that the words matter, beyond providing a collection of singable phonemes:

> GILDA: Oh quanto dolor! quanto dolor! . . . che spremere sì amaro pianto può? quanto dolor! quanto dolor! . . . che spremere sì amaro pianto può? Padre, non più, padre, non più, padre, non più, non più, calmatevi, mi lacera tal vista, non più vi calmate, non più, mio padre, ah, vi calmate, padre, mi lacera, padre, mi lacera tal vista. Padre, non più, padre, non più, padre, non più, non più, calmatevi, mi lacera tal vista, non più vi calmate, non più, mio padre, ah, vi calmate, padre, mi lacera, padre, mi lacera tal vista.

RIGOLETTO: . . . Tu sola, sola resti al misero, sola, ah sì, tu sola resti al misero, sola resti al misero, sola tu resti . . . Dio, sii ringraziato, ringraziato. Ah sì, tu sola resti al misero, sola resti al misero, sola tu resti . . . Dio, sii ringraziato, ringraziato.

Verdi also changes words (Rigoletto's *Tu sola, sola resti al misero* rather than *Sola or tu resti al misero*; Gilda's *vi calmate* rather than *calmatevi*) and adds to them (Rigoletto's *ah sì*; Gilda's *ah*) to fit the music. But here Gilda and Rigoletto are hardly communicating with each other even though they are singing together.

The problem continues through the *tempo di mezzo* and the *cabaletta*. In the play, Triboulet summons Dame Bérarde (the equivalent to Giovanna); he interrogates her on whether anyone sees him when he enters the house; he says farewell to Blanche; he turns again to the duenna to ask whether the door is kept locked; he hears a sound from the street and goes to investigate, leaving the door half open (which allows the King to enter surreptitiously); and he keeps running to and fro with his questions and instructions until he finally leaves, closing the door carefully (but too late). The latter part of the scene is observed by the King (hiding behind a tree), who is immensely amused to realize that the man he has in the past seen entering Blanche's house is in fact Triboulet, and still more to discover that Blanche is his daughter.

Piave more or less follows Hugo, save that the Duke's double discovery passes without the character's elaborating on it. The entrance of Dame Bérarde/Giovanna would seem well suited for a *tempo di mezzo*, as for that matter would that of the King/Duke. The question, however, is how, and where, to fashion a *cabaletta* from a situation that does not seem to allow of one: there is nothing about which Rigoletto and Gilda can sing together. Following Giovanna's entrance and interrogation, Piave comes up with two stanzas for Rigoletto (each of four eight-syllable lines) asking Giovanna to tend to Gilda like a flower (*Veglia, o donna, questo fiore*), and two matching stanzas for Gilda where she comments on her father's love and seeks to assure him that the protection of her mother in heaven will ensure that this flower will not be uprooted or broken (*non fia mai divelto o infranto / questo a voi diletto fior*). This is some kind of *cabaletta*, if not a conventional fast-paced one, and Verdi sets it as an *Allegro moderato assai*, although it does speed up in the typical way. Piave then creates a separate scene (I.11) for the business that allows the Duke to gain admission to the courtyard before Rigoletto exits. This scene is in *versi sciolti*—breaking away from

Rigoletto and Gilda's eight-syllable lines—and so on the face of it would seem to be the start of a new *scena*.

One suspects that here Piave and Verdi found themselves between a rock and a hard place. Placing the Duke's entrance within the *tempo di mezzo*—where it might seem logically to belong—would create problems both for a *cabaletta* (what would Rigoletto and Gilda sing about?) and by way of one (once the Duke enters, the action needs to move on). But Piave's next scene means that Rigoletto makes only a weak exit, and that his interaction with Gilda lacks dramatic and musical closure. Verdi's solution is to bring that next scene back into the *cabaletta*, separating the latter's two halves. That second half differs from the first in two ways: Gilda drops her comment (both deceitful and indelicate) that her flower will never be uprooted or broken; and an additional *addio* gets tacked on at the end. This way, the Duke observes only half a *cabaletta*, and Rigoletto gets his applause on exiting. Dividing a *cabaletta* by way of some action is not unusual: we have already seen the case of the courtiers' intervention in the Duke's "Possente amor mi chiama." There, however, the courtiers' text was in the poetic meter of the *cabaletta*, whereas here it is not. In this case, at least, Verdi seems not to have minded.

There is no such problem with Rigoletto and Gilda's second duet, at the very end of Act II and therefore with no further action to complicate matters, although the two characters still have difficulty singing off the same page, as it were. The *tempo cantabile* concerns Gilda's confession of meeting her young lover in church (*Tutte le feste al tempio*), then (in her third stanza) of her kidnap, which Rigoletto cuts short:

GILDA

. . .   . . .

| e a forza qui m'addussero | 7s | and brought me here by force |
| nell'ansia più crudel. | 7t | in the most cruel state of anxiety. |

RIGOLETTO

Non dir . . . non più, mio angelo.	7s	Do not say it . . . no more, my angel.
(T'intendo, avverso ciel!	7t	(I understand you, adverse heaven!
Solo per me l'infamia	7s	Infamy only for myself
a te chiedeva, o dio . . .	7	did I ask from you, o God . . .

Rigoletto's two lines beginning *Non dir . . . non più, mio angelo* could in principle have served to allow him and Gilda to sing their couplets together, although there are problems with it: the first line ("Do not say it . . . no more, my angel") suggests that Gilda is about to reveal something to which the censor might take objection, while the second ("I understand you, adverse heaven!") is the start of an aside which Gilda is not meant to hear. Verdi drops these two lines, and gives Rigoletto a new start (after a connecting *Ah!*) at *Solo per me l'infamia* (which, again, Gilda should not hear): they sing together only as he invites her to weep and she seeks consolation (*Piangi, fanciulla, e scorrere*).

In the *tempo di mezzo* (the text shifts to *senari doppi*), the Count of Monterone crosses the stage on the way to jail and speaks to the Duke's portrait, prompting Rigoletto to declare that the old man will have revenge after all. Here ends the parallel act (III) in Hugo's play. But Piave and Verdi need a *cabaletta*, and we are also at a point that seems suitable for a no less conventional revenge duet, or would if both characters desired revenge. Rigoletto certainly follows the trope:

Sì, vendetta, tremenda vendetta	10	Yes, revenge, tremendous revenge
di quest'anima è solo desio . . .	10	is the sole desire of this soul . . .
di punirti già l'ora s'affretta,	10	of your punishment now rushes the hour
che fatale per te tuonerà.	10t	which will chime fatefully for you.
Come fulmin scagliato da dio,	10	Like a lightning bolt hurled by God,
il buffone colpirti saprà.	10t	the jester will know how to strike you.

This works well enough, though Verdi changes the last line to the slightly less elegant *te colpire il buffone saprà*, perhaps to provide a consonant rather than a vowel for the singer's initial attack (the meaning stays the same). But Piave has more difficulty coming up with a matching stanza for Gilda. Hugo has already had Blanche state in an aside—as Triboulet curses the King (before the play's equivalent of Monterone appears)—that God should not listen because she is still in love (*Ô Dieu! n'écoutez pas, car je l'aime toujours!*). Piave picks up on the hint but needs to construct something more substantial:

O mio padre, qual gioia feroce	10	O my father, what fierce joy
balenarvi negli occhi vegg'io! . . .	10	do I see flashing in your eyes! . . .
Perdonate, a noi pure una voce	10	Forgive him; we may also receive
di perdono dal cielo verrà.	10t	a word of forgiveness from Heaven.
(Mi tradiva, pur l'amo; gran dio!	10	(He betrayed me, yet I love him. Great God!—
per l'ingrato ti chiedo pietà!)	10t	I ask you for mercy for the ingrate!)

This is not entirely straightforward, however, and it was a matter of some discussion between Verdi and Piave. According to the first edition of the libretto, Rigoletto is addressing the portrait of the Duke (as Monterone has just done), which makes sense. But matters are less clear for Gilda. Her last two lines are placed in parentheses, the conventional indicator for an aside, which is appropriate: she seeks divine mercy for the Duke because she still loves him. But the 1851 libretto marks the first line (and so by implication, the whole) of Gilda's six-line stanza *da sé*, that is, also as an aside. This will not work for Verdi: Gilda addresses her *Perdonate*—"Forgive (him)"—directly to Rigoletto, and he answers with a resounding *No!* That Gilda should seek forgiveness for the Duke from Rigoletto, and mercy for him from above, is plausible enough given how operatic heroines are meant to behave—they also establish the ground for Gilda's self-sacrifice in the coming act—and indeed this could be an excuse for some kind of prayer-scene. As a *cabaletta* of a revenge duet, however, it hardly seems appropriate. Nor is it possible to finish with an aside. For the typical faster conclusion, Verdi has to cobble something together from Piave's verse to get to the end:

> GILDA: A noi pure il perdono dal ciel verrà, a noi pure il perdono dal ciel verrà, a noi verrà, ah, perdonate, perdonate.
>
> RIGOLETTO: [-prà,] colpire te il buffone, te colpire saprà, colpire il buffone, te colpire saprà, sì, sì, colpire, te colpire il buffone, saprà.

Rigoletto's fierce threat to "strike" the Duke is all well and good, but Gilda's plea for forgiveness, this time round, is surely lost in the fortissimo chords and applause as the curtain comes down on the act.

Rigoletto and Gilda are at odds even to the extent of being unable to share a common rhyme (at least as Verdi sets the text). The distance between the one's rage and the other's compassion is too great for the genre to handle, at least within any plausible bounds of convention. Should Piave and Verdi need an excuse, it probably lies in the position of the duet at the end of an act, and also in the fact that it is for the two principal characters (and singers), who therefore need a blockbuster conclusion. But both the composer and the librettist were perfectly capable of doing something more radical in different circumstances, the most significant of which are perhaps revealed by the duet between Rigoletto and Sparafucile in Act I, scene 7.

Here Piave translates Hugo's Act II, scene 1—where Triboulet encounters the hired assassin Saltabidil—quite literally, save for typical compressions and cuts. But he does so not by way of the *versi sciolti* of recitative:

RIGOLETTO		
(Quel vecchio maledivami!)	7s	(That old man cursed me!)
SPARAFUCILE		
Signor? . . .	→	Sire? . . .
RIGOLETTO		
Va', non ho niente.	7	Go away, I don't have anything.
SPARAFUCILE		
Né il chiesi . . . a voi presente	7	Nor have I asked for it . . . here before you
un uom di spada sta.	7t	stands a man of the sword.
RIGOLETTO		
Un ladro?	→	A thief?
SPARAFUCILE		
Un uom che libera	7s	A man who frees
per poco da un rivale,	7	people from a rival for little money,
e voi n'avete . . .	→	and you have one . . .
RIGOLETTO		
Quale?	7	Who?
SPARAFUCILE		
La vostra donna è là.	7t	Your lady is inside there.

The text continues in four-line stanzas (another six following the two given above) each ending with a *verso tronco*.

The poetic choice comes close to a series of alexandrines (if one pairs the lines as *settenari doppi*), but it seems a little odd in musical terms. It is hard to see what else Piave might have done, however: this is not a *scena* that can lead to an aria or duet (what could Rigoletto and Sparafucile sing together about?), and it is not in itself a scene that can plausibly be subdivided into a *tempo cantabile*, *tempo di mezzo*, and *cabaletta*. Verdi therefore takes middle path: after beginning in the manner of a *recitativo stromentato* (for Rigoletto's *Quel vecchio maledivami!*), Sparafucile's entrance is marked by a lugubrious melody played by a solo cello and double bass (both muted) accompanied by lower woodwinds (clarinets and bassoons) and low strings (violas, cellos, and double basses)—the scoring is quite striking. Over this melody, Rigoletto and Sparafucile have declamatory phrases that occasionally turn into something more lyrical. Yet the *versi tronchi* clearly demarcate the phrase structure, and Verdi's decision to have the lugubrious melody return precisely at the point where Rigoletto asks Sparafucile to explain further how he manages to lure his victims to his house (*E come in casa?*) serves to emphasize a point that anticipates what will occur in Act III.

This kind of relatively formless *arioso* has been taken by some critics as a harbinger of a new Verdian style moving beyond the conventions of the time: less tuneful, more responsive to dramatic nuance, and held together by what happens in the orchestral accompaniment. Some have even gone so far as to see hints of what Wagner later called "endless melody," though if there are such hints, one probably should not lose sight of the irony of their being associated with an assassin for whom Rigoletto as yet has no use. Fewer have realized, however, that this and other novel features of operas such as *Rigoletto* emerge by default, as it were, given the then current tendency of the genre to make a musical meal out of every dramatic moment.

ARIAS AND MONOLOGUES

As Verdi himself noted, *Rigoletto* is very much designed as an opera of duets: having three in succession in Act I (Sparafucile and Rigoletto, Rigoletto and Gilda, Gilda and the Duke) is quite striking. Acts II and III both end with duets for Rigoletto and Gilda, and one might argue that even the larger ensembles in Act III are structured in effect as two duets superimposed (the quartet, with the Duke and Maddalena inside the inn and Rigoletto and Gilda outside), or a duet plus one (the trio, with Gilda as the outsider). Whether or not this was a result of fights with the censors (the duets limit potentially dangerous personal statements), it has the consequence of driving the action forward even as it leaves unanswered questions in its wake, such as what happens to Gilda in the palace in the middle of Act II: Verdi later wrote of the "magnificent duet" he could have written for a scene in the Duke's bedchamber, as he would surely have done had he been able to keep the parallel scene in Hugo's play. The focus on ensembles also leaves productions somewhat uncomfortable with the arias that remain: the *cabaletta* for the Duke's aria at the beginning of Act II, "Possente amor mi chiama," is (or at one time was) a standard cut, leaving him only with the *tempo cantabile*, plus two pieces identified as "real" songs—his Act I *ballata*, sung during the opening ball ("Questa o quella per me pari sono"), and "La donna è mobile" (a *canzone*) in Act III, both of which relate to songs cued in Hugo's play.

Gilda's aria, "Caro nome del mio cor" (in fact, just a *tempo cantabile*), cannot be so easily dismissed, although critics have not always found favor with it. Any singer who takes the role has a hard time in Act I: "Caro nome" comes after two duets that have already pushed the high notes. For the text, Piave expands upon a brief remark in the play (II.5) where Blanche muses briefly on what she has discovered is the name of her would-be lover, asking for it to be engraved on her heart (*Gaucher Mahiet! nom de celui que j'aime, / Grave-toi dans mon cœur!*), while she is observed by the courtiers who have come to kidnap her. Piave takes Hugo's couplet, then builds a two-stanza text expanding on the idea:

Gaultier Maldè! . . . nome di lui sì amato.	11	Gualtier Maldè!—name of him so beloved,
scolpisciti nel core innamorato!	11	engrave yourself on my enamored heart!
Caro nome che il mio cor	8t	Dear name which gave my heart
festi primo palpitar,	8t	its first palpitations,
le delizie dell'amor	8t	the delights of love
mi déi sempre rammentar!	8t	should you always make me remember.
Col pensiero il mio desir	8t	My desire in its thoughts
a te ognora volerà,	8t	will all the time fly to you,
e pur l'ultimo sospir,[2]	8t	and even my very last sigh,
caro nome, tuo sarà.	8t	dear name, will be yours.

Gilda's kidnap by the courtiers then forms the *tempo di mezzo*, but there is no conventional *cabaletta* for her: the chorus ending Act I stands in its place.

On the face of it, "Caro nome del mio cor" would seem to be just an excuse for coloratura singing; it is an unusual (for *Rigoletto*) lyric interlude that—apart from its obvious audience appeal—seems to serve only the purpose of leaving time between the departure of the Duke and the arrival of the rest of Gilda's band of kidnappers (Ceprano and Borsa are already onstage if not yet in sight of Gilda). But its sheer conventionality plays up what will happen to Gilda, who has nothing so conventional later in the opera. It also becomes emblematic of one of the more striking features of *Rigoletto*: that so much of the action is observed by characters in the wings, as it were. Gilda moves from the courtyard to a terrace (where she can be seen from over the

---

2. Verdi has *a te sempre volerà / e fin l'ultimo sospir* (will always fly to you / and until my very last sigh), which makes slightly less sense in terms of the final line of the text.

wall); the courtiers fill the street as she repeats the strains of her song; and they remark on her beauty before getting on with the task of kidnapping her. Thus the aria, or at least its conclusion, takes place in real time and helps resolve one of the several paradoxes of opera as the characters watch other characters perform: they become voyeurs just like the audience, thereby providing a rationale—or is it an excuse?—for the performance itself, and also vindicating our position as watchers of it. The issue will come to a head in Act III of the opera, where things overheard enable Gilda to decide her fate.

Rigoletto's Act II aria is far less conventional in design. In the play, as Triboulet enters the palace in search of Blanche—observed with amusement by the courtiers—he sings the stanza of a song (responding to singing from one of the courtiers); Piave and Verdi opt instead just for his vocalizing in seeming nonchalance (*La-rà, la-rà*). The *scena* (in *versi sciolti*) continues as Rigoletto tries to engage with the courtiers while searching for evidence of Gilda, until an exchange with the page makes him realize that she is with the Duke; this prompts the jester to reveal, in turn, that Gilda is his daughter. His following diatribe becomes what should probably be called the *tempo d'attacco*:

Cortigiani, vil razza dannata,	10	Courtiers, vile, damned mob,
per qual prezzo vendeste il mio bene?	10	for what price have you sold my dear one?
A voi nulla per l'oro sconviene! . . .	10	There is nothing you will not do for gold! . . .
Ma mia figlia è impagabil tesor.	10t	But my daughter is a treasure beyond any price.

The key (C minor), the harmonic language (rich in diminished-seventh chords), and Rigoletto's harping on the note C all have strong echoes of the music associated in the opera with Monterone's curse, which is now in motion to be fulfilled.

Rigoletto's text—and the *tempo d'attacco*—continues in stanzas of ten-syllable lines, although the tempo slows in a second section as Rigoletto tries to appeal to Marullo's better side (*Ebben, piango . . . Marullo . . . signore*), and the music becomes still more lyrical in a third as he pleads with the courtiers as a group:

Miei signori . . . perdono, pietate . . .	10	My lords . . . forgive me, have mercy . . .
al vegliardo la figlia ridate . . .	10	give the old man back his daughter . . .
ridonarla a voi nulla ora costa,	10	to give her back costs you nothing now,
tutto al mondo è tal figlia per me.	10t	but such a daughter is everything in the world to me.

In the first and second of these sections, Rigoletto's melodic line breaks down into declamation as he tries to open the door into the Duke's chamber and asks Marullo whether Gilda is indeed in there. As for the more lyrical third, while Piave seems to want to close it off (with the *verso tronco*, like the others), Verdi extends it into a cadenza as Rigoletto begs for mercy (*ell'è per me. Pietà, pietà, signori, pietà, signori, pietà*). One might well ask if the *tempo d'attacco* has somehow changed into the *tempo cantabile*. But it would in one sense miss the point to do so: any *tempo cantabile* here, such as it might be, never reaches a well-formed conclusion. Piave has simply translated Hugo, if cutting a large number of lines in the process. The most telling aspect of the process, however, is that he and Verdi did not feel the need to add to the text to create a more conventional structure, with a clear distinction—metrical or otherwise—between a *tempo d'attacco* and *tempo cantabile*, then heading toward a *cabaletta*. The jester, so articulate when making fun of the courtiers in more social settings, seems lost both for words and for a musical form in which to contain them. His one big aria in the opera does not seem so very much like an aria.

If a term is needed to label a movement like "Cortigiani, vil razza dannata," it probably again has to be "arioso." But Verdi has not quite—or not yet—removed all the distinctions between different formal operatic elements. Rigoletto's other speech condemning courtiers, in Act I, scene 8, occurs in the *scena* following his duet with Sparafucile (scene 7), as Rigoletto returns to his house. *Pari siamo!*—he muses: he and Sparafucile are alike in being assassins for hire, one with the tongue and the other with the dagger. But his thoughts keep returning to Monterone's curse (*Quel vecchio maledivami!*)—Piave repeats the line from the beginning of scene 7 (as does Hugo in the play). Then Rigoletto's fury breaks out:

O uomini! . . . o natura! . . .	7	O men! . . . o nature! . . .
vil scellerato mi faceste voi! . . .	11	You have made me vilely wicked! . . .
Oh rabbia! . . . esser difforme! . . . esser buffone! . . .	11	Oh what fury! . . . to be deformed! . . . to be a jester! . . .
Non dover, non poter altro che ridere! . . .	11s	To be obliged, to be able, to do nothing but laugh! . . .
Il retaggio d'ogni uom m'è tolto . . . il pianto!	11	The right of every man is taken from me . . . tears!

The text is in *versi sciolti,* and Verdi adopts the musical gestures associated in earlier opera with *recitativo stromentato*: punctuating and sustaining chords, scale fragments, tremolandos, and an occasional lyric moment (when Rigoletto says that he is a changed man when he returns home: *Ma in altr'uom qui mi cangio*). This is still recitative rather than *arioso*, and it can be recognized as such both textually and musically. But if stanzas of ten-syllable lines (in "Cortigiani, vil razza dannata") can be treated so fluidly as to break down typical formal boundaries, and if *versi sciolti* are constantly elevated into *recitativo stromentato*, the purpose of any distinction between them becomes increasingly obscure.

A QUARTET . . . A STORM . . . AND A DEATH

My argument thus far would seem to suggest that at least some aspects of those features of *Rigoletto* that modern commentators assume make the opera "great"—the prominent duets, the musical-dramatic flow, the lack of conventional forms—might rather be due to accidents of design (the treatment of Hugo's play) and of realization (as the censors intervened). But the presumed greatness of *Rigoletto* has also tended to discourage some harder-hitting interpretative questions as well.

It is almost certainly a mistake to expect operatic characters to behave logically even within the parameters of the drama through which they are created. But when they do not, one has to wonder why. For example, what prompts Rigoletto to kill the Duke? The beginning of Act III of the opera is somewhat unclear, as, for that matter, is the play. The jester has brought his daughter to Sparafucile's inn, but first he interrogates her:

E l'ami?		→	Do you love him?
GILDA			
Sempre.		→	Always.
RIGOLETTO			
Pure	7		Yet
tempo a guarirne t'ho lasciato.		→	I have given you time to heal yourself of it.
GILDA			
Io l'amo.	11		I love him.
RIGOLETTO			
Povero cor di donna! . . . Ah il vile infame! . . .	11		Poor heart of woman! . . . Ah the vile wretch! . . .
Ma avrai vendetta, o Gilda . . .	7		But you will be avenged, o Gilda . . .

GILDA

Pietà, mio padre . . .   →   Have mercy, my father . . .

RIGOLETTO

 E se tu certa fossi   11   And if you were certain
ch'ei ti tradisse, l'ameresti ancora?   11   that he might betray you, would you
           still love him?

GILDA

No 'l so . . . ma pur m'adora.   7   I don't know . . . but he does indeed
           adore me.

Rigoletto promises Gilda vengeance—as Triboulet does Blanche (*Je te vengerai*)—but for what? The conventional reading would be a good father's response to a daughter's illicit seduction (or rape) and subsequent dishonor. But the question seems to have worried Piave.

 The version of the libretto that Piave produced (as *Il duca di Vendôme*) in immediate response to the ban on the opera in December 1850—which is the earliest version of the text that survives—opens with Rigoletto saying, in an aside, that he "knows" that the Duke is in the inn and that he is trying to offer Gilda "final proof" of the Duke's infidelity (*So ch'egli è la . . . tentiam l'ultima prova*), suggesting that he has tried before. He also gives her more information:

Povero cor di donna! . . . Ei t'ha   11   Poor woman's heart! . . . He has set
 sprezzata . . .   you aside . . .
Ad altra pensa . . . ma ne avrai   11   He thinks about another . . . But you
 vendetta.   will be avenged.

GILDA

Padre, nol credo.   →   Father, I don't believe it.

RIGOLETTO

 E se tu certa fossi   11   And if you were certain
. . .   . . .

Here the revenge is not for Gilda's seduction, but for the fact that she has been dropped by the Duke (if yet without her knowledge), whose eye now wanders elsewhere. Perverse though it might appear in the context of the opera, it seems that Rigoletto would not take action against the Duke if the latter remained faithful to his daughter: his revenge has a proximal cause more in keeping with the conventional plot lines of nineteenth-century Italian opera—seduction can be condoned, but not infidelity.

This exchange is an addition to the play, but in operatic terms—and also as a way of appeasing the censors—it is a logical corollary to events in it that are omitted from the libretto. Both versions of Piave's text—*Il duca di Vendôme* and the final one—leave two questions unanswered. First, how much time has Rigoletto given Gilda to "cure herself" of her love for the Duke; and second, how can Gilda be so sure of the Duke's affections? A third question is raised by the text in *Il duca di Vendôme*: how does Rigoletto "know" that the Duke is in the inn? In all these cases, the play is clear. Blanche has been living openly as the King's mistress for a month, and with Triboulet's apparent approval (although he says that he has been feigning it while laying his trap); and she knows that the King loves her because he has behaved in so kindly a manner. As for Triboulet's knowledge of his employer's whereabouts, it emerges in a subsequent conversation between the King and Maguelonne that their first encounter was a week ago in town, and engineered, precisely, by Triboulet. In other words, Triboulet has set in train the plan suggested by Saltabidil on their first encounter: to use the charms of the assassin's sister to lure intended victims to the inn.

There are only vague echoes of all this in the final version of the libretto, almost all of which seem like accidental leftovers from the process of translation. Piave can be a little careless at times. For example, in Act II, scene 6, as Rigoletto commiserates with Gilda, he notes how everything has changed in "a single day" (*E tutto un solo giorno cangiare poté*)—a line taken from the play—although in fact it has been two days since the start of the opera: in Act I, scene 5, at the ball, the Count of Ceprano asks his fellow courtiers to meet him "tomorrow" and "at night" so as to take their revenge on the jester, and Act II, scene 6 takes place the morning after the kidnap. While the play is more precise—Blanche's kidnap (in Act II) takes place at night on the same day as the court ball that begins Act I (and Triboulet meets Saltabidil in the late afternoon, it seems)—the discrepancy hardly matters save as an example of a problem. But the timing of Act III is more crucial. As we have seen, Piave is vague at the beginning of the act, although at the start of Act III, scene 8, as Rigoletto returns to Sparafucile's inn toward midnight, we discover (in lines translated from the play) that the jester has been waiting thirty days for revenge, weeping tears of blood while still playing the fool (*Della vendetta alfin giunge l'istante! / Da trenta dì l'aspetto, / di vivo sangue a lagrime piangendo, / sotto la larva del buffon*). The reference to "thirty days" might easily pass us by, as it has those many commentators who have failed to consider the consequences of Gilda's spending a month in the Duke's bed, focusing instead on the violence done to her by the Duke the morning after her kidnap. But given the changes earlier in the act, it seems that Piave would not want us to think about those consequences too much.

As for the Duke's previous encounter with Maddalena—engineered in the case of the King and Maguelonne by Triboulet—this is reduced by Piave to a vaguely remembered conversation as the Duke initiates the *tempo d'attacco* for the Act III quartet:

Un dì, se ben rammentomi,	7s	One day, if I remember well,
o bella, t'incontrai . . .	7	o fair one, I met you . . .
mi piacque di te chiedere,	7s	It pleased me to ask you,
e intesi che qui stai.	7	and I understood you to live here.
Or sappi, che d'allora	7	Now know that from that day on
sol te quest'alma adora.	7	this soul has adored only you.

This seems to have been a point of issue with the censors: Verdi complained that the King/Duke needed some reason to come to the inn by way of a rendezvous, although the final agreement approving the staging of *Rigoletto* stated that it would be left vague. But again, do we need to know how and why the Duke should end up there? Some would consider it idle, and fruitless, speculation. Others, however, might feel that the timing has an impact on how to interpret Gilda's apparent folly in loving and then sacrificing herself for a libertine, while Rigoletto's involvement in luring the Duke to the inn will affect any reading of his involvement in a crime leading to his daughter's death, and therefore the blame attaching to him for Gilda's demise.

At least Piave could follow Hugo straightforwardly in one aspect of the first part of Act III. In the play, the King enters and demands from Saltabidil two things on the spot, "your sister and my glass" (*Ta sœur e mon verre*). He then sings a ditty, the first two lines of which quote an epigram often, if somewhat wrongly, attributed to the real François I:

Souvent femme varie,	Often a women changes her mind,
Bien fol est qui s'y fie!	he who trusts her is mad!
Une femme souvent	A woman is often
N'est qu'une plume au vent!	nothing but a feather in the wind.

Piave has to accommodate the censors: the Duke asks for "a room and some wine" (*una stanza e del vino*); later versions toned it down still more to "something to sit on and some wine" (*da sedere e del vino*). But as for the King's ditty, it translates quite easily into the Duke's *canzone* in the same poetic meter (but for which Piave provides an additional three stanzas). This plays as a "real" song heard by all the characters as such, also with a nice rhetorical touch in the third line:

La donna è mobile	5s	Woman is fickle
qual piuma al vento,	5	like a feather in the wind,
muta d'accento—e di pensier.	5 + 5t	she changes her tune and her mind.

The decision to create a quartet out of the Duke's flirting with Maddalena (inside the inn) observed by Rigoletto and Gilda (outside) posed greater challenges, however. Hugo made quite a meal of the King-Maguelonne episode but kept Triboulet and Blanche silent for a good while, so for the *tempo d'attacco* (in seven-syllable lines, mixing *versi sdruccioli*, *piani*, and *tronchi*) Piave needed to cut down the text and also to add a line for Rigoletto at the end, as well as an interjection for Gilda (*Iniquo traditor!*—Unjust traitor!), which Verdi repeats, and to which he himself adds (*Ah, padre mio!*—Ah, my father!). Some invention was also required for the *tempo cantabile*, which Piave first wrote in ten-syllable lines but then recast in more compressed eights. In the play, the King's protestations of love reach a climax but then collapse into stage business with Maguelonne as Blanche finds her voice:

LE ROI
Quelle fille d'amour délicieuse et folle!

What a delicious and mad daughter of love!

(*Il la prend sur ses genoux et se met à lui parler tout bas. Elle rit et minaude. Blanche n'en peut supporter davantage; elle se retourne, pâle et tremblante, vers Triboulet.*)

(*He takes her on his knee and begins to speak to her in a low voice. She smiles and simpers. Blanche cannot take any more; she turns, pale and trembling, toward Triboulet.*)

TRIBOULET (*après l'avoir regardée un instant en silence*)

(*after having looked at her for a moment in silence*)

Hé bien! que penses-tu de la vengeance, enfant?

So! What do you think about vengeance, child?

BLANCHE (*pouvant à peine parler*)

(*scarcely able to speak*)

Ô trahison!—L'ingrat! Grand Dieu! mon cœur se fend!

O betrayal! The ingrate! Good God! My heart is torn in two!

Oh! comme il me trompait! Mais c'est qu'il n'a point d'âme!	Oh! how he deceived me! But it's that he has no soul!
Mais c'est abominable! Il dit à cette femme	But it is abominable! He says to this woman
Des choses qu'il m'avait déjà dites à moi.	things which he had already said to me.
(*Cachant sa tête dans la poitrine de son père*)	(*Hiding her head in her father's breast*)
Et cette femme, est-elle effrontée!—oh!	And this woman, she's shameless! Oh!

TRIBOULET (*à voix basse*)   (*in a low voice*)

Tais-toi.	Be quiet.
Pas de pleurs. Laisse-moi te venger!	No tears. Let me avenge you!

BLANCHE

Hélas!—Faites	Alas!—Do
Tout ce que vous voudrez.	everything you might wish.

This will not work for Piave. By report the quartet is the part of the opera that Hugo particularly admired when he saw it in Paris, precisely because the music allowed four characters to speak at once. The voice types helped: the soprano (Gilda), alto (Maddalena), tenor (Duke), and baritone (Rigoletto) formed a typical four-part ensemble without any duplication of vocal ranges. But Piave also needed to come up with words for them to sing.

In the case of the Duke, he picks up on the King's line, *Quelle fille d'amour délicieuse et folle!*

Bella figlia dell'amore,	8	Beautiful daughter of love,
schiavo son de' vezzi tuoi;	8	I'm a slave to your charms;
con un detto sol tu puoi	8	with a single word you can
le mie pene consolar.	8t	console my torment.
Vieni e senti del mio core	8	Come and feel my heart's
il frequente palpitar.	8t	fast beating.

This is the typical language of seduction used by all noblemen to charm the lower classes: all those torments to be consoled, those exhortations to "come and feel," had been used by countless Don Giovannis to get their Zerlinas into bed, and Maddalena has already said that the Duke seems to be a "libertine" (*Ha un'aria il signorino / da vero libertino*). She also accuses him of joking with her (*vi piace canzonare?*), using the typical pun that invites comparison with song (we saw Valletto use a version of it in Act I of *L'incoronazione di Poppea*). But Piave does not seem to think that the Duke needs to work very hard at it: after the first four lines (ending in a *verso tronco*) we have just another two, not four. Verdi, however, gives him more lyrical space: the six lines are set as if they were eight in an ABCB form (lines 1–2, 3–4, 5–6, 3–4).

Piave has to provide equivalent stanzas (same meter and rhyme) for the other three characters. For Gilda, he can adapt Hugo:

Ah così parlar d'amore	Ah, speaking thus of love
a me pur l'infame ho udito!	have I heard the wicked one do to me!
Infelice cor tradito,	Unhappy, betrayed heart,
per angoscia non scoppiar.	do not break for anguish.
Perché, o credulo mio core,	Why, o credulous my heart,
un tal uom dovevi amar!	should you have loved such a man!

Hugo also provides some basis for Rigoletto, if not quite enough:

Taci, il piangere non vale;	Be quiet, weeping is to no avail;
ch'ei mentiva or sei secura . . .	now you are sure that he lied . . .
Taci, e mia sarà la cura	Be quiet, and mine will be the care
la vendetta d'affrettar.	to hasten the revenge.
Pronta fia, sarà fatale,	It will be ready, it will be fatal,
io saprollo fulminar.	I will know how to strike him down.

Maddalena causes still more difficulties, however, because Hugo has her just simpering silently on the King's knee, so Piave has to invent something from scratch:

Ah! ah! rido ben di core,	Ha! ha! I truly laugh from my heart,
ché tai baie costan poco;	for such jokes cost little;
quanto valga il vostro giuoco,	how much your game is worth,
me 'l credete so apprezzar.	believe me, I know how to value it.
Sono avvezza, bel signore,	I am accustomed, fine signore,
ad un simile scherzar.	to similar jesting.

This creates a dramatic problem (and also a directorial one) in terms of whether Maddalena's comments are to be staged as being addressed directly to the Duke (as marked in the libretto) or as an aside (as Verdi might seem to set them).

Things cannot be left so ambiguous for Gilda, however. Hugo has Blanche inveigh against her lover and then permit her father to take whatever revenge he wishes. Later she will repent (and will choose to die to save the King, as Gilda does the Duke), but for the moment, at least, she seems glad to be rid of him. Piave's reworking of Blanche's *Ô trahison!* speech repeats the idea that Gilda is hearing words of love she thought spoken just to her, and also the reference to her heart breaking. But for lines 5–6, Piave adds a question not present in Hugo: "Why, o credulous my heart, / should you have loved such a man!" It seems a plausible enough thing to ask, but also a dangerous one: should Gilda provide the answer and realize its consequences, she would never take the next, fateful step of self-sacrifice. Moreover, while Gilda's first four lines are presumably meant to be heard by Rigoletto, the last two, where she addresses her "credulous heart" (*o credulo mio core*), appear to function as an aside. Verdi seems to have been bothered by the issue: he omitted those two lines, giving Gilda just four lines rather than six. He also needed to come up with a way of rounding off her and the others' texts. Piave's last words for Gilda, Maddalena, the Duke, and Rigoletto (respectively, *scoppiar*, *scherzar*, *palpitar*, and *fulminar*) are not particularly characterful. Verdi comes up with a better conclusion: *ah no!* (Gilda), *ah sì!* (Maddalena), *vieni!* (Duke), *taci!* (Rigoletto). The women have new exclamations (but it is not clear what Maddalena is saying "yes" to), and the men, imperatives drawn from earlier in their texts ("come!" and "be silent"). Gilda is also neatly isolated from the rest by virtue of her non-rhyme.

As was the case in Rigoletto and Gilda's Act I duet, there is still some action that needs to take place before the drama can move on: Piave moves to *versi sciolti* as Rigoletto orders Gilda to flee to Verona and she leaves. This is the end of scene 3 in the libretto, and could in principle be treated as a *tempo di mezzo* prior to the quartet's *cabaletta*, although it is hard to imagine what such a *cabaletta* might contain. Rather, the quartet is left just as a *tempo cantabile*, and Verdi treats the final *versi sciolti* as the start of a new *scena* that will eventually lead to a trio (*terzetto*) ending with a *tempesta* (storm music). Rigoletto negotiates with Sparafucile, and the Duke decides to stay the night—he falls asleep singing "La donna è mobile" (Piave adds this repetition of the Duke's *canzone* to the play). In the trio—beginning at Maddalena's *È amabile in vero cotal giovinotto* (in *senari doppi*)—Maddalena and Sparafucile start to argue over killing the Duke; Gilda returns and listens in (through the same chink in the wall); she overhears their eventual plan to substitute for the Duke anyone who knocks at the door before midnight; and she decides to save the Duke. Throughout all this, a storm has been building, reaching its height as Gilda bangs on the door of the inn; she is stabbed by Sparafucile as the lightning bolts and thunderclaps are at their peak.

Once more, the poetic distinctions have less impact on the music than one might expect; there is not much musical difference between Verdi's setting of the *versi sciolti* (before the reprise of "La donna è mobile") and the *senari doppi* (after)—in part because Verdi uses similar musical ideas in the orchestra in both sections—and the "trio" only comes into focus as an actual trio (Sparafucile, Maddalena, and Gilda singing together) at two points, when each character is given a couplet culminating in a *verso tronco*. Their first exchange is when Sparafucile proposes substituting whoever might arrive before midnight, Maddalena complains that the night is too stormy to expect anyone to come, and Gilda comes up with the idea of sacrificing herself. The second is after Gilda has knocked: Maddalena urges Sparafucile into action, he tells her to open the door, and Gilda asks for forgiveness for them and also for herself. As with the quartet, Verdi also comes up with new final words for the three characters: *perdonate* for Gilda and *entrate* for Maddelena and Sparafucile. This time they rhyme.

Verdi carefully notates in his score when the stage machines creating lightning, thunder, and rain should operate, choreographing them quite precisely to orchestral gestures (accented chords, rushing scales, low tremolos, and the like); he also places the male chorus in the wings, humming chromatic harmonies to imitate the sound of the wind. This kind of sonic imitation of natural phenomena became something of a game in nineteenth-century opera (and some instrumental music): storms were particularly appropriate, although Verdi has some difficulty with finding a musical equivalent for lightning (he opts for arpeggios on a flute and a piccolo). But as Hugo also realized, the storm's rising and then dying down serves as more than just a natural metaphor for the deeds onstage: it also provides a plausible way to light the scene, not least when it comes to the jester's discovery about the body delivered to him in a sack by the assassin.

Rigoletto enters, delighted that the moment of vengeance is at last at hand. But he discovers the truth when he hears the Duke's voice in the distance singing his *canzone*. This *coup de théâtre* was Hugo's, whose stage directions also make clearer how it arises: the King is ushered out of the inn by Maguelonne—he is unaware of what has happened—and he goes back to the palace, singing the while. Rigoletto's cry of joy turns to horror as he realizes that there is indeed a body in the sack but it cannot be the Duke, then some convenient lighting flashes (more flute and piccolo) reveal his daughter.

Onstage deaths, especially of the female variety, would become something of a specialty in nineteenth-century opera. In *L'incoronazione di*

Poppea, Seneca goes offstage to die, as (according to our knowledge of history) does Ottavia. In *Giulio Cesare in Egitto*, Tolomeo is mortally wounded by Sesto but collapses without saying a word, lying dead and unacknowledged while Cornelia sings an aria about how her fortunes have changed for the better. The classical model of Greek tragedy would normally require acts of violence to occur out of sight—and recounted by a narrator (a messenger or the like)—so as not to offend the audience as well as for the sake of verisimilitude, and to avoid the inconvenience of dead bodies hindering stage movement (not to mention the problem of getting them offstage). However, the Greeks could then wheel in a corpse if one were needed to generate some reaction from the other characters (and the audience), as at the end of Aeschylus's *Agamemnon* (the first play of the *Oresteia*). But it took a nineteenth-century sensibility to enjoy a drawn-out death of a "good" kind, which usually involved some act of contrition, a plea for forgiveness, a prayer for those remaining, and a vision of heaven. The powerful, transgressive female characters that dominated opera were therefore brought back into line, offering the audience an object lesson in proper behavior (or in the perils of the improper) as well as a voyeuristic erotic thrill.

Accordingly, Gilda is not yet quite dead; indeed, Rigoletto thinks for a brief moment that she might be saved. But her return to consciousness lasts just long enough to fulfill the convention. The text shifts from *versi sciolti* to ten-syllable lines, of which Gilda first has a couplet:

V'ho ingannato . . . colpevole fui . . .	10	I have deceived you . . . it was my fault . . .
l'amai troppo . . . ora muoio per lui! . . .	10	I loved him too much . . . now I die for him! . . .

and then (following Rigoletto) a quatrain:

Ah, ch'io taccia! . . . a me . . . a lui perdonate! . . .	10	Ah, let me be silent! . . . Forgive me . . . him! . . .
Benedite . . . alla figlia . . . o mio padre . . .	10	Bless . . . your daughter . . . o my father . . .
Lassù . . . in cielo! . . . vicina alla madre . . .	10	There . . . in heaven! . . . alongside my mother . . .
in eterno per voi . . . pregherò.	10t	in eternity for you . . . will I pray.

Those six lines cover the conventions very efficiently. The first three come directly from Hugo (at which point Blanche dies); the last three are more operatic in origin, and they lard the scene with somewhat mawkish sentiment. Rigoletto has another quatrain (matching Gilda's in meter and rhyme-scheme) that is still more mawkish. The text then breaks down into fragments that Piave lays out as *versi sciolti*, but surely only out of a sense of poetic self-respect:

GILDA

Non più . . . a lui . . . perdo- . . . nate . . .	7	No more . . . for- . . . give . . . him . . .
mio padre . . .ad- . . .dio! (*Muore.*)	→	my father . . . fare- . . .well! (*She dies.*)

RIGOLETTO

Gilda! mia Gilda! è morta! . . .	11	Gilda! my Gilda! she is dead! . . .
Ah! la maledizione!	7	Ah! the curse!

Not that Verdi pays much attention to the poetic niceties, and he wants Gilda's last word to be something other than *addio!* He draws out her final gasps (also interspersing them with interjections from Rigoletto not given here):

Non più . . . A lui . . . perdonate . . . mio padre . . . Addio! . . . Lassù in ciel! . . . lassù in ciel . . . pregherò . . . per voi preghe . . .	No more . . . Forgive him . . . my father . . . Farewell! . . . There in heaven! . . . there in heaven . . . will I pray . . . for you will I pr . . .

At this point, Hugo has a long concluding scene where Triboulet calls on passers-by for help, remembers his daughter as a child, hears a doctor confirm that Blanche is indeed dead, and (for the last line of the play) cries out in pain *J'ai tué mon enfant! j'ai tué mon enfant!* (I have killed my child!) before collapsing. Piave had the sense to cut thing short. After Gilda dies, Rigoletto tears his hair and falls on his daughter's body. His *Ah! la maledizione!* allows for a final return of musical ideas associated with Monterone's curse at several points in Act I, starting with the prelude. But we are not given too much time to ponder the fact: it made sense to drop the curtain as quickly as possible.

For Gilda to die with a half-formed prayer on her lips—rather than a simple *addio!*—offers the possibility of some kind of redemption to a character whose blamelessness would no doubt have been a matter of debate in terms of nineteenth-century moralities. Piave's return to the curse in Rigoletto's last line also seems to be part of a strategy of exculpation. The theme tends to get forgotten in the play, and Triboulet ends with a more honest statement

(*J'ai tué mon enfant!*). But displacing the blame for Gilda's death onto *la maledizione* does not just minimize her own agency; it also tends to avoid one of the more obvious problems of *Rigoletto*—the stature of its protagonist. Rigoletto certainly behaves badly in Act I—even the Duke warns him against going too far—and he is foolish to think that standing next to royalty offers him permanent protection. Triboulet acts in an even worse manner—because he has much more to say—in the equivalent act in the play, and as for later, one is unlikely to sympathize with his sixty-five lines crowing over the sack containing what he thinks is the King's dead body (Piave reduces them to eight). When Hugo was forced to defend *Le Roi s'amuse* against the accusation of immorality—by way of his preface to the printed edition—his argument hinged on Triboulet's receiving just retribution. His wickedness might be caused by his being deformed, in poor health (so Hugo says), and a court jester, but he is wicked all the same, and his circumstances do not justify the hypocrisy of his double life: pimping for the King at court while claiming something better for his daughter. Hugo points out the ironies: Triboulet thinks he is helping kidnap another woman for the King, but it is his daughter; he thinks he has had the King killed, but ditto. However, Hugo does not—at least in this context—claim that Triboulet deserves sympathy; nor does he encourage any reading of the character as tragic. Indeed, as a play *Le Roi s'amuse* subverts nearly all the requirements of tragedy according to any classical definition of the term.

When Verdi complained about the censorship of his opera and the attempt to remove the jester's hump, he claimed that "I thought it would be beautiful to portray this extremely deformed and ridiculous character who is inwardly passionate and full of love." This sidesteps—no doubt deliberately—the main problem of the opera: Rigoletto's behavior and our sympathy (or not) for its consequences. Verdi may have enjoyed the idea of an antihero—he later (1853) called *Rigoletto* "the best subject I have set to music so far"—but his music, and our idealized reading of it, inevitably works in Rigoletto's favor and also Gilda's, while the silencing of the Duke—as he fades into irrelevance—might also be seen as a form of judgment. Viewing those characters through the prism of Triboulet and Blanche prompts a harsher analysis that many critics would claim illegitimate, though if, as invariably occurs, judging *Rigoletto* involves imagining some kind of back story for its main characters so as to explain their behaviors in the opera itself, then it would seem illogical not to use the play as the primary source. But whether or not one reads *Rigoletto* in the light of *Le Roi s'amuse*, the opera seems to contain something less noble or sublime than we might want from the genre. Nor is the alternative—to suspend moral judgment altogether—any more attractive if *Rigoletto* is to hold its place in the pantheon of great, and therefore morally good, art.

In spite of, or perhaps because of, these problems, *Rigoletto* has often been subject to the updatings and other machinations associated with so-called *Regietheater* (director's theater), whether locating the opera among the New York Mafia in the 1950s (as did Jonathan Miller for the English National Opera in 1982) or among the Las Vegas "rat pack" in the early 1960s (Michael Mayer for the Metropolitan Opera in 2013). The usual justification is that the opera somehow deals with universal themes applicable across times and places. What these and other updatings most clearly reveal, however, is the nature of *Rigoletto* and other operas of its kind as bourgeois melodramas: not comic, nor tragic, nor epic in any classical senses of those terms, but seeking different dramatic form and outcomes. One danger of melodrama, however, is that it suspends judgment in favor of sentiment. And there is a greater danger still. The closer opera is assumed to come to "real" life, the more problematic appear its moral and aesthetic dilemmas. If we dig deep into them, we may not always like what we find.

FURTHER READING

The circumstances surrounding the creation of *Rigoletto*, and Verdi's comments in his letters quoted here, are well enough known from the standard studies such as Charles Osborne, *The Complete Operas of Verdi* (New York: A. A. Knopf, 1970); Mary-Jane Phillips-Matz, *Verdi: A Biography* (Oxford and New York: Oxford University Press, 1993); and Julian Budden, *Verdi*, 3rd ed. (Oxford and New York: Oxford University Press, 2008). Also useful for a broader overview are the essays in Scott L. Balthazar, ed., *The Cambridge Companion to Verdi* (Cambridge: Cambridge University Press, 2004). Catherine Clément's *L'Opéra, ou La Défaite des femmes* (1979), published in English as *Opera, or The Undoing of Women* (Minneapolis: University of Minnesota Press, 1988), is the classic study of opera's use, or abuse, of female characters. Information on performances at the Teatro La Fenice, a reproduction of the 1851 libretto of *Rigoletto*, and other relevant documents can be found in the theatre's archival resources available online at www.archiviostoricolafenice.org/ArcFenice/Index.aspx.

CHAPTER 6

Giuseppe Giacosa, Luigi Illica, and Giacomo Puccini, *La Bohème* (Turin, 1896)

GIACOMO PUCCINI, GIUSEPPE GIACOSA, AND LUIGI ILLICA

Puccini collaborated with Giacosa and Illica on La Bohème, Tosca *(1900), and* Madama Butterfly *(1904), usually, though not always, on friendly terms.*

Torre del Lago, Museo Villa Puccini. AKG-IMAGES/De Agostini Picture Library/A. Dagli Orti.

Rodolfo, a poet: Evan Gorga (tenor)
Mimì, a seamstress: Cesira Ferrani (soprano)
Marcello, a painter: Tieste Wilmant (baritone)
Musetta, a singer: Camilla Pasini (soprano)

Schaunard, a musician: Antonio Pini-Corsi (baritone)
Colline, a philosopher: Michele Mazzara[1] (bass)
Benoît, their landlord: Alessandro Polonini (bass)
Alcindoro [di Mitonneaux], a state councillor: Alessandro Polonini (bass)
Parpignol, a toy vendor: Dante Zucchi (tenor)
A customs official: Felice Fogli (bass)
Students, working girls, townsfolk, shopkeepers, street vendors, soldiers, waiters, and children

SETTING: Paris, about 1830.
SOURCE: Henri Murger (1822–1861), *Scènes de la vie de bohème* (1845–49, 1851).

FIRST PERFORMED: Turin, Teatro Regio, 1 February 1896. The opera spread quickly across Italy—it was performed at the Teatro Argentina in Rome on 23 February, and in Palermo on 24 April—and then abroad (Buenos Aires, 16 June 1896). The next year saw openings in Alexandria (Egypt; 6 January 1897), Moscow (1 February), Lisbon (11 February), Manchester (England; 22 April), Berlin (22 June), Rio de Janeiro (2 July), Mexico City (22 August), Vienna (5 October), Los Angeles (14 October), and The Hague (19 October); in 1898 it appeared in Prague, Barcelona, New York, Athens, Paris, Valparaiso, Warsaw, Zagreb, Smyrna, and in Malta.

TABLEAU I. (*In an attic.*) Marcello, a painter, grows frustrated at his canvas of *The Crossing of the Red Sea*; Rodolfo, a poet, gazes out of the window at the chimneys of Paris (*Nei cieli bigi / guardo fumar da mille / comignoli Parigi*). The two friends are cold—but not as cold, Marcello says, as the heart of his lover, Musetta—and Rodolfo decides to stoke the fire with the manuscript of his latest play (*A te l'atto primo*). Colline, a philosopher, enters, carrying his books, and warms his hands. As evening falls, the door suddenly opens. Two boys carry in food, wine, cigars, and firewood, followed by Schaunard, a musician, who throws some coins to the ground. He was hired by an English lord who wanted a musician to play long

---

1. Not Michele Mazzini, as appears in some secondary sources.

enough to kill a garrulous parrot (*Un inglese . . . un signor . . . lord o milord*). Schaunard did so for three days, but then came up with the idea of persuading a chambermaid to give him some parsley, which he fed the bird, poisoning it. The friends hardly pay attention to the story, so overwhelmed are they by the food and wine on the table. Schaunard is annoyed: they should save the food for later, meanwhile going out to spend this Christmas Eve eating in the Latin Quarter. The landlord, Benoît, enters to collect the rent, but the bohemians distract him by wine and conversation (*Dica: quant'anni ha / caro signor Benoît*). They pretend to be scandalized by his tales of chasing women and throw him out of the room. Marcello, Schaunard, and Colline decide to head off to the Latin Quarter—Rodolfo will stay behind so as to finish off an article for the newspaper (*Io resto / per terminar l'articolo*)—and they make a rowdy exit, promising to wait for him in the street. Rodolfo finds it hard to get down to writing (*Non sono in vena*) and hears a knock at the door: it is Mimì, whose candle had gone out as she climbed the stairs to her own room. Rodolfo invites her in, and she is overwhelmed by coughing: he invites her to sit down, sprinkles water on her face, and offers her some wine. She recovers and makes to leave but realizes that she does not have her key (*Oh! sventata / la chiave della stanza*). Her candle goes out again, and Rodolfo blows his out as well, leaving the two of them scrabbling around in the dark; he finds the key but pretends still to search for it, and they touch. Rodolfo is surprised at how cold her hand is (*Che gelida manina!*). He introduces himself (*Chi son? Sono un poeta*), as does Mimì (*Mi chiamano Mimì*), who tells of her simple life as an embroiderer. The other bohemians call up from the courtyard; Rodolfo admits that he is no longer alone and says that he will meet them at the Café Momus. Rodolfo turns back to Mimì, whom he sees in the moonlight, and waxes lyrical (*O soave fanciulla, o dolce viso*); they embrace, and although Rodolfo would rather stay in, Mimì proposes going with him to the Latin Quarter. Rodolfo offers her his arm (*Dammi il braccio, mia piccina*), and they declare their love for each other.

Tableau II. (*In the Latin Quarter.*) In a bustling street scene, vendors sell Christmas fare as people mill around. Schaunard buys a hunting horn, even though it will not sound the note he wants, and Colline a secondhand overcoat; Marcello eyes up the ladies; and Rodolfo takes Mimì into a haberdashery to buy a bonnet. The other bohemians meet up at the Café Momus and, annoyed at there being no free table outside, go in. Mimì asks Rodolfo if the bonnet suits her, then admires a coral necklace, although Rodolfo says that given that he has a millionaire uncle, he would want to buy her something prettier. Colline, Marcello, and Schaunard emerge from the café carrying a table, followed by a waiter bearing chairs. Meanwhile, Rodolfo gently chides Mimì for glancing over at a group of students: "Are you jealous," she asks (*Sei geloso?*), and Rodolfo replies that men who are happy in love are always suspicious. They meet Marcello and company at the café just as Parpignol, the toy seller, is heard announcing his wares offstage. Rodolfo introduces his new friend to the others (*Questa è Mimì*). As the waiter comes to take their order, Parpignol enters, surrounded by children with their grumbling mothers in tow. Marcello asks Mimì what Rodolfo has bought her: a pink lace bonnet she has long wanted, she replies (*Una cuffietta / a pizzi, tutta rosa, ricamata*), praising Rodolfo for having intuited her desires; Rodolfo waxes poetical, but Marcello gripes, and when Mimì is worried that she has offended him Rodolfo explains that he is in mourning (over Musetta). Schaunard and Colline quickly change the subject, proposing a toast, although Marcello continues to grouse that he is drinking poison. The reason becomes clear when Musetta appears with her latest beau, Alcindoro, following behind carrying all her packages; she decides to take the table next to the bohemians and orders "Lulù" to sit down. Marcello explains to Mimì who she is (*Il suo nome è Musetta*) while Musetta ostentatiously tries to attract his attention, if in vain. The onlookers enjoy the scene as Alcindoro tries to hush her by appealing to their dignity; she refuses and sings a waltz tune (*Quando men' vo soletta per la via*). Alcindoro is scandalized; Marcello is furious but cannot resist her song; Mimì is sorry for him and realizes that she loves Rodolfo all the more. Musetta decides to rid herself of Alcindoro by claiming great pain in her foot, forcing him to go off and buy her new shoes; Marcello realizes that he cannot escape his love for her; the friends remark that the comedy is stupendous (*La commedia è stupenda*). Marcello and Musetta embrace each other as the waiter brings the bill, and a military band is heard in the distance. The bohemians are short of money, and even Schaunard's recent earnings have been spent, so Musetta takes the bill and says that the man who was with her (Alcindoro) will pay. The military band enters, leading a troop of soldiers returning to barracks, and all the vendors, grisettes, students, children, and passers-by flock to the parade. The bohemians take advantage of the confusion to make a quick escape, with Marcello and Colline carrying Musetta on their shoulders, since she cannot walk barefoot. Alcindoro returns carrying a pair of shoes, sees the bill, realizes that he has been left alone, and sits dumbfounded.

TABLEAU III. (*The Barrière d'Enfer.*) The scene reveals one of the toll gates to the city of Paris leading from the road to Orléans; on the left is a tavern bearing a sign that has converted Marcello's painting from Act I, *The Crossing of the Red Sea*, into "At the Port of Marseilles." It is dawn. Street sweepers, milk sellers, and other vendors await the opening of the gate by customs officers, while carousing is heard from the tavern, including Musetta singing her signature waltz. Mimì enters and asks the customs sergeant for directions to the hostelry where a painter works (*Sa dirmi, scusi, qual'è l'osteria*); he points out the tavern; a maid comes out of it, and Mimì asks her to fetch Marcello. Bells sound matins as some couples leave the tavern. Marcello emerges and tells Mimì to come inside, but when she learns that Rodolfo is there, she says she cannot. She asks Marcello for help (*O buon Marcello, aiuto!*): her life with Rodolfo has changed—he loves her but is constantly jealous and keeps telling her to leave. Mimì has a coughing fit but then reveals more: they fought last night, and Rodolfo came to the tavern to sleep it off, which is why she is here. Marcello looks inside the tavern and sees Rodolfo waking up; he urges Mimì not to make a scene, telling her to go home. Rodolfo enters—as she watches from the side—and tells Marcello that he has decided to separate from Mimì: he is jealous, and she flirts constantly (*Mimì è una civetta*), most recently with a young viscount. But Rodolfo then quickly admits the real reason for his being unable to bear staying with her: she is so very ill (*Mimì è tanto malata!*), getting worse every day and clearly dying; he cannot give her the care she needs, and his poverty clearly does not help. Mimì is shocked to overhear all this; she succumbs to a fit of coughing again, revealing her presence, and Rodolfo rushes over to her. He begs her to enter the tavern, but she says that it would be too stuffy in there. They embrace as Marcello hears Musetta laughing and goes back inside to check on her. Mimì bids farewell to Rodolfo (*Donde lieta uscì / al tuo grido d'amore*): she will return to living alone and will send a porter to fetch her possessions, although Rodolfo can keep the lace bonnet as a memento. They reminisce fondly over their good and bad times together (*Addio dolce svegliare alla mattina*). Marcello and Musetta enter bickering: he accuses her of flirting with the tavern's customers, Musetta complains that Marcello is behaving too much like a husband rather than a lover, and they get into a full-blown argument. Mimì and Rodolfo are oblivious; they decide to stay together until spring (*Ci lascieremo alla stagion dei fior!*).

TABLEAU IV. (*The attic.*) Marcello and Rodolfo are back living together in their attic, the one working at his easel, and the other at his desk. Rodolfo has seen Musetta in a carriage dressed in much finery; Marcello has seen Mimì in similar circumstances. They pretend not to care, but neither can forget his lover: Marcello surreptitiously pulls out a ribbon from his pocket and kisses it, and as Rodolfo laments Mimì's absence (*O Mimì, tu più non torni*), he gazes on the bonnet that she left behind. Schaunard enters with four loaves of bread, and Colline carries a small package, which he ceremoniously opens to reveal a single herring: this will be their lunch, accompanied by a bottle of water. The friends joke: Schaunard is going to a ball that evening, while Colline has been appointed minister to the king. Schaunard begins a speech but is shouted down by the others, and he proposes instead an impromptu dance (*La danza / con musica vocale!*), which descends into a mock duel. Musetta suddenly enters in great agitation, saying that Mimì has collapsed on the stairs (*C'è Mimì che mi segue e che sta male*). Rodolfo rushes to bring her in, and the friends place her on the bed. Musetta fetches her a glass of water; she recovers slightly and embraces Rodolfo, asking whether he wants her there (*O mio Rodolfo!*); Rodolfo says a passionate "yes" and arranges the pillow under her head. Musetta tells the story: she had heard that Mimì had left the viscount and was mortally ill; she searched everywhere for her and found her half dead on the street; and Mimì asked to be brought to Rodolfo. Mimì says that she feels better (*Mi sento assai meglio*) and looks around, happy to be back in a familiar place. Musetta asks what food and drink there is in the house—none, Marcello replies—while Schaunard predicts that Mimì will be dead within half an hour. Mimì's hands are cold, and she wishes she had a muff; she coughs repeatedly, then seems to fall asleep. Musetta gives Marcello her earrings so that he can buy medicine and find a doctor; she then decides to go with him to procure a muff. Colline will give up his overcoat—to which he sings a morose lament (*Vecchia zimarra, senti*)—and he and Schaunard leave the lovers alone. Mimì opens her eyes: she was only pretending to be asleep because she wanted to be just with Rodolfo (*Sono andati? Fingevo di dormire*). The two lovers recall their first encounter and the happy time they had buying the lace bonnet. The friends gradually return, and Mimì enjoys the muff, especially when Musetta kindly tells her that Rodolfo paid for it: love has been found again, her hands are warm, and she can sleep. Marcello tells Rodolfo that the doctor is coming; Musetta warms medicine over a spirit stove and murmurs a prayer for Mimì (*Madonna benedetta*), which she briefly interrupts to ask Marcello to improvise a shade around the candle to stop the flame from flickering (he uses a book). Rodolfo hopes that things are not too serious, but Schaunard realizes that Mimì has died. Colline returns with money, then helps Rodolfo try to hang Musetta's cape over the window to shield Mimì's face from the sunlight. Rodolfo still thinks that Mimì is just sleeping, but when he sees the looks Marcello and Schaunard are giving each other, he realizes the truth. He throws herself on her body, crying out in despair (*Mimì . . . Mimì . . .*); Musetta lets out a cry and runs to the bed, falling to her knees on the opposite side from Rodolfo; Schaunard collapses into a chair; Colline goes to the foot of the bed, stunned by the speed of the catastrophe; and Marcello sobs, turning his back on the audience.

ANYONE SCANNING the advertisements in the Turin newspaper *La stampa* on Saturday 1 February 1896 in search of an evening's entertainment had a number of options: Bizet's *Carmen*, followed by the ballet *Il conte di Montecristo*, at the Teatro Vittorio Emanuele; a Spanish *zarzuela*, *El duo de La Africana*, by Manuel Fernández Caballero, at the Carignano; Beaumarchais's play *Il matrimonio di Figaro* (i.e., *Le Mariage de Figaro*) at the Alfieri; an equestrian circus at the Balbo; or, for lucky subscribers and guests of the opera season at the Teatro Regio, the opening of a new opera by Giacomo Puccini (1858–1924): *La Bohème*. For the previous fortnight, the Teatro Vittorio Emanuele had been performing Pietro Mascagni's *Cavalleria rusticana* (1890) and Ruggero Leoncavallo's *Pagliacci* (1892), usually in the typical double bill, while the Regio featured performances of its other main works of the 1895–96 season: Wagner's *Il crepuscolo degli dei* (*Gotterdämmerung*;

TITLE PAGE OF THE VOCAL SCORE FOR *LA BOHÈME* (1902)

The "Stile Liberty" (Art Nouveau) design by Adolf Hohenstein seems to emphasize the pleasures of bohemian life for the opera's six main characters more than its pains.
AKG-IMAGES.

1876), Verdi's *Falstaff* (1893), and Natale Canti's *Savitri* (1894).[2] By coincidence (or not), on the night before the opening of *La Bohème* the Teatro Alfieri staged Théodore Barrière's *La Vie de bohème* (1849) as a benefit performance for the actor Libero Pilotto. This play, co-authored with Henri Murger, had played an important role in spreading the nineteenth-century fascination with Murger's serial novel *Scènes de la vie de bohème*.

The choice of Turin for the premiere of *La Bohème* was in part due to the intense competition between Giulio Ricordi (Puccini's publisher) and his archrival, Edoardo Sonzogno, who was also director of the Teatro alla Scala in Milan from 1894 to 1897. This also has a bearing on the competing setting of Murger's novel on which the Sonzogno-supported composer Ruggero Leoncavallo was working concurrently. But the Teatro Regio had already seen two Puccini premières: *Le villi* (1884) and his most recent success, *Manon Lescaut*, which opened exactly three years before *La Bohème* on 1 February 1893, conducted by Alessandro Pomè. *La Bohème* was led by the Regio's new principal conductor, Arturo Toscanini (1867–1957), who had conducted *Manon Lescaut* in Pisa in March 1894.

Ricordi argued, perhaps on financial grounds, that the opera needed a "homogenous" cast rather than one consisting of superstars; and Luigi Illica (the co-librettist of *La Bohème*), who directed the production, later

---

2 Although Wagner's *Der Ring des Nibelungen* had been performed in German in Venice and Bologna in 1883, this was the first production of part of the tetralogy in Italian.

took credit for persuading Puccini that it was more important for the singers to be good actors. The first Mimì, Cesira Ferrani (1863–1943), had created the title role in *Manon Lescaut*; her other roles included Gilda (*Rigoletto*) and Marguerite (Gounod's *Faust*), and she was to be the first Italian Mélisande (in Debussy's opera *Pelléas et Mélisande*; performed at La Scala under Toscanini in 1908). Evan Gorga (1865–1957; Rodolfo) was to be the first Marcello in Leoncavallo's *La Bohème* (Venice, 1897). Tieste Wilmant (Marcello) had sung in *Manon Lescaut* at La Scala (during the 1893–94 season) and later was an Alberich and a Iago there; Puccini felt that he was by far the weakest of the *La Bohème* cast. Camilla Pasini (Musetta) had been a Violetta and a Desdemona, and Suzel in Mascagni's *L'amico Fritz* (1891; a role also played by Cesira Ferrani); Puccini much preferred the singer who played Musetta in Rome later in February 1896, Rosina Storchio. Antonio Pini-Corsi (Schaunard) premiered the role of Ford in Verdi's *Falstaff* at La Scala in 1893, the same year in which he played Rigoletto there; in 1894 he took the role of Lescaut in Puccini's *Manon Lescaut* in London, and he was also well-known for such comic baritone parts as Bartolo in Rossini's *Il barbiere di Siviglia* and Dr. Dulcamara in Donizetti's *L'elisir d'amore*. Alessandro Polonini (Benoît, Alcindoro) was the first Geronte de Revoir in *Manon Lescaut* and the surgeon in Verdi's *La forza del destino* (St. Petersburg, 1862); he was Beckmesser in the Teatro Regio's first performance (in Italian) of *Die Meistersinger von Nürnberg* (1893).

The first-night reviews of *La Bohème* were somewhat mixed, although the opera did well enough during its twenty-four performances in Turin, and the immensely powerful Ricordi had already secured enough stagings elsewhere in Italy to create a success. The opera was done on its own at the premiere, but by the third performance (on 4 February) it was followed by the pantomime-ballet *Fidès*, by Georges Ernest Street (first performed at the Opéra-Comique in Paris in 1894). By 11 February this had been replaced, much to the relief of the Turin critics, by the ballet *La fata delle bambole*, that is, Josef Bayer's *Die Puppenfee* (*The Fairy Doll*; 1888), which remained associated with Puccini's opera: the two works were also coupled at the opening of Puccini's *La Bohème* in Venice on 26 December 1897. As we saw in the case of *Rigoletto*, pairing an opera with a ballet was common practice in nineteenth-century Italian opera houses, although it also reflects the fact that *La Bohème* runs somewhat short for a full evening's performance. In 1925–26, the Metropolitan Opera in New York solved the problem by adding Stravinsky's ballet

Petrushka, perhaps prompted by the apparent musical connection with Puccini's Act II opening. However, *La Bohème* was originally meant to be longer, we shall see.

BOHEMIAN RHAPSODIES

The title of *La Bohème* refers to that artistic countercultural space known as "bohemia," although it is often translated as "Bohemian Life" in reference to its source, the *Scènes de la vie de bohème* (Scenes of Bohemian Life) by the French author Henri Murger (1822–1861). The *Scènes* first came out as series of short stories (*Scènes de la bohème*) in the Paris magazine *Le Corsaire–Satan* from March 1845 to April 1849; they were published in book form in 1851, and translations followed in German (1851), Italian (1859), and English (1887), although for the Italian, the version made by Felice Camerone (published in 1872 and reprinted in 1890) became more standard. The stories, which draw on Murger's own experiences as a budding writer in a bohemian underworld, form a loose narrative sequence but are largely episodic: the main focus falls on two coquettes, Musette and Mimi (also called Lucile), and their sometime lovers, respectively the painter Marcel and the poet Rodolphe. Alexandre Schaunard, a musician, and Gustave Colline, a philosopher, have their own occasional mistresses, and are joined by a much larger cast of bohemian characters, including Jacques, a sculptor, who falls for a young seamstress named Francine. Musette and Marcel, and Mimi and Rodolphe each have on-and-off relationships, and Mimi takes up with the *vicomte* Paul, though they, too, split up, and Mimi lives briefly on her own until she can no longer pay the rent. Penniless and ill with tuberculosis, she returns to Rodolphe but then admits herself to the hospital, where she dies alone (so Rodolphe discovers only later, and after an awkward mix-up when her death is reported before it occurs). The final story, "La Jeunesse n'a qu'un temps" (chapter 23, "There Is But One Youth"), is set a year after Mimi's death, with Marcel and Rodolphe still sharing an apartment. But they and Schaunard have found artistic success and financial stability; Marcel has more or less put Musette behind him; and he and Rodolphe decide that they now prefer bourgeois respectability, leaving behind their bohemian life as mere youthful indulgence.

Shortly after the serialization of the stories, the playwright Théodore Barrière collaborated with Murger to produce a stage drama drawing loosely on the stories. *La Vie de bohème*, first performed at the Théâtre des Variétés in Paris on 22 November 1849, was advertised as a "pièce en cinq actes, mêlée de chants" (play in five acts, mixed with songs), the *chants* being mostly popular songs or snatches from well-known operas (the text also cues incidental orchestral music). While *La Vie de bohème* took its characters from Murger's *Scènes* (Rodolphe, Marcel, Schaunard, Colline, Musette, Mimi), it created a somewhat different, and less morally reproachable, version of the Rodolphe-Mimi story: Rodolphe's rich uncle, Durandin, has plans to marry him to a respectable widow, Césarine de Rouvre; Durandin pressures Mimi to leave his nephew so that he can have a better future; she does, but on being hospitalized for tuberculosis, she decides to return; Durandin and de Rouvre realize the power of such young love and relent, but Mimi dies almost immediately.

Both the stories and the play have numerous intertextual resonances. The name "Mimi" (for Lucile) is associated with Alfred de Musset's short story about the grisette Mimi Pinson (published in *Le Diable à Paris* in 1845); Murger's "Musette" also makes the connection with the author's older friend. As for *La Vie de bohème*, it shares obvious similarities with *La Dame aux camélias* by Alexandre Dumas *fils*, a novel published in 1848 (the year before Barrière and Murger's play) and itself the basis for a play first staged at the Théâtre du Vaudeville in Paris on 2 February 1852. Thus Rodolphe is akin to Armand Duval, in love with Marguerite Gautier, while his rich uncle (present also in Murger's novel but unnamed, and a more benign figure) matches Duval's stern father; Mimi is also described as having skin the velvet-white color of camellias (the description is also included in the quotations prefacing the score of Act I of *La Bohème*). An earlier model for the leading of young men astray by loose women was Abbé Prévost's famous novel *L'Histoire du chevalier des Grieux et de Manon Lescaut* (1731), which Théodore Barrière had also turned into a play in 1851 (with Marc Fournier). Puccini had adopted this book for his *Manon Lescaut* of 1893, evidently relishing a contest with the French composer Jules Massenet's *opéra comique* on the same subject, *Manon* (1884; it was done at La Scala in 1895). Puccini (represented by Ricordi) may have felt in competition with Massenet (represented in Italy by Edoardo Sonzogno): Massenet had also composed some incidental music for a reprise of the play *La Vie de bohème* in 1875. But Puccini had other reasons to avoid the Murger-Barrière play, even though he clearly knew it: it was still in copyright (unlike the novel, he noted), and the parallels with Dumas were too dangerous given that *La Dame aux camélias* had provided the basis for Verdi's opera *La traviata* (1853). Puccini and his collaborators worked hard to avoid the obvious comparisons between Mimì and the *demimonde* courtesan Violetta Valéry (the opera's equivalent of Marguerite Gautier), which, we shall see, led to some oddities in the portrayal of their own heroine.

La Bohème is divided into four *quadri* (pictures or tableaux)—although I use the term "acts" for convenience—which acknowledges the episodic nature of Murger's "scenes." Each is played on a single set, and there are no scene divisions corresponding to the entrance or exit of individual characters. The libretto describes the sets in great detail and also is full of very specific stage directions—presented sometimes in even greater detail in the score—written, it seems, by Illica, who also used them to compensate for particular cuts made to the libretto by Puccini that left numerous loose ends (Illica ties them up by mute action). We have already seen in the case of *Rigoletto* how such descriptions and directions reflect the industrialization of nineteenth-century Italian opera (not least, by the Ricordi publishing house). They also leave little room for directorial maneuvering. In addition, each act is preceded by a series of quotations from Murger's novel (in Italian translation) providing background information and some sense of context, albeit mostly about Musetta, who is more finely drawn than she appears in the opera. There is also a preface drawing on Murger's own preface to his novel and outlining some of the features of a bohemian life, which is both gay and dreadful (*Vita gaia e terribile*)—an adjectival coupling that seems slightly more frenetic, and less enchanting, than Murger's *vie charmante et vie terrible*. The preface has a footnote explaining that the authors of the libretto thought it better not to follow Murger's novel step by step—also because of the demands of the theater and, above all, music—but wanted, rather, to capture the essence of "this bizarre book," and one that is "perhaps the freest in modern literature." This also provides the justification for their having merged multiple characters into one, not least Mimi and Francine, who, so the footnote says, might rather be given a single name, "Ideal" (*Ideale*). It further explains why the operatic Mimì needs to introduce herself at such length: "Mi chiamano Mimì," she sings, but she is not the character that audiences familiar with the novel might expect.

One might reasonably ask what "ideal" the combined Mimi-Francine represents. But that exculpatory footnote was also necessary for anyone familiar with the novel (and, eventually, with Leoncavallo's more literal treatment of it). Murger paints Mimi as a coquette very similar to Musette, whereas Francine is much softer and a more typical *femme fragile*. It is Francine's love affair with the sculptor, Jacques, and then her affecting death (recounted in chapter 18, "Francine's Muff"), that provide the detail for Rodolfo and Mimì in Acts I and IV. The opera also draws on the novel's chapters 11 ("A Bohemian Café"; for Act II) and 22 ("Epilogue of the Love Affairs of Rodolphe and Mademoiselle Mimi"), plus elements from chapters 9 ("The Violets from the Pole"; Rodolfo burning his play in Act I), 15 ("*Donec gratus*," referring to Horace's Ode 3.9; Mimi leaves Rodolphe for *vicomte* Paul and Musette leaves Marcel, but the latter two meet on the street and reunite), 16 ("The Passage of the Red Sea"; Marcel's painting eventually becomes a shop sign), 17 ("The Toilet of the Graces"; Schaunard's dead parrot), 19 ("Musette's Whims"; the landlord comes for the rent, herring for dinner, etc.), and 20 ("Mimi Wears Feathers"; the Mimì-Marcello discussion in Act III).

Murger and his French colleagues were writing in dangerous times, around the 1848 Revolution; *La Bohème* shifts the action slightly earlier and more squarely in the reign of King Louis Philippe to play down any revolutionary overtones. Its version of bohemia is not particularly political, being populated by male artists happily slumming it as they revel in their inability to live off their art, and by a range of *demimonde* women free with their sexual and other favors: the stories are frank and also titillating in ways that are hardly toned down in the opera. As the final chapter of the novel reveals, this is just an adolescent stage of life; likewise, the play ends with Rodolphe's sad admission that his youth will lie buried with Mimi, although in the novel she is but one of a series of his lovers (he starts out with Louise before falling for his cousin, Angèle, and then, during one of his breaks from Mimi, he becomes enamored of Juliette). There is more than a whiff of self-indulgence in this bohemian life—despite the obvious critique of bourgeois hypocrisies—and even if Murger's characters needed toning down for any opera (as they did for the play), it is hard to know how much they deserve our sympathy.

Like Murger, Puccini had himself experienced—and even perhaps enjoyed—some of the bohemian life, in his case as a poor music student in Milan: he drew on one of his compositions from that time, the *Capriccio sinfonico* (1883), for the opening of *La Bohème*. Moreover, in the early 1890s he rented lodgings with his mistress (later wife), Elvira Bonturi, in Torre del Lago, near the Lago di Massaciuccoli (just south of Viareggio in the province of Lucca). Here he became associated with a group of artists linked to the so-called Macchiaioli school of Tuscan rural impressionists. One of them, the painter Ferruccio Pagni (one of Puccini's early biographers), gave a lively account of their bohemian japes during the composer's stays there. Pagni claimed that he himself was the model for Colline and that Marcello was based on the painter Francesco Fanelli (just as Murger's characters were reportedly modeled on the author's friends and associates). *La Bohème* has also been associated with the broader Italian artistic movement known as the Scapigliatura, comprising writers, artists, and musicians from the mid 1860s through the 1880s of a decidedly radical, nonconformist bent modeled on the French bohemians and their successors (including Baudelaire and Poe) who also engaged in the political struggles for Italian unification and its aftermath. But there is little of this in *La Bohème* save perhaps an elegiac nostalgia for times past.

It is probably this sense of nostalgia that sets *La Bohème* apart from the works of Puccini's Italian competitors in the 1890s. As we have seen, Mascagni's *Cavalleria rusticana* (1890) and Leoncavallo's *Pagliacci* (1892) were playing in Turin around the same time as *La Bohème*, and both works were, and still are, regarded as landmarks in the new Verismo (Realism) school. Verismo opera drew on broader naturalist trends in Italian literature from the 1870s on to portray lower-class characters in a harshly realistic way, usually culminating in a violent death. *La Bohème*, however, takes a more sugarcoated view of things: it is set in a picture-postcard bohemia that appears suavely urbane rather than grittily urban; Rodolfo and his friends seem to be just playing at poverty; and Mimì's demise is genteel rather than harrowing. The common view—and one that led to significant criticism of Puccini even during his lifetime—is that the composer sold out for the sake of international success; a more charitable one is that he got caught on the horns of various late nineteenth-century operatic dilemmas.

A PUBLISHER, TWO LIBRETTISTS, AND A RIVAL

For his first two operas, *Le villi* (1884) and *Edgar* (1889), Puccini set librettos by one of the Scapigliatura poets, Ferdinando Fontana. His third, *Manon Lescaut*, had a more problematic genesis. Puccini first worked with the playwright Marco Praga, who brought in the poet Domenico Oliva; however, Puccini grew dissatisfied with Praga's work, asked the composer (and librettist) Ruggero Leoncavallo to draft new scenarios for parts of the opera, and then engaged the librettist Luigi Illica (1857–1919) to revise the entire text, although Illica did not take credit for it in the published libretto. Illica did not particularly relish that experience, criticizing Puccini's tendency to turn poetry into "lines of doggerel," and in January 1893 he said that he did not want to work with the composer again. But they stayed together for Puccini's next projects, also bringing in the Italian playwright Giuseppe

Giacosa (1847–1906); the three of them worked together on *La Bohème*, *Tosca* (1900), and *Madama Butterfly* (1904).

Behind the scenes in all these collaborations was Giulio Ricordi (1840–1912), head of the famous music-publishing house following the death of his father, Tito, in 1888: the Ricordi firm was in effect the chief publisher and distributor of Italian operas from Rossini on. Just as Tito's father (Giovanni) and Tito himself had taken Verdi under their wing, so did Giulio with Puccini, actively involving himself in the creation of his operas by way of meetings with the composer and his librettists, as well as maintaining a voluminous correspondence with them. Likewise, the Casa Ricordi took charge of many aspects of the production, including having its art director, Adolf Hohenstein, design the sets and also the advertising material. Giulio Ricordi later claimed some paternity over *La Bohème*, not just as a facilitator but also in terms of the direct suggestions he made for its structure and content, and his letters reveal him urging, cajoling, and even forcing Puccini, Giacosa, and Illica into action. At least one of his ideas bore tangible fruit: the offstage reprise of Musetta's waltz in the Barrière d'Enfer act (he suggested it on 20 June 1895). Others did not, including his request, made around the same time, that the same act should end with a memorable phrase for Mimì on a par with Violetta's "Amami, Alfredo." But Ricordi's willingness to compete with Verdi was not going to be shared by Puccini and his collaborators.

Illica was a perfectly capable librettist in his own right: his single-authored librettos include *La Wally* (Catalani, 1892), *Cristoforo Colombo* (Franchetti, 1892), *Andrea Chénier* (Giordano, 1896), and *Iris* and *Le maschere* (Mascagni, 1898 and 1901), among others. Giacosa had less experience in the genre but was well-known as a poet and playwright. As Italian production models shifted from theater-specific commissions, there was no longer an obvious role for the in-house poet/librettist, as Francesco Maria Piave had been for La Fenice in Venice. Double-team librettists were also not unusual in France. Bringing Giacosa and Illica together seems to have been a matter of expediency on the one hand (they were busy people), and on the other, of seeking a cumulative wisdom that was all the more useful in the cutthroat world of late nineteenth-century Italian opera.

The common view of a clear division of labor between Illica and Giacosa in the case of *La Bohème*—the former providing the dramatic outline and the latter turning it into singable verse—does not bear scrutiny in the light of materials now being uncovered concerning the creation of the opera. Giacosa was in on the discussions from very early on; Illica provided a great deal of poetry for it, much of which was reworked by Giacosa but some

ADOLF HOHENSTEIN'S SET DESIGN FOR ACT II OF *LA BOHÈME*

Hohenstein joined the Ricordi publishing house in 1889, becoming its art director and designing productions and costumes (e.g., for Verdi's Falstaff *and Puccini's* La Bohème *and* Tosca*) as well as advertising material. His striking set for the Latin Quarter takes a literal approach that is hard to avoid for the opera.* Milan, Casa Ricordi. AKG-IMAGES/Joseph Martin.

of which stayed intact; and when it came to subsequent revisions, Puccini and Ricordi turned to one or the other depending on who was available or might be most useful. As he started to sketch out the music, Puccini also frequently intervened in the text; he was perfectly capable of writing verse (as he often did in humorous letters to his collaborators), and at times he would send his librettists what one might call dummy lines (nonsense phrases to indicate meter, accent, and rhyme) to fit a precomposed melody, or to create additional space for some musical or dramatic action.[3] Failing a proper critical edition of the score and a reasoned account of all its prior textual and musical sources—rendered still more complex by Giulio Ricordi's need

3 The oft-cited example is Puccini's *Coricò, coricò, bistecca* for Musetta's waltz, "Quando men' vo soletta per la via," the melody of which had been used for an earlier piano piece (*cocoricò* is the sound a rooster makes, and *bistecca* is beefsteak). However, the story (from Puccini's sometime librettist and early biographer Giuseppe Adami) may be apocryphal, and the nonsense words do not quite fit the melody as Puccini first conceived it.

to start typesetting text and engraving music piecemeal, before composition was complete—it is almost impossible to identify which words came when and at whose instigation.

Clearly Ricordi had a significant hand in the inception of the opera. The first official news comes from late March 1893, when a brief article in the 19 March issue of the *Gazetta musicale di Milano* (a Ricordi periodical) announced that Puccini was at work on a *La Bohème* with two (unnamed) librettists. On the 20th, *Il secolo*—a newspaper published by Edoardo Sonzogno—claimed precedence for Leoncavallo, whose *Bohème* opera had been in progress "for some months" and was projected to have its premiere in 1894. Puccini (actually Illica) responded briefly in the *Corriere della sera* on 21 March staking out his own position, prompting Leoncavallo to provide more information in *Il secolo* the next day (22 March): his own opera was under contract, and when Leoncavallo told Puccini of the project "a few days ago," the latter admitted that he had only come up with the idea of his own *Bohème* on returning from Turin (from the première of *Manon Lescaut* on 1 February) "a few days ago" and that Illica and Giacosa had not yet finished the libretto. Given that Leoncavallo had recently had his greatest success with *Pagliacci* (premiered under Toscanini in Milan on 21 May 1892), one might expect Puccini to have taken a softer line. Matters were also rendered more complicated by the rumor (which emerged later) that Leoncavallo had in fact offered Puccini his own *La Bohème* libretto a year before the present controversy. But as *Manon Lescaut* had already revealed, Puccini was never shy of a fight, and he threw down the gauntlet: if Leoncavallo had told him earlier than "the other evening" about his plans, then surely he would have given way, but he had been working on his own idea "for about two months" since the premiere of *Manon Lescaut* and had made no secret of it: "Let him compose and I will compose. The public will judge."

Given that Illica had completed a prose outline of *La Bohème* by 22 March 1893, when Giacosa wrote to him praising it, things had clearly been underway for a while. Ricordi's intense rivalry with Sonzogno surely had a part to play in all this, and in the end, probably neither publisher thought things bad for business. The problem with Puccini, however, was that he spent much of the second half of 1893 and the first of 1894 traveling to oversee other performances of *Manon Lescaut*, and he was also pursuing ideas for a different operatic project based on *La lupa* by the Verismo novelist Giovanni Verga. He dropped *La lupa* in July 1894 but then started making secret overtures to the poet and playwright Gabriele d'Annunzio for another opera. Verga, who was also associated with the Macchiaioli, was the author of the short story and play that formed the basis for Mascagni's *Cavalleria rusticana* (1890). Puccini's apparent indecision may have been due to the fact that he was now caught between his biggest rivals, Mascagni on the one hand, and Leoncavallo on the other. It is unclear how Puccini thought he might best compete.

Meanwhile, Illica and Giacosa pressed on. The *Gazetta musicale di Milano* reported on 2 July 1893 that the libretto of *La Bohème* was finished, although in fact the authors were still hard at work (Act IV had not even been begun, it seems). Clearly they were facing difficulties with it, for Giacosa proposed resigning from the project in October because the Latin Quarter scene (Act II, although at this point it was the finale to Act I) was proving impossible, and later that month Puccini himself proposed abandoning the opera. This placed matters in some kind of crisis toward the end of 1893, leaving Ricordi to try and pick up the pieces. Illica also became deeply upset at what he thought was Puccini's shabby treatment of him in terms both of his criticisms of his draft texts and of his tendency to pursue other projects (with Verga and d'Annunzio, we have seen). Nevertheless, work on the libretto continued through 1894, and Puccini got down to drafting the music for Act I that summer. Again, however, there were delays: Act I was finished and orchestrated from 21 January to 6 June 1895; Act II was completed on 19 July and sent to Ricordi on 9 August; Act III was done by 18 September; and Act IV was finished by 10 December. One further episode was added to Act II even after the Turin opening (possibly in May 1896), where Marcello asks Mimì what Rodolfo has bought her—a lace bonnet, she replies (*Una cuffietta / a pizzi, tutta rosa, ricamata*)—then the friends acknowledge his talents in both poetry and love, and the group offers a toast, although for Marcello (who sees Musetta) it is a bitter moment. Other adjustments to the end of Act II were also made around this same time, including (it seems) the removal of some final words for Alcindoro.

Leoncavallo's *La Bohème* was eventually premiered in Venice on 6 May 1897 (conducted by Alessandro Pomè, who had led the premiere of Puccini's *Manon Lescaut*), eight months before Puccini's opera reached there. It adheres more closely to Murger's novel: the four acts are based broadly on chapters 11, 6, 15, and 22 (but Mimì dies in the garret). It had some success over the next decade, although Puccini, perhaps inevitably, derided its inflated conventionality. Leoncavallo knew in the end that he had lost the battle: in 1913 he revised his opera as *Mimì Pinson* to avoid the competitive title—and perhaps to divert attention away from Murger toward Musset—but it was not enough to rescue it.

A MISSING ACT

Illica and Giacosa became frustrated at the constant changes to the scenario for *La Bohème*. The original plan was for four acts: the first in the bohemians' attic and then the Latin Quarter (eventually Acts I and II; the division was made in September 1894); the second at the Barrière d'Enfer (eventually III); the third in the courtyard of Musetta's lodgings (from where she is just being evicted); and the fourth back in the attic. The "courtyard" act was finally removed—after fierce debate—in February 1894, and even in July 1894 Puccini still favored dropping the Barrière d'Enfer one. Arguments over Act IV continued until quite late in the day, even as Puccini was composing the score (in the last few months of 1895). A mock political-campaign speech by Schaunard had already been removed by the spring of 1895. But later in the year Puccini and his collaborators were still discussing a facetious *Credo* for Schaunard inveighing against women, and a *brindisi* in praise of water: the former would probably have come too close to Verdi's *Otello* (Iago's "Credo" in Act II), and the latter—although it was a very common trope—to *La traviata* (Alfredo's *brindisi* in Act I), *Otello* (Iago's in Act I), or *Cavalleria rusticana* (Turiddu's in scene 9). Instead, they continued with the rather fatuous mock dance sequence (gavotte, minuet, *pavanella*, fandango, quadrille) descending into a duel, which serves only to heighten the catastrophe as Musetta enters with the dying Mimì. The main problem with the second half of the opera, however, was whether Mimì should separate from Rodolfo: for a long while Puccini thought not (and he wanted the final act just to focus on her death), although Illica insisted that some form of separation was essential to the story. Indeed it is, to follow Rodolphe's on-and-off relationship with Mimi in Murger's novel, although, given that the operatic Mimì had more in common with Murger's Francine (who stays faithful to her Jacques), one can see how the difficulty arose.

Combining Mimi with Francine means that the operatic Mimì remains a somewhat ambiguous character. It further explains the debates over the courtyard act, elaborating on chapter 6 of Murger's novel ("Mademoiselle Musette") and also set by Leoncavallo. This played in the *cortile* of a house at Via Labruyère 8, the residence of Musetta supported by her new lover—who, however, has just dropped her, leaving her in penury. The bailiffs come to remove the furniture, stacking it for sale in the courtyard; Marcello, Rodolfo, Schaunard, Colline, and Mimì arrive, and with Musetta they turn the space into a ballroom for a final party for her and her neighbors. Musetta finds a ballgown for Mimì to wear and introduces her to a group of students, urging them to invite her to dance. One who plucks up the courage to do so is *visconte* Paolo (introduced in Murger's chapter 12: "A Reception in Bohemia"), who, so Musetta whispers to Mimì, is rich, noble, and young (*Ricco! Gentile! Nobile!*). Rodolfo is smitten with jealousy:

SCHAUNARD (*ai suonatori*)		(*to the instrumentalists*)
Una quadriglia! I cavalieri qua	11t	A quadrille! The gentlemen here
conducete le dame.	→	should lead the ladies.
RODOLFO (*non crede ai suoi occhi. Le si avvicina e la chiama.*)		(*he does not believe his eyes. He approaches her and calls to her.*)
Mimì!	→	Mimì!
(*Mimì si svolge.*)		(*Mimì turns.*)
È lei! . . .	11	It's her! . . .
(*A Mimì con l'ira*)		(*To Mimì, angrily*)
Che fate?	→	What are you doing?
SCHAUNARD (*sempre in faccenda colle coppie dei ballerini*)		(*still preoccupied with the pairs of dancers*)
Attenti!	→	Watch out!
MIMÌ		
Danzo!	→	I'm dancing!
RODOLFO (*entra in mezzo alla coppie*)		(*goes amongst the couples*)
Chi v'ha detto	11	Who told you
d'abbigliarvi così?	→	to dress yourself up like this?
SCHAUNARD (*impazientito*)		(*impatient*)
Rodolfo, via!	11	Rodolfo, get out!
MUSETTA, MARCELLO		
Via! S'incomincia.	→	Get out! We're starting.
RODOLFO		
Al diavol la quadriglia!	11	Damn the quadrille!
(*A Mimì*)		(*To Mimì*)
Non voglio che balliate.	→	I do not want you to dance.
TUTTI		
Via, Rodolfo!	11	Get out, Rodolfo!

This leads to the staging of a complex quadrille (divided into its various parts) over which Rodolfo vents his vexation, calls out for a drink, says that he is drowning in bile, and complains about women (*Dammi da bere! Ancora! ancora! ancora! / La bile ho che m'affoga, ora! Oh le donne!*), while Marcello tries to get back together with Musetta. Secondhand dealers enter to auction off Musetta's furniture, Schaunard offers them an ironic toast, and the act ends in an ensemble, with the auction in full swing, while Rodolfo is in his cups:

	Come sopra una croce	7	As over the cross
	d'un bianco camposanto,	7	of a white gravestone,
	levo ancora la voce,	7	I raise again my voice,
	canto l'ultimo canto!	7	I sing my final song!
5	Odi, canta il mio cor.	7t	Listen, my heart sings.
	(*Con immenso slancio*)		(*With great passion*)
	Esci solo! Coi raggi,	7	You [Mimì] leave alone! With the rays
	sulla fronte, del sole,	7	of the sun on your face,
	quando sembra la vita	7	when life seems
	una plaga fiorita	7	a flowery field
10	sparsa di rose e viole	7	strewn with roses and violets
	e di giunchiglie in fior!	7t	and with jonquils in bloom!
	(*Con tristezza*)		(*With sadness*)
	Ma il verno . . . nei misteri,	7	But in winter . . . in mysteries,
	fra il tepor della seta,	7	in the warmth of silk,
	vivi! . . . Tu sei un fiore	7	you live! . . . You are a flower
15	di serra! . . . Fa terrore	7	of the hothouse! . . . Your cough
	la tosse all'ex poeta	7	terrifies this ex-poet-king[4]
	cesareo del tuo cuor!	7t	of your heart.
	(*Scoppia in un lungo singhiozzo; Schaunard e Colline lo trascinano via.*)		(*He bursts into a prolonged sobbing; Schaunard and Colline lead him away.*)

Illica and Giacosa fought hard to keep the act, and for good reason: it explains how Mimì comes to leave Rodolfo for a viscount (unnamed in the final version of the opera), only to return on the verge of death. In the opera we have only a hint of Mimì's flirtatiousness in the final Act III (at the Barrière d'Enfer)—save for the briefest reference in Act II that probably passes most audiences by—where Rodolfo complains about a certain *viscontino* who has been giving her the eye before admitting that this

---

4 *Poeta cesareo* ("imperial poet") was a position appointed by the Habsburg emperor: Pietro Metastasio, for example, held the title.

is just his excuse because he is more worried about what her perpetual coughing might portend for such a hothouse flower (a concern brought in from the end of the passage from the courtyard act just quoted). Then there is a rather strange and very brief account at the beginning of Act IV, where Marcello describes seeing Mimì in a carriage dressed like royalty. Matters hardly become clearer when, later in the last act, Musetta leads in the dying Mimì and explains the circumstances sotto voce to her friends (letters or words in square brackets, below, are omitted in Puccini's setting):

Intesi dire che Mimì, fuggita	11	I heard say that Mimì, having fled from
dal viscontino, era in fin[e] di vita.	11	the *viscontino*, was on the verge of death.
Dove stia? Cerca, cerca . . . [Or or] la veggo	11	Where is she? Searching, searching . . . [Now] I see her
passar per via	5	passing on the street
trascinandosi a stento.	7	dragging herself with effort.
Mi dice: "Più non reggo . . .	7	She says to me: "I cannot hold up any more . . .
Muoio, [muoio,] lo sento . . .	7	I am dying! [I am dying,] I feel it . . .
(Agitandosi, senz'accorgersene alza la voce.)		*(Becoming agitated, she raises her voice without realizing it.)*
Voglio morir con lui! Forse m'aspetta . . .	11	I want to die with him! Perhaps he is waiting for me . . .
M'accompagni, Musetta? . . .	7	Will you accompany me, Musetta? . . .

Events in the dropped courtyard act therefore explain a lacuna in the final version of the opera that certainly seems very odd, even if (we shall see) there is good reason for it.

That "missing" act also served another function in terms of defining the timescale of the opera. The final Acts I and II are set on Christmas Eve (remember that Act II was originally the conclusion to Act I), and Act III in February (according to its initial stage direction), with Rodolfo and Mimì deciding to stay together until the spring. The courtyard act is set in autumn—Musetta refers to the autumn mists already darkening the streets (*Ecco, l'autunno annebbia già le vie*)—so Rodolfo and Mimì have lasted together longer (although in the courtyard Mimì tells Musetta that they are falling short of money and even of love). And Mimì dies in winter—as she does in the novel (but Francine dies on All Saints' Day)—so one can plausibly assume from the setting, and the temperature, of the final act; an early draft of the libretto for the final act has Rodolfo note that it is

Epiphany, that is, 6 January. This means that the opera spans roughly a year of bohemian life, which is less clear in the final version.

Puccini's arguments in favor of dropping the courtyard act are not known, but one can perhaps guess some of them. The Café Momus and Barrière d'Enfer had already given the composer a chance to show his virtuosity in hustle-and-bustle crowd scenes: one more would have been redundant. Staging action over a dance (with onstage musicians) was a common enough operatic convention, if perhaps a rather tired one by now: we have already seen it at the end of Act III of *Le nozze di Figaro* and in the first scene of *Rigoletto* (the latter also with its echoes of the Act I finale of *Don Giovanni*). While the act reveals a key element of the Rodolfo-Mimì story, it also focuses largely on Musetta, who in the end needs to remain a less prominent character if she is not to compete with the *prima donna*. And perhaps most important, a coquettish Mimì dancing with other men is closer to Murger's Mimi than to his Francine. If the operatic Mimì is to retain our sympathy—and she must as her death comes nigh—she cannot afford to be too promiscuous with her sexual and other favors. For all the antibourgeois sentiment of *La Bohème*, its moral compass is set firmly in line with the bourgeoisie, whether onstage or in the audience.

VERSE AND MUSIC

The text of the courtyard act survives complete, but so far as we know, Puccini never set it to music in any extended manner. One striking thing about that text, however, is that its poetic structure is perfectly clear and straightforward (seven- and eleven-syllable *versi sciolti* and occasional *quinari doppi*). The same is true of the scene removed from the last act, where Schaunard plays satirically at being a candidate for political office (mostly in seven-syllable lines, with a few eleven-syllable ones). Here, at least, Giacosa and Illica did little to break the typical patterns of poetry for Italian opera.

Exactly the same is true of the rest of the libretto for *La Bohème* as Ricordi printed it in 1896: Giacosa and Illica kept their carefully crafted verse intact. However, the text as set in the music appears far less regular, in large part because Puccini changed, reordered, or dropped words and phrases, weakening its poetic integrity. Musetta's Act II waltz, for which Puccini drew on an earlier piano piece, provides a simple example. In the libretto, it has two four-line stanzas, a couplet, and a final stanza, all in quite regular meter (and some might claim that the fourteen lines vaguely echo the form of a sonnet):

Quando men' vo soletta per la via,	11	When I go alone on the street,
la gente sosta e mira,	7	people stop and stare,
e la bellezza mia—ricerca in me	11t	and my beauty do they seek out
tutta da capo a piè.	7t	wholly from head to foot.
5 Ed assaporo allor la bramosia	11	And then I savor the desire
sottil, che dai vogliosi occhi traspira,	11	so subtle, which passes through avid eyes,
e dai vezzi palesi intender sa	11t	and knows how to move from surface charms
alle occulte beltà.	7t	to hidden beauties.
Così l'effluvio del desìo m'aggira,	11	Thus the flood of desire rushes over me,
10 e delirar mi fa!	7t	and makes me delirious!
E tu che sai, che memori e ti struggi	11	And you who know it, who remember and pine,
com'io d'amor, da me tanto rifuggi?	11	like me, for love, do you so much avoid me?
So ben: le angoscie tue non le vuoi dir,	11t	Well do I know it: you do not want to speak of your pains,
ma ti senti morir!	7t	but you feel yourself dying!

Puccini makes a large number of alterations:

> lines 3–4: *tutta* shifted to *e la bellezza mia tutta ricerca in me / da capo a piè* (and all my beauty do they seek out / from head to foot)
>
> line 6: *vogliosi* omitted
>
> line 7: *palesi vezzi* instead of *vezzi palesi*
>
> line 9: *tutta* added to *Così l'effluvio del desìo tutta m'aggira* (. . . rushes all over me)
>
> line 10: *felice mi fa* (makes me happy) rather than *e delirar mi fa* (and makes me delirious)
>
> line 12: *com'io d'amor* omitted

We shall see below the musical reasons for that last change. As for the others, they might be seen as sharpening the text, though a poet's view would be that they damage not just the meter but also the syntax, and even someone not a poet might regret the loss of Musetta's reference (*com'io*) to her own love for Marcello.

We have already seen composers taking legitimate licenses with their librettos, but nowhere near to this extent. As noted above, Illica was resigned to Puccini's tendency to mangle librettos; the poet later rationalized it by claiming that when it came to writing for opera, strong words were more important than strong meters. For Giacosa, honor would have been satisfied by a careful printing of the libretto, which Ricordi certainly provided in 1896 even at the expense of confusing the reader or listener following the text alongside the music. More recent editions of the libretto of *La Bohème*, however, have preferred to follow the score, silently accepting Puccini's alterations and then attempting (or, more often, not) to make some kind of poetic sense of them. This means that save by going back to the 1896 edition of the libretto (or subsequent ones based on it)—and to Giacosa and Illica's prior drafts—it is hard to recover what Puccini had in front of him when starting to compose *La Bohème*, and therefore to see and understand what he did with it.

Giacosa and Illica themselves had varying views on what kinds of verse might best suit an opera libretto. Illica had a tendency to favor the *settenari doppi* that were now a standard part of the librettist's toolbox (the beginning of Verdi's *Falstaff* of 1893—to a libretto by Arrigo Boito—provides a good example); they are also known as *versi martelliani*, after the Baroque poet Pier Jacopo Martello, or as *alessandrini*, because of their similarity to the French alexandrine, and they usually take the form of rhyming couplets. Illica's first version of the passage in Act III when Mimì explains to Marcello her current problems with Rodolfo is precisely in this meter (7 + 7):

Sapete chi è Rodolfo . . . carattere impastato	You know who Rodolfo is . . . someone made up
d'ira e di gelosia . . . Credete! Avvelenato	of anger and jealousy . . . Believe it! Poisoned
è il viver nostro! . . . Amore n'ebbe e n'ha . . . ancor . . . ma via!	is our life! . . . He felt love and does so . . . still . . . but goodness!
è troppo insopportabile quella sua gelosia!	this jealousy of his is too unbearable!

Giacosa's reworking of Mimì's complaint started out by using the same meter:

Rodolfo m'abbandona, e mi ama e si tormenta	Rodolfo abandons me, and he loves me and yet torments himself
con una gelosia ingiusta e violenta.	with an unjust and violent jealousy.
È geloso di tutto: ogni passo, ogni detto,	He is jealous of everything: every step, every word,
un vezzo, un nastro, un fiore gli è causa di sospetto.	a glance, a ribbon, a flower is for him a reason for suspicion.

However, he then opted for the more flexible combination of mixed verses found elsewhere in Boito's librettos for Verdi, such as the eleven-, seven-, and five-syllable lines (some *tronchi*) seen in Iago's "Credo" in Act II, scene 2 of *Otello* (1887). Puccini called them "versi rotti" (broken verses), and when Giacosa wanted similar poetry from his co-librettist, he rather playfully asked for "illicasillabi." Thus Mimì's outpouring becomes more natural—and is made even more so by Puccini's word shifting and repetitions (and an added *Ahimè*—"alas"—in the penultimate line)—although the rhyming couplets remain (the version here is the final one, although Giacosa took a few stages to get there):

	Rodolfo m'ama, Rodolfo si strugge	11	Rodolfo loves me, Rodolfo is consumed
	di gelosia e mi fugge.	7	by jealousy and avoids me.
	Un passo, un detto,	5	A step, a word,
	un vezzo, un fior lo mettono in sospetto . . .	11	a glance, a flower make him suspicious . . .
5	onde corrucci ed ire.	7	hence vexation and anger.
	Talor la notte fingo di dormire	11	Sometimes at night I pretend to be asleep
	e in me lo sento fiso	7	and I feel him staring at me
	spiarmi i sogni in viso.	7	to spy on my dreams.
	Mi grida ad ogni istante:	7	He shouts at me all the time:
10	Non fai per me, prendete un altro amante.	11	"I don't need you: take another lover."
	In lui parla il rovello;	7	It is anger that speaks in him;
	lo so, ma che rispondergli, Marcello?	11	I know that, but how should I reply to him, Marcello?

For the most part, this kind of poetry is reasonably familiar from the *versi sciolti* of earlier recitatives, although like Verdi, Puccini treats portions of the text for moments of lyrical expansion moving far beyond any declamatory style.

Settenari doppi have the advantage of leaving options open: these longer lines will have greater or less metrical definition depending on the syntax, the internal rhyme (assonance, etc.), and the strength or weakness of the mid-line caesura. Thus at times they can seem very poetic indeed, and at times much more akin to prose. In the latter case, the meter is hardly noticeable, especially when the line is divided between characters. For example, when Rodolfo is left alone by his friends in the middle of Act I, he hears a timid knock at the door:

Chi è la?	Who's there?
Mimì (*di fuori*)	(*from outside*)
Scusi.	Excuse me.
Rodolfo (*alzandosi*)	(*getting up*)
Una donna!	A woman!
Mimì	
Di grazia, mi si è spento il lume.	Please, my candle has gone out.
Rodolfo (*corre ad aprire*)	(*runs to open the door*)
Ecco.	Here.
Mimì (*sull'uscio, con un lume spento in mano ed una chiave*)	(*on the threshold, with an unlit candle in her hand and a key*)
Vorrebbe . . . ?	Would you . . . ?
Rodolfo	
S'accomodi un momento.	Sit down for a moment.

These seven exchanges take up just two lines of *settenari doppi*:

> *R.* Chi è la? *M.* Scusi. *R.* Una donna! *M.* Di grazia mi si è spento
> il lume. *R.* Ecco. *M.* Vorrebbe . . . ? *R.* S'accomodi un momento.

The text continues in this proselike manner until it shifts to eight-syllable lines as Mimì admits to being a nuisance (*Importuna è la vicina*) and Rodolfo hits his poetic stride, picking up her rhyme upon touching her cold hand (M: *Ah!* R: *Che gelida manina!*). He then adopts more formal eleven-syllable lines, with yet craftier internal rhymes, as he says that it is useless to search for the key in the dark (*Cercar che giova?—Al buio non si trova*) despite the good fortune of the moonlit night (*Ma per fortuna—è una notte di luna*). Thus he reveals his profession, charming Mimì in the process, even before he explains it to her: his *Chi son?—Sono un poeta* sets the seal on the poetic deal by way of seven three-line stanzas in seven-syllable lines (*abb, acc, bdd, bee,* etc.). As one might expect, Mimì's response is far less "poetic" in that metrical sense, but clearly Giacosa and Illica thought that Rodolfo should dazzle her both with his command of meter and of rhyme, and with his rich, sometimes archaic vocabulary, which contrasts with the rather earthy vernacular of his friends. That stanzaic structure is hardly apparent in Puccini's setting: he must have assumed that it was music that needed to do the work of seduction, and he added and changed words toward the end of Rodolfo's text in order to meet what seem to be purely musical needs.

Giacosa and Illica provided Rodolfo with even more "poetry" in their drafts of *La Bohème*, but it got progressively removed. Even that which remains is consistently undercut by Puccini's more proselike approach in the music. Rodolfo waxes poetic again in Act III, when he tells Marcello of his anxieties over Mimì's health, not realizing that she is within earshot:

RODOLFO

Mimì è tanto malata!	7	Mimì is so very ill!
Ogni dì più declina.	7	Every day she gets worse.
La povera piccina	7	The poor little girl
è condannata.	5	is condemned.

MARCELLO (*sorpreso*)   (*surprised*)

Mimì?	–	Mimì?

MIMÌ (*fra sé*)   (*aside*)

Che vuol dire?	–	What does he mean?

RODOLFO

Una terribil tosse	7	A terrible cough
l'esil petto le scuote,	7	strikes her frail breast,
e già le smunte gote	7	and already her emaciated cheeks
di sangue ha rosse . . .	5	are red with blood . . .

Rodolfo has three more stanzas in the same pattern (*abba⁵, cddc⁵,* etc.), while the ongoing interjections for Marcello and Mimì are nonmetrical (and in the 1896 libretto are printed in separate columns not quite with the words set in the score). The idea seems to have been fixed early on: Illica's first version of this passage has the same stanzaic structure (but different words), yet with no interjections (so who added them?). As for the music, the stanzas certainly influence the phrase structures, with some treated in a more declamatory fashion and others in a more lyrical one. We shall see that there is also a certain analytical advantage to be gained by looking closely at how Puccini uses the rhyme-words to construct and anchor his larger melodic arches: this also helps the singer direct the phrasing to longer-term goals. But again, the poetry only weakly determines the musical setting.

Those ametrical insertions for Marcello and Mimì are justified by the fact that in Marcello's case they are conversational interpolations, and in Mimì's they are asides. Thus the musical focus remains just on Rodolfo, while the other two voices have little melodic identity. But even when characters are kept distinct by more formal poetic means, the results can be similar. In the quartet at the end of Act III, Mimì and Rodolfo bid tender farewell to their past (*Addio dolce svegliare alla mattina*): their melody comes from a song, "Sole e amore," that Puccini wrote in 1888. Meanwhile, Musetta and Marcello argue rancorously and decide to separate. The two pairs of characters pay no attention to each other, and the libretto keeps them separate: Rodolfo and Mimì have *versi sciolti*; Marcello and Musetta, eight-syllable lines. The technique is quite different from, say, that of the quartet in Act III of *Rigoletto*, although the musical results are not dissimilar. What is most striking, however, is that the *versi sciolti* generate the most lyrical melodies, whereas for an earlier period one would expect the more regularly patterned eight-syllable lines to do so. Puccini's melodic invention seems to have favored verse with a lesser degree of structure rather than a greater one.

But presumably it still mattered to him that the libretto should exhibit various types of patterning. Act I proceeds quite logically in sections matched to the action that are delineated by poetic meter:

Marcello and Rodolfo banter about their living conditions: *versi sciolti* (7/11) then *settenari doppi* (7 + 7)
Rodolfo decides to burn the manuscript of his play: ten-syllable lines
Colline enters: *settenari doppi* (7 + 7)
Rodolfo burns Act II of his play: *quinari doppi* (5 + 5)
Marcello notes that the fire is dying down again: nine-syllable lines
Rodolfo calls for wood: eight-syllable lines

Schaunard enters: six-syllable lines
Schaunard tells the story of the English lord and his parrot: *versi
      sciolti* (7/11)
etc.

The shifts of meter are obvious and even preserve some vestige of their function
in earlier librettos: *versi sciolti* for everyday interactions (Marcello and Rodolfo)
or for narratives (Schaunard and the parrot), and other meters to mark a change
of pace or rhetoric. Those shifts also have some impact on the music, at least by
offering different rhythmic possibilities (of which Puccini takes full advantage).

But yet again there seems to be a mismatch—at least in so far as what one
might expect from earlier operatic practice—between these poetic and musical
structures. The act begins in mid-stream in those conversational *versi sciolti*:

MARCELLO (*seduto, continuando a dipingere*)		(*sitting, continuing to paint*)
Questo *Mar Rosso*—mi ammollisce e assidera	11s	This *Red Sea* enervates and chills me,
come se addosso—mi piovesse in stille.	11	as if it were raining down my back drop by drop.
(*Si allontana dal cavalletto per guardare il suo quadro.*)		(*He moves away from the easel to look at his painting.*)
Per vendicarmi, affogo un Faraon[e]!	11	To avenge myself, I drown a pharaoh!
(*Torna al lavoro. A Rodolfo*)		(*He goes back to work. To Rodolfo*)
Che fai?	→	What are you doing?
RODOLFO		
Nei cieli bigi	7	In the gray skies
guardo fumar dai mille	7	I see smoking from its thousand
comignoli Parigi,	7	chimneys Paris,
(*additando il camino senza fuoco*)		(*pointing to the fireplace without a fire*)
e penso a quel poltrone	7	and I think of this sluggard
di un vecchio caminetto ingannatore	11	of an old, treacherous fireplace,
che vive in ozio come un gran signore.	11	which lives in luxury like a great lord.

However, Puccini treats Rodolfo's *Nei cieli bigi* as a moment for lyrical
expansion—matching the poet's gaze over the chimneys of Paris and his rather
extravagant image of the fireplace as an indolent nobleman—with a powerful

melodic idea (taken from the aborted opera *La lupa*) that, we shall see, recurs in various contexts. This is all well and good, and Puccini's flexible musical prose has an undeniable power as well as, one might argue, a greater degree of dramatic naturalism. The problem that follows, however, is how this treatment of the text might square with any need to generate plausible musical structures.

FORMLESS FORMS?

We have already seen the issues come into play in Verdi's *Rigoletto*, and they were much debated in the course of the later nineteenth century, both in Italy and in France: it would probably be a mistake to view *La Bohème* as exceptional in any way. In the early stages of work on it, Giulio Ricordi was excited by the idea of producing something genuinely new ("un'opera veramente nuova," as he wrote to Puccini in early June 1893). Illica's later claim that *La Bohème* was of a new kind ("genere nuovo") may also reflect a somewhat resigned acceptance that the old ways were long gone. But absent the traditional musical forms of Italian Romantic opera—or, perhaps, their increasingly ghostlike presence—the challenge was to build musical paragraphs that made some kind of structural sense. Puccini's text-setting runs the gamut from declamatory patter in the manner of recitative to lyrical passages akin to would-be arias (duets, etc.) with fairly clear beginnings, middles, and ends rendered coherent by way of melodic and other repetition. However, given that these latter passages are rarely created or defined by regular poetic structures, and still fewer stanzaic ones, Puccini has to find other clues within the text. Some are metrical, and some based on content. For the former, when in Act II Mimì tells Rodolfo's friends how he bought her a lace bonnet, pink and embroidered (*Una cuffietta / a pizzi, tutta rosa, rica-mata*)—an episode added to the opera after the premiere—the text falls into fairly regular eleven-syllable lines, meaning that Mimì's initial melody can be reused intact at various points throughout this episode, culminating in Mimì's, Rodolfo's, and Marcello's proposing to cast cares aside and to raise their glasses and drink: their *E via i pensier, / alti bicchier! / beviam! . . . beviam!* is made up of three five-syllable *versi tronchi*, but the shorter lines can fit into the longer phrase.

Such musical repetition to different words sometimes raises other issues, however, as two examples for Mimì in Act I reveal. First she loses her key (the text here begins with the second half of a *settenario doppio*):

RODOLFO (*l'accompagna fino all'uscio*)		(*he accompanies her to the doorway*)
Buona sera.	→	Good evening.

(*Ritorna subito al lavoro.*)		(*He returns quickly to work.*)

MIMÌ (*esce, poi riappare sull'uscio che rimane aperto.*)		(*she leaves, then reappears in the doorway, which stays open.*)
Oh! sventata!	+ 7	Oh! I am so thoughtless!
La chiave della stanza dove l'ho lasciata?	7 + 7	The key of the room, where have I left it?

Five lines later, after her and Rodolfo's candles have gone out, she apologizes for being an importunate neighbor (*Importuna è la vicina*). Puccini chooses to repeat the musical idea devised for Mimì's *Oh! sventata*, adapting for eight syllables something originally created for fourteen by removing an upbeat pattern and slurring some of the shorter notes (syllables in italic are on the downbeats of the 2/4 measures):

Oh!	sven-	*ta-*	ta,	sven-	*ta-*	ta!	La	*chia-*	ve	del-	la	*stan-*	za
	Im-	por-	-		*tu-*	na_è	_	*la_*	_		vi-	- *ci-*	na

The melodic connection makes sense: Mimì is first careless and then importunate. The final -*a* rhyme may also have been a factor in Puccini's thinking: there are parallels in other such cases when the composer seems to have associated melodies with recurring vowels or phonemes. The only inconvenience—and it is a minor one—are the long notes on -*por*- in *Importuna* (where the accent comes on -*tu*-) and on *la*.

There is nothing surprising about this kind of calculation—which would have come as second nature to Puccini—but the need for repetition has significant structural consequences. Musetta's waltz in Act II is performed as "real" music: her escort, Alcindoro, calls it *quel canto scurrile*—that scurrilous song—and tries to silence her. It falls into a clear ternary form in sections of equal length, the first two (AB) each sixteen measures long, and the last (A') a slightly curtailed fifteen, although a pause in the penultimate measure balances things out. The search for this kind of patterning helps explain Puccini's deviations from the libretto noted above (the text below is taken from the score):

A	Quando men' vo soletta per la via, / la gente sosta e mira, / e la bellezza mia tutta ricerca in me / da capo a piè . . .	When I go alone on the street, / people stop and stare, / and my beauty do they seek out / wholly from head to foot . . .

B   ed assaporo allor la bramosia / sottil, che da gli occhi traspira, / e dai palesi vezzi intender sa / alle occulte beltà. / Così l'effluvio del desìo tutta m'aggira, / felice mi fa!

    and then I savor the desire / so subtle, which passes through those eyes, / and knows how to move from surface charms / to hidden beauties. / Thus the flood of desire rushes all over me, / [and] makes me happy!

A′   E tu che sai, che memori e ti struggi, / da me tanto rifuggi? / So ben: le angoscie tue non le vuoi dir, / ma ti senti morir!

    And you who know it, who remember and pine, / do you so much avoid me? / Well do I know it: you do not want to speak of your pains, / but you feel yourself dying!

This tripartite musical structure splits the text into 4 + 6 + 4 lines as prompted by the content: (A) Musetta is always admired in the street; (B) she enjoys the attention; (A′) she wonders why her lover avoids her. The return of the A section (rather than setting this ABC) is cued by the direction of Musetta's argument: the "they" of the first section (those who admire her in the street) are contrasted with the "you" (Marcello) addressed in the final section (whereas the middle section concerns "I"). However, to allow for the musical return—that is, the same music to different words—Puccini had to change the libretto, turning line 12 (the second line of the A′ section) from an eleven-syllable line (*com'io d'amor, da me tanto rifuggi*) to a seven-syllable one (omitting *com'io d'amor*) so as to match line 2 (*la gente sosta e mira*).

Shortening a line for musical balance is straightforward enough. But Puccini's free treatment of the libretto created other problems for him. The A and B sections are formed of eight-measure phrases, each spanning two lines of text:

	A		B			A′	
lines:	1–2	3–4	5–6	7–8	9–10	11–12	13–14
phrases:	x	x'	y	y'	z	x	x''

The case of x' (in the first A section) and x'' (in the final one) is revealing. In the libretto, lines 3–4 and 13–14 match each other (an eleven-syllable *verso tronco* and then a seven-syllable one, so ten and then six actual syllables). However, Puccini repositioned the *tutta* from line 4 to line 3 (the libretto has *e la bellezza mia—ricerca in me / tutta da capo a piè*), giving line 3 thirteen actual syllables and line 4, four. Furthermore, he then set line 3 with an internal repetition so as to produce seventeen actual syllables:

> e la bellezza mia tutta ricerca in me, ricerca in me
> da capo a piè . . .

Therefore in the final section, he extends line 13 from ten syllables to sixteen (then six for line 14):

> So ben: le angoscie tue non le vuoi dir, non le vuoi dir, so ben,
> ma ti senti morir!

Although the repeated *so ben* at the end of that line serves for emphasis ("Well do I know it: you do not want to speak of your pains, you do not want to speak of them, well do I know it, / but you feel yourself dying"), there is also another reason for it. At the equivalent point in the first A section, *ricerca in me*, Puccini has Musetta move to a held high note (on the first *me*). If Puccini repeated the pattern in the final A section, that high note would occur on *dir*, a closed vowel, which is much harder to sing than an open one: putting it on *ben* solves the problem nicely, and Puccini has Musetta repeat the flourish in the next measure—to the same high note on the same vowel sound—at "*sen*-ti morir."

This closed ABA form allows Musetta's waltz to stand as a complete unit, and one that can be extracted for performance outside the opera house (removing the interventions of the other characters); Ricordi published it separately in the *Gazetta musicale di Milano* as a teaser for the premiere of *La Bohème*. It helps that the text is generic: while the "you" to whom Musetta refers toward the end points at Marcello, it could be read as applying to any recalcitrant lover. Other portions of *La Bohème* might seem less amenable to such extraction, given their localized dramatic references, but that has not prevented tenors from showcasing Rodolfo's "Che gelida manina," or sopranos doing the same with "Mi chiamano Mimì" or "Donde lieta uscì."[5] Puccini and Ricordi would have expected it—the royalties were not to be sniffed at—even if the lack of clear beginnings and endings makes removal from the opera difficult.

---

5. Take, for example, the problem of whether to include in any concert performance Mimì's *Sì* at the beginning of "Mi chiamano Mimì" (it is just a positive answer to Rodolfo's question about whether she feels better).

In the case of "Mi chiamano Mimì," however, Puccini takes still further the techniques seen in Musetta's "Quando men' vo." The text is mostly in seven- and eleven-syllable *versi sciolti*, with occasional five-syllable lines (text in angled brackets, below, indicates Puccini's repetitions):

A (4 mm.)	Mi chiamano Mimì, / ma il mio nome è Lucia.	They call me Mimì, / but my name is Lucia.
B (5)	La storia mia / è breve: a tela o a seta / ricamo in casa e fuori.	My story / is brief: linen or silk / do I embroider at home or away.
A (4)	Son tranquilla e lieta, / ed è mio svago / far gigli e rose.	I am contented and happy, / and it is my pleasure / to make lilies and roses.
C (5 + 5)	Mi piaccion quelle cose / che han sì dolce malìa, / che parlano d'amor, di primavere, / <che parlano> di sogni e di chimere, / quelle cose che han nome poesia.	I love those things / that have such sweet enchantment, / that speak of love and springtimes, / <that speak> of dreams and visions, / those things that are called poetry.
	. . .	[brief exchange with Rodolfo]
A (4)	Mi chiamano Mimì, / [ed] il perché non so.	They call me Mimì, / why I do not know.
D (8)	Sola mi fo / il pranzo da me stessa. / Non vado sempre a messa / ma prego assai il Signor.	All alone I make / my own supper by myself, / I do not always go to Mass, / but I pray to the Lord often enough.
—(2)	Vivo sola, soletta.	I live alone, alone.
D (8)	Là in una bianca cameretta / guardo sui tetti e in cielo.	There in a white little room / I look over the roofs and to the sky.
E (11)	Ma quando vien lo sgelo / il primo sole è mio, / il primo bacio dell'aprile è mio! / <il primo sole è mio.>	But when the thaw comes / the first sun is mine, / the first kiss of April is mine, / <the first sun is mine.>
C (10)	Germoglia in un vaso una rosa . . . / foglia a foglia la spio! / Così gentile / il profumo d'un fiore! / Ma i fior' ch'io faccio, ahimè! non hanno odore.	A rose grows in a pot . . . / I watch it leaf by leaf! / So delicate / is the perfume of a flower! / But the flowers I make, alas, have no smell.

In effect, Puccini creates three melodic phrases of increasing intensity: a rising line (A) for "Mi chiamano Mimì" that returns twice; a more extended passage (C)—Puccini marks it *dolcemente* (sweetly)—in the middle coming back at the end; and a more emotionally intense one (E) that clearly forms the melodic climax of the piece—it is marked *con molta anima* (with great spirit) and then *con grande espansione* (with great expansion). Section B is declamatory, and D is a simpler melody (*con semplicità*). The melodic climax (E) comes as Mimì thinks of spring—and as the text starts to revel in fluid *-io* sounds—and Puccini needs to repeat words to provide enough to bring things back down from that high point for the final C section. This last part may seem anticlimactic—and it makes it difficult to end the piece as a concert item—but it establishes an important connection between Mimì and flowers (Rodolfo returns to the image in Act III), and also suits the moment: Mimì needs to remain grounded, even musically modest.

So constructivist an approach is carefully calculated, and as we have seen already, Puccini has no compunction about varying the libretto to suit his purpose. In the B section of "Mi chiamano Mimì," Puccini shortens the text for the sake of balanced phrases—the libretto has two extra, if redundant, lines (in italic here):

La storia mia	My story
è breve. A tela o a seta	is brief. Linen or silk
ricamo in casa e fuori,	do I embroider at home or away,
in bianco ed a colori.	*in white and in colors.*
Lavoro d'ago,	*I work at the needle,*
son tranquilla e lieta	I am contented and happy

Similarly, in the second D section, Puccini subverts the syntax by beginning in mid-sentence: *Là in una bianca cameretta* is a prepositional phrase attached to *Vivo sola, soletta*, while Mimì's looking out over the rooftops and to the sky is a separate clause. Meanwhile, the libretto printed for the premiere in 1896 has a different reading still:

Vivo sola, soletta	I live alone, alone
nella mia cameretta	in my little room
che guarda i tetti e il cielo,	which looks out over the roofs and heaven,

In the case of Puccini's setting, presumably he was attracted by the potential parallels in terms of meter and accent between *Sola mi fo / il pranzo da me stessa* and *Là in una bianca cameretta*: hence the two D sections. His change from the printed libretto here also makes a difference: if Mimì, rather than her room, looks out over the roofs of Paris, then she is not so different from Rodolfo, who muses on Parisian chimney tops.

The kind of fluid setting seen in "Mi chiamano Mimì" is more dynamic than a static ABA form. It is also processive and what one might call recursive as individual melodic segments return—ABACADEC . . . —allowing the drama and the music to keep moving forward while containing enough repetition to maintain coherence. And it depends on Puccini's creating long-breathed melodies that can be accommodated to different poetic line lengths (and different numbers of syllables) either by subdividing notes or by slurring them. This recursive technique can work on both the small scale (the whole of "Mi chiamano Mimì" lasts seventy-one measures) and the larger one. For example, at the end of Musetta's waltz in Act II, Alcindoro continues his attempt to silence Musetta, Rodolfo tells Mimì that Marcello once loved Musetta, Schaunard and Colline comment on the situation, Musetta enjoys Marcello's discomfort, Mimì tells Rodolfo that she loves him, Musetta tries to attract Marcello's attention even more, and then she decides to get rid of Alcindoro. As Musetta shrieks in pretended agony over her painful shoes (*Sciogli, slaccia, rompi, straccia*), Puccini reprises the last two strains of her waltz melody (x, x''), this time giving it to Marcello and forcing yet another change to the libretto as he sings about his youth that is not yet dead: Puccini has *Gioventù mia, tu non sei morta* rather than the libretto's *La giovinezza mia non è ancor morta*, perhaps because Marcello thus starts on a stronger consonant. Musetta's "real" song has been turned into something else: in effect, Marcello is repeating what he has heard Musetta sing, but he is speaking to himself. These fifteen measures carry some twenty-four lines of text in total: Marcello says that his youth is not yet dead, nor his memory of it, and that if Musetta knocked at his door, his heart would run to open it; Musetta and Alcindoro bicker over the shoe; Rodolfo and Mimì comment on how obvious it is that Musetta still loves Marcello; and Schaunard and Colline note what a stupendous comedy this all is (*la commedia è stupenda*, bringing in a line given earlier in the libretto rather than setting what is actually there at that point). It is virtually impossible to distinguish all these words, and opera-house supertitles will gloss over them. We are lost in a wash of sound that comes back into focus only toward the end when, inevitably, Musetta and Mimì get that climactic high note of the melody, Musetta on *va!* and Mimì on "Mar-*cel*-lo" (again, open vowels). But in the process, Puccini has plugged an extraordinarily good tune.

The technique can extend even further. We first encounter Rodolfo in Act I as he gazes over the smoking chimneys of Paris (*Nei cieli bigi . . .*). This is another of those moments where Puccini treats *versi sciolti*, rather than more structured poetry, as an excuse for melodic expansion, giving Rodolfo a lyrical theme for six and a half lines of verse that recurs a number of times in Act I, either in the voice or in the orchestra: when Rodolfo decides to burn his play (*Aguzza / l'ingegno. L'idea vampi in fiamma*; four ten-syllable lines); when he hands Marcello its first act (*A te l'atto primo*) and they enjoy the warmth (two ten-syllable lines); when he tells his friends that he is staying behind to finish his article while they make a rowdy exit (*Io resto / per terminar l'articolo*; six or so lines of *versi sciolti*); when he tells Mimì how despite his poverty he still lives like a lord, building dreams, chimeras, and castles in the air (*In povertà mia lieta*; six seven-syllable lines). Mimì even gets a melodic idea closely related to it when she loses her key (*Oh! sventata*), even though she has not yet heard Rodolfo's tune. Again we see the adaptability of Puccini's melodies to quite different textual (and metrical) situations. Some of these repetitions appear thematic—representing Rodolfo the poet—while others seem more just for convenience. But as we shall see, they help create a surprisingly taut musical structure for the opera as a whole.

OPERATIC REALISMS

Schaunard's and Colline's comment toward the end of Act II on the "stupendous" comedy (between Marcello and Musetta) playing out before their eyes is a typical moment of operatic self-awareness: we have seen Lorenzo da Ponte playing the same trick in *Le nozze di Figaro*, although for Puccini, Leoncavallo's *Pagliacci* was probably a more pertinent example. The orchestra then repeats the first strains of Musetta's waltz melody—just in case we had forgotten it—under dialogue as Schaunard continues his theatrical analogy: "We've reached the final scene" (*Siamo all'ultima scena!*), he says. But while we are under no illusion as to the theatrical artifice of what we are seeing, the waltz is abruptly curtailed in mid-phrase by the sound of a military band coming from the distance, and the music once more becomes "real" as the bohemians plot their escape from the Café Momus, leaving the hapless Alcindoro to pay the bill.

The arrival of that onstage military band marks the culmination of an act notable for its street scenes and crowd effects, starting with its bustling parallel chords as the curtain rises on hawkers extolling the virtues of their oranges, dates, hot chestnuts, and other Christmas fare. Such virtuosic merging of scenic and musical effect is typical of late nineteenth-century French and Italian opera: several have also noted the parallels with the beginning of Act IV of Georges Bizet's *Carmen* (1875), which is a similar street scene. The musical effect of that opening is also similar to one that Igor Stravinsky later used for the Shrovetide fair in his ballet *Petrushka* (1911)—which is not to say that he knew *La Bohème*, though he certainly met Puccini in Paris. The realism continues as Schaunard buys a hunting horn that resolutely refuses to sound his desired D (we keep hearing a dissonant combination of E flat and D flat instead)—the idea is taken from the beginning of Murger's novel, where Schaunard is working at a piano with an out-of-tune D—and then children pursue the toy seller Parpignol. All this caused Puccini's librettists numerous headaches: Giacosa almost gave up on *La Bohème* in October 1893 because of the difficulties of this scene, and Illica felt it necessary (on 5 February 1894) to send Ricordi a diagram of the staging so as to differentiate the characters and action. However, audiences are unlikely to apprehend the detail—how many hear the two women calling out for the child Emma? There are also some quite specific, and even necessary, stage actions that may get lost in the general hurly-burly, such as Colline's buying an overcoat (the one he will pawn in Act IV), or Rodolfo and Mimì's little tiff as he accuses her of being too interested in a group of students—the first hint we get of a jealous streak that, we discover in the next act, will threaten their relationship. There are times when Puccini might have been a bit more careful to accentuate points like this that matter for the drama.

Act III of *La Bohème* paints another large-scale canvas, a foggy dawn by the Barrière d'Enfer as tradespeople pass the customs post into the city of Paris, while from the interior of a tavern are heard carousing voices extolling the pleasures of drinking underneath the siren call of Musetta singing her waltz tune. The scene unfolds in an almost Impressionist haze, although Puccini is precise enough to provide sufficient instrumental music at the beginning—after the opening call-to-attention flourish—for the audience to be able to enjoy, and applaud, the stage set described (like all the others) in great detail in the initial rubric to the act. He also uses the orchestra quite carefully to provide atmosphere (the bare harmonies at the beginning to suggest the fog-covered scene), to supply the sounds necessary for the onstage effects (the bells sounding matins), and also at times to choreograph the action, as it were, by cueing it at precise moments by way of a musical gesture (for example, a sudden chord) that might even provide some kind of sonic approximation of it. Likewise, when in Act I Rodolfo tears up the second act of his drama to stoke the fire, or sprinkles water on Mimì's brow, what we hear in the orchestra mimics the (wordless) act in a manner not dissimilar to the technique in film scores known as "mickey mousing." Such careful musical attention to matters of production laid out in great detail can also be found in the later Verdi operas (the long orchestral prelude to the final scene of *Otello* and its accompanying stage directions provide a classic example); it involves more than just the evocation of natural sounds, as with the storm music in Act III of *Rigoletto*. It means that opera directors have scant leeway in deviating from such detail if the music is to relate in any sensible way to the action.

It is but a short step from the orchestra's choreographing or mimicking the action to its somehow helping tell the story, in effect acting as a wordless narrator to guide the audience or to focus its attention. In *Rigoletto*, we have seen, Verdi created a recurring musical idea associated with the Count of Monterone's curse, but Puccini goes further, crafting melodic fragments that seem to embody specific characters, places, or actions and then retain their associations when they recur. An obvious case is the repeat of the music for Rodolfo's "Che gelida manina" at the end of Act I when he invites Mimì to take his arm as they leave for the Café Momus: *Dammi il braccio, mia piccina* (note the shared -*ina* rhyme). We have also already seen the case of Rodolfo's poetic "Nei cieli bigi," mixing thematic and nonthematic recurrences, and there are numerous other examples: the energetic motive that begins the opera (Puccini marks it *ruvido*, i.e., rough, coarse, or harsh) and punctuates the subsequent action when the bohemians get boisterous; the jaunty idea marked *deciso* (decisive) that accompanies Schaunard's entrance with food, wine, and cigars; the coquettish and obstinately repetitive theme associated with Musetta's entrance in Act II, to be played *brillante, con fuoco* (sparkling, with fire). Sometimes their significance, if any, becomes clear only in retrospect at their second or subsequent hearings, and at times they can seem to be just a game for the composer: the obvious example is Schaunard's reference in Act I to the Latin Quarter music—anticipating the beginning of Act II—when he orders his friends to save all the provisions he has brought because it is better to go out on the town for Christmas Eve. While these motives remain discrete and are pieced together patchwork fashion, they can sometimes also appear to develop one into another, making still further dramatic and musical connections. The technique is often associated with Wagnerian leitmotifs, but it is common enough in much late nineteenth-century opera as a way of knitting together or connecting long segments of music that might otherwise seem to ramble because of the lack of clearly defined forms. Librettists were well aware of it, too: Giacosa worked quite hard in his drafts to find a way of enabling the return of the music of Rodolfo's "Che gelida manina" at the end of Act I. But once these musical ideas are recycled, they also gain a degree of semiotic power that can be put to dramatic use, if only to remind the audience of prior circumstances that then take a different direction. Puccini knew full well how to take advantage of the pathos that could be generated by such associations; indeed, Act IV makes its effect almost entirely because of them.

MIMÌ DIES

The "missing" act of *La Bohème* means that we lose a significant part of the Rodolfo-Mimì story (how she takes up with the viscount), and there are only brief references in the final act of the opera to make up for it. At some point, however, it hardly matters: Mimì is less a person than an "ideal" whose time must pass. Act IV begins with a compressed version of the musical opening of the first: the stage set is the same, so the audience does not need time to applaud it. Rodolfo and Marcello are at work bantering once more, and when Rodolfo tries to write before cursing his pen (*Che penna infame!*) and throwing it down in frustration, we hear in the orchestra the same music used for a similar moment in Act I, as the bohemians leave Rodolfo alone to finish off his article, though he has no mind for it (*Non sono in vena*). There is new music for Marcello and Rodolfo as each laments his lost love, but then we hear the old jaunty melody for Schaunard's (and Colline's) entrance, and so on through the bohemians' mock dancing, descending into a duel that is abruptly halted by the appearance of Musetta and then Mimì, the latter cued in the orchestra by the music for "Mi chiamano Mimì": the parallel with Act I (starting with jolly japes in the garret, then shifting tone at Mimì's entrance) are obvious enough. The orchestral reminiscence continues underneath Musetta's *parlando* explanation of how she found Mimì in the street in a state of collapse. There is no strong connection between Musetta's text and the one originally associated with this part of "Mi chiamano Mimì" (the C section). However, Mimì's interventions, such as when she says she feels better (*Mi sento assai meglio*), have sonic parallels with it (*di sogni e di chimere*), suggesting once again how Puccini sometimes conceives, or recalls, melodies in association with particular word sounds, also making it easier for singers to remember them. But his principal aim here is one of nostalgic evocation, as music from happier times returns in more tragic circumstances. Puccini had already used musical reminiscences from Act I (and briefly Act II) at Mimì's first farewell to Rodolfo, at the end of Act III. Now, however, the gestures have greater dramatic import.

This part of Act IV contains two "new" musical episodes: Colline's lament for his overcoat (*Vecchia zimarra, senti*)—to give the character something to sing on a par with Schaunard's account of the dead parrot in Act I—and an arialike moment for Mimì after she is left alone with Rodolfo. Here she asks whether the friends have gone and says that she was just pretending to be asleep so that she could be alone with him (*Son andati? Fingevo di dormire*; in a nicely shaped six lines rhyming ABABCC). But as Mimì grows weaker, she lapses into reminiscences of how she and Rodolfo first met: how she lost her key; how Rodolfo took her frozen hand in his. All this is to echoes of their music in Act I: Puccini made a special request of Illica (in mid October 1895) to include text that would allow Mimì to reprise Rodolfo's "Che gelida manina." Likewise, the subsequent comings and goings of the other bohemians are matched, and staged, by fragments of their former music. The ending of Rodolfo's "Che gelida manina" recurs once more in the orchestra as Mimì warms her hands in the muff, but the music then shifts to sustained chords with only occasional rhythmic punctuation and three separate state-ments of the first few notes of the C section of "Mi chiamano Mimì." When Rodolfo realizes that Mimì is dead, the orchestra plays *fortissississimo* (and *tutta forza*, with all force) the melody from Mimì's "Son andati? Fingevo di dormire"—her sleep is no longer a pretense. That reprise leads to a final three-measure cadence taken from the end of Colline's lament for his over-coat, after he had just said farewell (*addio*) to it. The fanciful reading is that this *addio* now applies to Mimì; the mundane one is that Puccini needed an ending. The audience is unlikely to notice either way, given that the falling curtain invariably prompts premature applause.

The libretto has some eighteen lines of verse after Mimì's fragmentary final words about her warm hands enabling her to sleep (*Le mani . . . al cal-do . . . e . . . dormire . . .*), and Puccini stretches them out over forty-five slow measures, the main musical focus, such as it is, being Musetta's prayer to the Madonna—a gesture to another operatic convention. At this point, the score is littered with still more elaborate, and lengthy, stage directions (even more than in the 1896 libretto): Rodolfo is reassured by Mimì's falling asleep; he cautiously moves away from her, and, having made a sign that the others should be quiet, he steps next to Marcello (and asks him what the doctor said); Musetta warms medicine on a spirit stove; Rodolfo speaks sotto voce with Marcello and Schaunard (they have no text or music) while occasion-ally moving over to Mimì; Marcello positions a book around a candle on the table to stop its flickering in the draft; Rodolfo moves next to Musetta while Schaunard tiptoes over to Mimì and makes a grieving gesture before returning to stand next to Marcello; Marcello likewise heads toward the bed and steps back in fright; Colline enters with the money he has received for his overcoat and places it on the table; a ray of sunlight shines through the window onto Mimì's face, and Rodolfo tries to create some shade, for which Musetta offers her cape; Rodolfo thanks her with a glance, steps on a chair, and tries to find a way to hang it over the window; Colline goes to help Rodolfo with the cape and asks him how Mimì is ("Peaceful," Rodolfo replies, speaking rather than singing); Rodolfo turns and sees Musetta, who signals that the medicine is ready, so he steps down from the chair but in moving toward Musetta sees Marcello and Schaunard's strange demeanor and asks what it means; Marcello, unable to contain himself, runs to embrace Rodolfo ("Courage," he says); Rodolfo rushes to the bed and lifts and shakes Mimì, crying out with the greatest desperation (*Mimì* . . .), but he realizes that she is dead and throws himself on her body, weeping (*Mimì* . . .). Rodolfo's are the last words we hear, but the action continues, with still more stage directions detailing precisely what Musetta, Schaunard, Colline, and Marcello are meant to do as the curtain slowly falls.

There is no musical mickey mousing here; indeed, the relative neutrality of the music would seem to suggest that Puccini felt that understatement was a better musical option at this point in the opera, save for the none-too-subtle (as Puccini himself admitted) orchestral *fortississimo* reprise of the music of "Sono andati?" Likewise, he gives the characters mostly rhythmicized speech, as if there is nothing more to sing about. What is most striking about all these stage directions, however, is that they do not state when Mimì dies. Puccini marked the moment clearly in his autograph score with a skull and crossbones, at the long silent pause after her final *dormire*, itself set to an unfinished musical phrase. But it takes a good long while for the others to recognize her passing. All that subsequent stage business described at length above (from where Rodolfo asks Marcello about the doctor) is in the end just a distraction: this is not how operatic heroines are meant to go from this world to the next.

Puccini's letters to Ricordi reveal that he was worried about Mimì's dying and what it stood for. Part of the problem lies in the character, both for herself and, we have seen, in terms of her being an amalgamation of different women in Murger's novel. There, the death is Francine's—in the presence of Jacques and a doctor—and the relevant chapter (18) continues the narrative through her funeral, its aftermath for the sculptor, his gaining a commission and briefly finding new love (with Marie), and then his own death, with his plan to create a statue for Francine's tomb left unfulfilled. For the opera, Puccini and his collaborators needed to cut the story short, and also to find business that keeps all the other characters occupied: thus it is Musetta who buys the muff (Jacques does so in the novel). As for Mimì, however—and still more after the removal of the courtyard act—she is not a "bad" woman who somehow needs to take a redemptive turn at the end. That role is taken, instead, by Musetta, whose actions invented for the libretto—caring for Mimì and her final, too-late prayer—present a very different side to the hard-hearted coquette we have seen in Acts II and III, and even suggest, perhaps, that she will reform, turning to more appropriate forms of feminine behavior (this was a transformation that emerged gradually in the creation of *La Bohème*, it seems). Nor is Mimì's death a necessary sacrifice to allow her lover, Rodolfo, to gain a better future with a different wife, and it appears to offer no transcendent message to the audience. As we saw in the case of Gilda in *Rigoletto*, redemption, sacrifice, or transcendence would have allowed Mimì some final musical word: indeed, operatic convention would have demanded it. Her silent demise might instead be viewed as a dramatic masterstroke.

The fact that Puccini resisted any perimortal indulgence for Mimì stands in contrast to the prolonged demise of his Manon Lescaut and may reflect the abrupt deaths—absent dying-breath arias—typical of other Verismo operas of the time that preferred reality over convention. But it was also probably a move to preempt invidious comparisons with other tubercular operatic heroines, not least, of course, the Violetta of Verdi's *La traviata*. The drafts of the libretto for *La Bohème* further suggest that a differently dangerous operatic heroine, Carmen, was another intertextual resonance to be avoided. But there may be yet another anxiety in play here. Puccini referred in his letters to how *La Bohème* needed to drive toward its goal, the "Tod von Mimì." Whether whimsical or not, this is a clear reference to the final "Liebestod" in Wagner's *Tristan und Isolde* (1865; first performed in Italian in Bologna in 1888): Isolde spends the last six minutes of that opera seeking a love-death transfiguration with her beloved, if now dead, Tristan. Mimì dies silently in fewer than six seconds. But the *Tristan*esque chords that accompany Mimì's entrance in Act IV turn that anxiety of influence into a snub as Italian opera seeks to confirm its anti-Wagnerian credentials. The third performance of *La Bohème* at the Teatro Regio in Turin on 4 February 1896 was followed on the 5th by *Il crepuscolo degli dei* (*Gotterdämmerung*). Puccini and Wagner went head to head again, as it were, on 8 and 9 February. Comparisons, of course, are futile. But one still wonders who won.

FURTHER READING

The best English-language accounts of *La Bohème* are Arthur Groos and Roger Parker, *Giacomo Puccini: "La Bohème"*, Cambridge Opera Handbooks (Cambridge: Cambridge University Press, 1986)—this also gives the text for the dropped courtyard act and for Schaunard's Act IV political rally—and in Michele Girardi, *Puccini: His International Art* (Chicago: University of Chicago Press, 2000), 99–144 (there is an updated version at www-5.unipv.it/girardi/saggi/2008_MG_Pavarotti.pdf). Further details of the creation of the opera are in Mary Jane Phillips-Matz, *Puccini: A Biography* (Boston: Northeastern University Press, 2002), 80–105; while Alexandra Wilson, *The Puccini Problem: Opera, Nationalism, and Modernity* (Cambridge: Cambridge University Press, 2007) covers important issues of reception history. For Puccini and Leoncavallo, and their use of Murger, see Jürgen Maehder, "Paris-Bilde: Zur Transformation von Henry Murgers Roman in den 'Bohème'-Opern Puccinis und Leoncavallos," *Jahrbuch für Opernforschung* 2 (1986): 109–76; this has also been translated as "Immagini di Parigi: la trasformazione del romanzo *Scènes de la vie de bohème* di Henri Murger nelle opere di Puccini e Leoncavallo," *Nuova rivista musicale italiana* 24 (1990): 402–56. My comments on (and examples of) the draft versions of the libretto are drawn from Virgilio Bernardoni, *Verso "Bohème": gli abozzi del libretto negli archivi di Giuseppe Giacosa e Luigi Illica*, Centro Studi Giacomo Puccini: Testi e documenti 1 (Florence: Olschki, 2008). For a broader view of the handling of the end of the opera, see Helen Greenwald, "*Ars moriendi*: Reflections on the Death of Mimì," in *The Arts of the Prima Donna in the Long Nineteenth Century*, edited by Rachel Cowgill and Hilary Poriss (Oxford and New York: Oxford University Press, 2012), 167–85.

CHAPTER 7

Afterthoughts

MIMÌ SPENDS MORE TIME singing about a lost key than she does about her own death. As opera moved toward greater so-called realism, it had to engage with the mundane on the one hand, and with the improbability of perimortal swan songs on the other. While comedy had often made a virtue of mundanity, tragedy was ostensibly made of sterner stuff, yet the intervention of bourgeois sentimentality threatened to overwhelm the genre. Much opera since 1900 has had to negotiate some kind of path between the banal and the overblown, either accepting the constraints of realist drama or returning to some version of myth.

The fact that *La Bohème* is the last opera covered in this book is not intended to treat it as the end of a line: Puccini still had six operas to go—eight if one counts the separate one-act components of *Il trittico*—with *Turandot* left unfinished at his death in 1924. And there were plenty of Italian operas composed in the twentieth century, although hardly any have entered the standard repertoire (as is true of much twentieth-century opera). But Puccini's collaborator, Luigi Illica, was clear on the changing nature of the librettist's art. As he wrote to Giulio Ricordi in October 1907, "I say, and I am persuaded, that it is the music that makes the form of a libretto, and that the composer should set to music not the poetry [*il verso*] but the idea [*il concetto*], the anguish of some suffering, the impression and the moment of a situation." "Poetry was fine in the period of cabalettas," he noted, but "what has true value in the libretto is the word: that the words should correspond to the truth of the moment (the situation) and of the emotion (the character)!" Illica's acceptance—somewhat grudging, it might be said—of an inevitability was cast in the form of a claim for both verisimilitude and naturalism. But while one can imagine, say, Pietro Metastasio making a similar appeal, he would not have given up the idea of poetry as poetry; nor would those composers who set Metastasio's librettos to music have denied the role of poetry in giving some kind of shape to their musical expression. One might assume that Pietro Mascagni and Ruggero Leoncavallo, the leaders of the late nineteenth-century school of Verismo opera, felt the same: in poetic terms, the librettos of *Cavalleria rusticana* (by Giovanni Targioni-Tozzetti and Guido Menasci; 1890) and *Pagliacci* (by the composer; 1892) differ little, if at all, from their predecessors.

Illica's emphasis on *il concetto* rather than *il verso*, however, prompted treating poetry in a manner akin to prose. It went hand in hand with breaking down the distinctions that traditionally characterized number opera (recitative, aria, duet, etc.) in favor of a continuous musical flow: we have seen the consequences both in *Rigoletto* and still more in *La Bohème*. This flow was somehow deemed more "natural" than any divide between musical speech and song and was also considered likely to promote greater dramatic cohesion. By now the impulse was associated with Wagner, and its close corollary was that the librettist became redundant: the composer could choose either to be the author of the text to be set to music (as did Wagner) or to treat some text conceived independently of any musical setting, such as a spoken play, with adjustments only to reduce the length, given that it usually takes longer to sing something than to say it. For example, although Tito Ricordi (son of Giulio) received credit for the libretto of Riccardo Zandonai's *Francesca da Rimini* (1914), the opera is drawn largely from Gabriele d'Annunzio's spoken tragedy of the same title, first performed in 1901: Ricordi cut down the play quite drastically but did little to the text (in *versi sciolti*) that remained.

Francesca da Rimini is an example of *Literaturoper*, which gained some force around 1900 as modernist opera reacted against Romanticism to claim greater dramatic pretensions. The medium of the libretto would depend on the medium of the source play: in the case of non-Italian examples, this could range from Maeterlinck's proselike but elevated *vers libres* in Claude Debussy's *Pelléas et Mélisande* (1902) through Oscar Wilde's prose-based *Salome* (Richard Strauss; 1905) to Georg Büchner's wholly prosaic *Woyzeck* (Alban Berg; 1925). Verdi's last two operas, *Otello* (1887) and *Falstaff*

(1893), tend not to be included within the genre because Arrigo Boito's verse librettos adapt Shakespeare in typical operatic ways, although they certainly set the bar high in terms of new approaches to drama through music. However, the Italian modernists often of the Generazione dell'Ottanta, reacting against Puccini, embraced D'Annunzio with a vengeance: his *La figlia di Iorio* (1904) was set by Alberto Franchetti (1906), his *Fedra* (1909) by Ildebrando Pizzetti (1909–12), *Sogno d'un tramonto d'autunno* (1898) by Gian Francesco Malipiero (1913), *La fiaccola sotto il moggio* (1905) by Pizzetti (as *Gigliola*; 1914–15), and *La nave* (1905–7) by Italo Montemezzi (1918), not to mention the French setting of *La città morta* (1898) by Raoul Pugno and Nadia Boulanger (1910–13). But by the 1920s and '30s, Malipiero (1882–1973), for example, preferred to source and write his own librettos: the main exceptions were his adaptations of Shakespeare (mostly in prose) for *Giulio Cesare* (1936), dedicated to Benito Mussolini, and *Antonio e Cleopatra* (1938), and of Carlo Goldoni (the three-act compilation *Tre commedie goldoniane*; 1926). However, he did engage—collaborate would probably be too strong a term—with Luigi Pirandello (1867–1936) on the latter's *La favola del figlio cambiato* (1930–32), which Pirandello adapted in *versi liberi* for Malipiero from his 1902 *novella*, although he desired no involvement in the musical setting (first staged in 1934) and designed it to all intents and purposes as a separate play, as it is performed today.

Malipiero was not the only composer perfectly capable of arranging and writing texts for musical setting. Luigi Dallapiccola (1904–1975) provided the words for all three of his operas, plus the *sacra rappresentazione* titled *Job*. He also seems to have been happy with librettos in a range of forms: his *Volo di notte* (1940; after the novel *Vol de nuit* by Antoine de Saint-Exupéry) is mostly in prose (as is *Job*); *Il prigioniero* (1949; after Auguste Villiers de l'Isle-Adam and Charles de Coster) mixes *versi liberi*, *versi sciolti*, and structured passages (such as the *ballata* in the prologue or the *aria in tre strofe* for the jailor in scene 2); and *Ulisse* (1968) has a classical—perhaps even intentionally archaic—mix of weighty *alessandrini* and eleven-syllable lines on the one hand, and *versi sciolti* on the other, although one might not always be able to tell the difference from the music. The advantage for the composer of self-authored librettos is obvious enough: the text can evolve and be revised as the music takes shape. The disadvantage is the risk of self-indulgence absent the discipline of a freestanding text, and also, perhaps, of a separate creative mind. Luigi Nono's *Intolleranza 1960* started out as a collaboration between the composer and the poet and Slavic-languages scholar Angelo Maria Ripellino, but Nono found the text intractable and reworked it so completely that Ripellino offered to remove himself from the project (instead, Nono came up with the formula that the opera was "after an idea" by Ripellino). The libretto became a collage of left-wing texts by Ripellino, Henri Alleg, Bertolt Brecht, Aimé Césaire, Paul Eluard, Julius Fučík, Vladimir Mayakovsky, and Jean-Paul Sartre, all "assembled by the composer." The result was political uproar at the 1961 Venice Biennale.

Intolleranza 1960 was called an *azione scenica*, in a typical shift of genre to avoid the connotations of opera, now viewed at least in some circles as a fossilized institution. Another collage-type libretto, Luciano Berio's *Un re in ascolto* (1984), is an *azione musicale*, a term with Wagnerian overtones (*Handlung für Musik*) perhaps via the French (*action musicale*, as adopted by Vincent d'Indy and others). Berio's (1925–2003) collaboration with the renowned Italian author, journalist, and intellectual Italo Calvino (1923–1985)—his second after *La vera storia* (1982)—seems to have been happier than Nono's with Ripellino, but again the composer "assembled" a range of texts from Calvino's scenario and other materials for the opera (and conversations with the author), and from texts related to Shakespeare's *The Tempest* by way of a late eighteenth-century adaptation (by Friedrich Wilhelm Einsiedel and Friedrich Wilhelm Gotter) and of W. H. Auden's poem *The Sea and the Mirror*, all superimposed in an intricate layer-upon-layer complex.[1] The libretto is partitioned into formal elements given titles with operatic associations (*Aria I, Duetto I, Concertato II con figure, Serenata,* etc.), although they are not marked poetically within the text, which is predominantly in polymetric (or ametric) *versi liberi*.

Like much recent opera—and perhaps like much opera in general when viewed in the abstract—*Un re in ascolto* is an opera about opera. Prospero is an aging theatrical impresario, the theater is his island, and the redemptive force is music. The idea is obvious enough, and the outcome might even seem trite were we inclined to doubt the composer's evident sincerity. As for the text, Berio claimed that Calvino himself was not very musical, indeed that he was intimidated by music and was in fact tone-deaf. This was not a problem for the composer, Berio said, because of his own aversion to "musical" texts: he preferred to rely on those lacking any musical intentions precisely because of the creative potentials for interpretative dissonance—the music was there not to illuminate the words but to leave them obscure,

1. The idea for *Un re in ascolto* went back to 1977, but Calvino published the short story that was one seed for the opera only after the premiere at the Salzburg Festival on 7 August 1984: it appeared in the Italian newspaper *La repubblica* on 12 August.

wrapped in convoluted webs of ambiguity. *Un re in ascolto* thematizes the whole issue as Prospero begins the work, struggling to hear something not quite remembered:

Ho sognato un teatro, un altro teatro,	I have dreamed a theater, another theater,
esiste un altro teatro,	there exists another theater,
oltre il mio teatro,	other than my theater,
un teatro non mio che pur io conosco,	a theater, not mine, but that I know.
5 io ricordo,	I remember,
ossia io ricordo d'aver dimenticato	or rather I remember having forgotten
solo questo	only this:
un teatro dove un io che non conosco canta.	a theater where an "I" whom I do not know, sings.
Canta la musica che non ricordo	It sings the music I do not remember
10 e che io adesso vorrei cantare	and that I now would like to sing,
non ricordo . . .	I do not remember . . .

These *versi liberi* mix lines of different lengths some of which can be measured in the normal way—the antepenultimate *Canta la musica che non ricordo* is a regular eleven-syllable line—while others cannot. Berio's setting, however, treats them all in the manner of prose, or as poetic only in their sententious gravity, also mixing words that are spoken (in italic below) and sung:

> *Ho sognato*, ho sognato un teatro, *un altro teatro*, ho sognato, ho sognato, ho sognato un teatro, *esiste*, esiste un altro teatro, oltre, oltre il mio teatro, *teatro*, un teatro . . .

Berio's evident interest in the sounds of words and their constituent parts is both musical and mystical. He also aids the singer in a manner not dissimilar to Puccini, oddly enough (or perhaps it is not so odd), by linking vowel sounds or phonemes to recurring pitches. This is particularly useful given his complex musical language. But it is another matter whether one can, or should, understand the text as it is delivered save by way of half-heard glimmers within a powerfully evocative soundscape.

One might of course argue that the same is true of all opera: that music sometimes—often?—appears to deconstruct the text to the point of inaudibility or even irrelevance. We have seen examples even in *Rigoletto* that seem to prove the point. Yet Calvino and Berio hardly underestimate the power of Italian versification. In the case of that eleven-syllable line, *Canta la musica che non ricordo* (It sings the music I do not remember), Berio has Prospero deliver much of it as speech. But while "the music" is unremembered, Prospero is presented as knowing full well the poetic meter to which it would have been sung. Whether intentional or not, this is an eloquent reminder of the operatic tradition that underpins Berio's enterprise even as he tries to resist it.

Berio's Prospero dreams of a theater that contains an "I" whom he does not recognize, singing music that he cannot recall. *Canta la musica*—the allusion to the prologue of Monteverdi's *Orfeo* (1607) seems clear, and it brings this book full circle back to its beginning. Berio certainly knew the work. His music-theatrical piece *Opera* (Santa Fe, 1970; revised for Florence, 1977)—which Berio described to the musicologist and critic Massimo Mila as "a little bit of exorcism of the opera and a little bit of the plural form of the opus"—used Alessandro Striggio's libretto as one of three elements within its improvisational collage (the other two were textual fragments related to the sinking of the *Titanic*, some by Umberto Eco and Furio Colombo; and the experimental theater piece *Terminal*, performed in New York by the group Open Theater, and directed by Joseph Chaikin collaborating with Roberta Sklar). For the 1984 Maggio Musicale in Florence (the same year as *Un re in ascolto*), Berio also arranged a spectacular outdoor "happening" based on *Orfeo* to complement the more "authentic" production of the original opera staged concurrently by the Early Opera Project (directed by Roger Norrington and Kay Lawrence) in the Palazzo Vecchio. However, his juxtaposition of an "old" and a "new" *Orfeo*—while typically radical—was not intended as iconoclasm in ways that might have formed the agenda of his *Opera* in 1970: rather, it celebrated the continuity of an art form so deeply embedded in Italian culture that it acts as a marker of national identity.

Berio wanted to suggest in parts of his *Opera* (according to the program note for the Santa Fe production) how "the operatic stage dreams its own past," whether in the throes of its death or in a constant stage of becoming. Likewise, the apparent deconstruction of the libretto in *Un re in ascolto* remains rooted in a tradition of *poesia per musica*—that telltale eleven-syllable line—that has always anchored the history of Italian opera. Nothing in this book has sought to deny the preeminently musical power exercised by the composers and performers who draw us to the opera house in the first place. I also began my Introduction with an example from Verdi—Violetta's *Amami, Alfredo, quant'io t'amo! Addio!*—that would seem to support the idea that music can (some might say, must) in some sense transcend the poetry it sets so as to work its magic. Thus we have seen Monteverdi, Handel, Mozart, Verdi, and Puccini move beyond the words even as I have argued that an understanding of how and why they did so rests on an awareness of poetic norms that are too often ignored in accounts of their operas. But the fact that these composers far more often follow, rather than override, the poetic structures of their librettos—so I have also shown—should give us pause. Monteverdi's recitatives, Handel's arias, Mozart's ensembles, Verdi's cabalettas, and Puccini's lyric flights all hinge on the verse their poets provided. They also remind us that not just the content but also the structure of opera librettos matters, even when we think they might not.

FURTHER READING

Illica's letter to Puccini is in Eugenio Gara, ed., *Carteggi pucciniani* (Milan: Ricordi, 1958), 358. The program book for the revival of Luigi Nono's *Intolleranza 1960* at La Fenice, Venice, in 2011 has extremely useful material on the opera's genesis: see www.teatrolafenice.it/media/libretti/114_6319intero_indd.pdf. For an overview of broader issues, see Raymond Fearn, *Italian Opera since 1945* (Amsterdam: Harwood Academic, 1997), from which I have also drawn the translation of the opening of *Un re in ascolto*. For Berio's views on Calvino, see his article "Le note invisibili" published in the Italian newspaper *L'Unità*, 12 January 1988, and as "La musicalità di Calvino" in the journal *Il Verri* (March–June 1988): 9–12. Berio's Santa Fe commission is discussed in Claudia di Luzio, "Opera on Opera: Luciano Berio's *Opera*," in *"Music's Obedient Daughter": The Opera Libretto from Source to Score*, edited by Sabine Lichtenstein, Textxet: Studies in Comparative Literature 74 (Amsterdam and New York: Rodopi, 2014), 463–81.

Index